the STRANGE *and* TRAGIC WOUNDS
of GEORGE COLE'S AMERICA

the STRANGE *and* TRAGIC WOUNDS *of* GEORGE COLE'S AMERICA

a TALE *of* MANHOOD, SEX, *and* AMBITION *in the* CIVIL WAR ERA

MICHAEL *de*GRUCCIO

 JOHNS HOPKINS UNIVERSITY PRESS BALTIMORE

© 2025 Johns Hopkins University Press
All rights reserved. Published 2025
Printed in the United States of America on acid-free paper
2 4 6 8 9 7 5 3 1

Johns Hopkins University Press
2715 North Charles Street
Baltimore, Maryland 21218
www.press.jhu.edu

Library of Congress Cataloging-in-Publication Data

Names: deGruccio, Michael E., author.
Title: The strange and tragic wounds of George Cole's America : a tale of manhood, sex, and ambition in the Civil War era / Michael deGruccio.
Description: Baltimore : Johns Hopkins University Press, [2025] | Includes bibliographical references and index.
Identifiers: LCCN 2024033466 | ISBN 9781421451541 (hardcover) | ISBN 9781421451558 (eBook)
Subjects: LCSH: Cole, George W. (George Washington), 1827–1875. | United States. Army—Officers—Biography. | United States—History—Civil War, 1861–1865—Veterans—Biography. | Murderers—United States—Biography. | Men—United States—Social conditions—19th century.
Classification: LCC E467.1.C595 D4 2025 | DDC 973.7092 [B]—dc23/eng/20240926
LC record available at https://lccn.loc.gov/2024033466

A catalog record for this book is available from the British Library.

ISBN 978-1-4214-5154-1 (hardcover)
ISBN 978-1-4214-5155-8 (ebook)

Special discounts are available for bulk purchases of this book. For more information, please contact Special Sales at specialsales@jh.edu.

I returned, and saw under the sun, that the race is not to the swift, nor the battle to the strong, neither yet bread to the wise, nor yet riches to men of understanding, nor yet favour to men of skill; but time and chance happeneth to them all.

—Ecclesiastes, King James Version

for my father
i miss your gentle & beautiful soul
i am still a boy
walking in your steps

CONTENTS

Acknowledgments ix
Prologue. A Domestic Tragedy (in an American Hotel) 1

Part I Bred in the Bone

Chapter 1 America, Republic without Grace 13
Chapter 2 To See Ourselves as Others See Us 24
Chapter 3 The False Dawn of Seneca Falls 34

Part II Delusions of Manhood

Chapter 4 Fog of War 47
Chapter 5 George Washington, Town Destroyer 56
Chapter 6 Below the Beast 70
Chapter 7 Tears for Uncle Tom 79
Chapter 8 A Good Deal of Trouble 90
Chapter 9 No Return 102
Chapter 10 The Resurrectionists 113
Chapter 11 Mutiny 130
Chapter 12 Family, the Inflammatory Stimulus 143

Part III Odyssey after War

Chapter 13 Homecoming 157
Chapter 14 Killing for Union 165
Chapter 15 Rising Men (Who Nearly Needed God) 176
Chapter 16 The Domesticated Prisoner 191

Chapter 17 Confessions		204
Chapter 18 Mary. Wife. Self.		214
Chapter 19 Life Imitates Art		224
Chapter 20 Some Magnetic Power		236
Chapter 21 Heroic Wounds		251
Chapter 22 Rings and Friends		261
Chapter 23 Schemes and Smoke		275
Chapter 24 Buried on the Brow of a Hill		286
Epilogue		297
Notes		311
Key to Sources Cited		349
Index		367

ACKNOWLEDGMENTS

At last, I get to come clean on how dependent I have been on others.

Nearly two decades ago I hit the road to gather traces left behind from the life of an obscure soldier. I traveled to archives in California, New Mexico, Pennsylvania, New York, Virginia, and Washington, DC. Stretching a meager grad school stipend, I slept in seedy hostels and in the backs of rental cars under the glare of gas station lights and Walmart signs. Feeling like I was searching for needles in distant haystacks, I wondered what I had gotten myself into. All I can tell you is that strangers, colleagues, mentors, friends, and family got me through.

This book would have been impossible without the research of dozens of scholars. I am especially indebted to Edward Longacre, Weymouth T. Jordan Jr., Gerald W. Thomas, David A. Norris, Norma Basch, Hendrik Hartog, Sharon Block, Leslie J. Reagan, Richard Bushman, Malcom Ebright, Clark S. Knowlton, Jim Downs, Margaret Humphreys, Ira Berlin, Joseph P. Reidy, Leslie S. Rowland, and Janet Farrell Brodie.

I wrote some of this book long ago in graduate school, where I was lucky to have the finest mentors. David Waldstreicher, with his infectious love for the craft of history, introduced me to the American Civil War era and challenged me to intervene in the biggest historical questions. My adviser,

Gail Bederman, was a true friend and support when I doubted myself; her scholarship on race and gender is a clinic on incisive, rigorous analysis of historical texts. I only hope that a little of her brilliance rubbed off on me.

Christopher Jones shared with me his unpublished, detailed work on the Third New York Cavalry. Dee Maguire, a descendant of Luther Harris Hiscock, shared her family history and her insights with me. Driven by the love of history, and on his own dime, Tom Tryniski singlehandedly scanned almost sixty million newspaper pages, mostly from the New York region (accomplishing something that well-funded libraries could not do); I simply could not have uncovered so many needles from George Cole's life without Tom's miracle: Fultonhistory.com.

It was Robert Brugger who read part of the earliest manuscript and convinced me to write an unconventional narrative for Johns Hopkins University Press. Other presses would not touch this story. Bob championed it from the start. I'll never forget how he met me at a train station in DC and, at a café table, told me to write the story as if I were sitting in a dark theater: "Black screen. Now fade in..." At Johns Hopkins University Press, Laura Davulis and Ezra Rodriguez got the scattered armies in my head marching in a line. At Westchester Publishing Services, Helen Wheeler and Ashley Moore helped me tame my feral endnotes and my prodigious output of malapropisms, misnumbered chapters, and typos. Thanks to the Credited Internships Program at Saint Peter's University, I was aided by a research assistant, Israel Cedeño, who helped me round up the images and the permissions. Our former provost, Marylou Yam, believed in my project and secured a needed sabbatical; my department chair and friend, David Gerlach, regularly needled me to quit making excuses about our heavy teaching load and push toward the finish line.

Multiple friends and colleagues read chapters or parts of the story and offered feedback: Mathew Mason, Shawn Miller, Jordan Bailey, James Goodman, Annie Skinner, Lauren Squillante, Jo Robertson, Kennan deGruccio, Cody Christopherson, Patrick Mason, and Norma Basch. William LaPiana gave me sage advice on the chapter about Mary Cole's inheritance. Krystyna von Henneberg read an early, sprawling version and offered vital criticism for an untamed manuscript. Martha Hodes sacrificed much of her summer to trudge through a bloated manuscript still in need of significant discipline. I had written at least three versions of this book; Martha helped me cut through the clutter of too many ideas. Bryan P. Luskey provided crucial feedback in the final stages. Peter Carmichael was my most loyal critic, urging me to allow for more redemption in the war while assuring me that this story needed to be told. (I miss you, Pete. I was ready to quit academia until you talked me down from the ledge.)

Gail Snyder, a local historian of the area where George and Mary Cole were born, sent me envelopes stuffed with historical notes; she took me around local cemeteries and allowed my family to sleep in her guest house. Without the work of William Griffing, who preserved the letters of his family, I would have not known that George Cole attended Wesleyan, or that he nearly died from depression. Nancy Anderson from the New Mexico Genealogical Society drove to the Mora region to confirm that I had not missed clues in the archives. After I had accepted that the only newspaper image of the Stanwix murder was ruined by ink spills, Gary Johnson at the Library of Congress tracked down a preserved edition and sent me photographs. (I almost fell out of my chair when I examined the image closely!) If not for David Burrows, an expert military collector who took time to educate a stranger (me), I would never have known that George Cole wore an identification disc in the war and that it had George Washington's image on it.

When Bryan Pickett and I trespassed on property in an isolated village of northern New Mexico, Decky Trambley, a cowboy-hatted rancher in his eighties, stood silently behind his door with his wife, Delicia, shotgun in his arms. He took a shine to us the next day and hauled us in his first-gen Ranger pickup to the General's grave site. Finally, Dan Irick—and generations of fellow Masons before him—preserved vital lodge records and sacred objects, even rescuing them from tornadoes, flood, and fire. A faithful Mason, Dan tracked down records from old feedstore warehouses, archives, and decaying boxes in the possession of aging brothers. Without these records I would not have known that George had engaged in intense rituals in New Mexico, near the end of his life, in a lodge filled with working men and soldiers.

Friends—too many to name here—humored me as I shared the strange scenes I hoped to weave into the story. Friends like Ernest Plange grilled me late into the night, after the scouts had finally gone to sleep in their tents, about narrative strategies. Mark Spicer helped me edit images and aided me with almost every IT-related problem I had, sending me spare laptops, monitors, and hard drives for storing thousands of archival images. Clyde and Linda Morse and Brad Haag opened their homes to me for my many visits to the National Archives. Sungah and Mark Thomas did the same during one of my trips to Los Angeles. And of course Bryan, who endured many nights of cheap motels and third-rate powder soup, helped me gather vital clues—especially the first tip that George had become a Mason—in the archives of New Mexico.

I am overwhelmed by how lucky I am.

My wife's parents, Boyd and Jo Robertson, raised the most marvelous girl on earth and helped us with our mortgage in the early days of grad school. And I am forever in debt to my parents—Eileen and Richard—who showed me how to love until the difficult end, to open our home to the marginalized, and to put duty before worldly ambitions. The irony is not lost on me that, to tell a story about an ambitious absentee father, I too often left the greater burden of caring for our young children—Gracie, Gabriel, and Ezra—to my wife, Kennan. If God gives me another thirty years to cook her meals, wash her dishes, rub her head, and make her crème brûlée, I will not have paid my debt for what she taught me over the first thirty trips around the sun: the true measure of the self is one's capacity for giving ordinary, consistent love to those in pain.

the STRANGE *and* TRAGIC WOUNDS
of GEORGE COLE'S AMERICA

George Washington Cole poses before a camera, likely in early 1864, proudly displaying his recent promotion in the Union army. He yearned for recognition in war as much as, if not more than, he did health, money, and life itself. He wears a field officer's frock jacket. The double row of buttons was an instant way to communicate one's status as a senior officer, somewhere from the grade of major to colonel. This was probably a proud moment after obtaining his colonelcy and taking command over a regiment of Black soldiers. He accentuates the two rows of buttons with his "hand-held-in" gesture, a cliché of nineteenth-century photography that aspiring common people used to communicate refinement and good breeding. His cuffs and collar appear to be made with dark velvet, an embellishment that was supposed to be unique to a general's jacket. It is also possible that he flipped down his collar to accentuate the dark lining, something that would have blurred the distinctions between a general's and colonel's jacket. On such distinctions, see article LI, "Uniform, Dress, and Horse Equipments," in *Revised United States Army Regulations of 1861* (Washington, DC: Government Printing Office, 1863), 462–81. *Photograph from author's collection*

PROLOGUE

A DOMESTIC TRAGEDY
(*in an* AMERICAN HOTEL)

MARY WEPT BEHIND HER VEIL. That is how fellow passengers remembered her the day of the dreadful event. They did not say if the veil was clipped into her hair or draped over a bonnet. They didn't say if it was sheer or if it was a crepelike material that hid her face. If they couldn't see her tears, they heard the sobs, as all remembered Mary Barto Cole crying on the train.

There was nothing unusual about a soldier's wife grieving in public, at least not since the destructive force of the recent war had begun cutting through American homes. Every adult on the train that day had seen young, weepy women in their widow's weeds.

Mary's husband, though, was sitting at her side. It was June 4, 1867, two years since the war had ended and over a year since he had returned home. The jostling railcar occasionally roused him from his vengeful stupor. He was dressed in thick gray woolen pants and a dark sack coat, the kind of clothes favored by laborers and soldiers. His eyes were bloodshot and swollen. The "General"—that's what George Washington Cole's friends often called him—at times rested his head against Mary's. At the St. Johnsville stop, he stepped from the train to get some food for her but took nothing for himself, though he had not eaten a meal for days.

He stared blankly. Tears occasionally welled up in his hornet-sting eyes as he tugged anxiously at the chevron mustache that covered his upper lip. Some passengers noted that blackish whiskers were scattered about his feet on the floor. The couple had boarded earlier that day in Syracuse, New York, where they had Mary's trunks, packed with two months of clothing, loaded onto the train. The General did not bring much besides a Colt revolver and a palm pistol. The couple was supposedly heading for Brooklyn, where Mary would remain until the trouble passed. She rightly sensed that her husband had something horrific brewing in his head. She dreaded the coming stop in Albany.

George was desperate to salvage himself—as he saw it, rescue his manhood—from the wreckage of the Civil War and the bleak life that had followed. His return to civilian life had brought one humiliation after the next. He had trouble finding and keeping a job. His war wounds nagged at him. They could not be heroically displayed before a camera or easily explained to acquaintances. He had nothing like an empty sleeve, pinned to his shoulder, to make plain to strangers what he had lost on some hallowed battlefield. Instead, his peculiar injuries traced back to insignificant skirmishes on nameless fields.

He and Mary were on the train because several days earlier, on a street in Syracuse, he had bumped into Luther Harris Hiscock, George's "bosom buddy" and family attorney. Hiscock had acted queerly, leaving George to nurse suspicions that his friend had dishonored him in some way. From trusted sources, the General eventually learned that during the war Mary had had sexual encounters with the lawyer. George could not be sure how often or how much Mary had consented; he only knew it had started while he had been fighting in Virginia and commanding mutinous Black soldiers in the borderlands of Mexico and Texas.

He had grown suspicious of a world where, in his mind, so little was given back to those most deserving. Hiscock had not fought in the war. Instead, he had recently won an election to the state assembly and by all accounts held a bright future. He was an ambitious man in a society that, fortunately for him, was robbed by war of many of its most talented men.

After the General confirmed his suspicions about his friend, he recalled that Hiscock was at Albany's state capitol, serving as a delegate for New York's constitutional convention, which was soon to convene. Desperate to humiliate Hiscock, George hatched a plot to take a train with Mary, track down his new enemy on the first day of the convention, corner him on the assembly floor, and make him beg like a dog for his life.

The train arrived in Albany too late for the General to make the sensational scene he had played out in his head. He checked Mary into a hotel, unsure for how long or where his bed would be that night. He met briefly with Mary's stepbrother, a convention delegate, who had never hidden his contempt for George's time serving over Black soldiers. The General left the meeting in frustration. With Mary's confession note in his jacket pocket—written in ink and amended in pencil—and two guns tucked away, he walked toward Albany's Stanwix Hall Hotel, where he spotted his nemesis in the lobby. In a circle of eminent men, Hiscock, who had just taken his evening tea and lounged in slippers, leaned against a pillar. Some claimed that he wore a set of shirt studs given to him during the war by Mary. The General stepped past the hotel front, slipped through the side door, and cut through a cluster of people, slackening his pace as he drew close. He raised his Derringer toward Hiscock's face and, stepping up to him, shot him point blank. Through the echoes of the explosion and confused gasps, the General exclaimed, "He's got it!"

That is, in the General's eyes, Hiscock had finally gotten what he had coming. Hiscock's large frame folded to the floor.

Friends recalled a sickening scene of contracting muscles, of spilt brains and black powder on his twitching face, of him rolling in blood on the black-and-white checkerboard floor of the lobby. Stunned, one of Hiscock's colleagues broke the silence, grabbing George by his shabby jacket and exclaiming, "Oh my God, General, what does this mean?" Almost every witness that evening would agree that the ex-soldier, while gesturing toward his coat pocket, calmly replied, "I considered that man one of my best friends, but he raped my simple, childlike wife while I was gone to war. . . . The evidence is clear, I have the proof!"[1]

With this single shot in an Albany hotel lobby, George Cole gained the fame that had eluded him in war.

★

MARY AND GEORGE COLE were born in neighboring villages in central New York, two generations after the American Revolution. They came of age in a place still marked with the brutal work of American empire: Relics in the dirt. Dispossessed Indians living on the margins of town. Swaths of forests felled by expeditions of conquest. Their grandparents had migrated to the Finger Lakes in the early days of the new United States to farm the fertile lands that had recently been seized from Iroquois tribes. In 1779, under order of General George Washington, American troops had razed every Indian village and all living quarters along a trail stretching hundreds of miles. Washington ordered his troops to extirpate the Iroquois, to achieve "total destruction and devastation" of their homes and villages; no peace agreements were to be made. Soldiers girdled orchard trees. They burned crops and seeds. They accomplished the extirpation, and immediately after the revolution, nearly two million acres were surveyed and mapped into square townships. In a show of reverence for ancient Greece and Rome, the townships were mostly named after ancient luminaries and war heroes like Pompey, Ovid, Scipio, Homer, and Hannibal.

Violence and war were part of the region's collective memory and inscribed on every map. Mary lived in a township named after Ulysses, the warrior in Homer's *Odyssey*. As the epic poem tells it, when Ulysses at last returns home from war to find men scheming to ensnare his wife, Penelope, he remorselessly butchers her suitors.

The celebrated violence of the ancient world was mapped onto Mary's little village. In 1851, Mary made vows in her parents' parlor to the young and handsome George Washington Cole, a mild-mannered, bookish doctor who had been named after America's venerated warrior. She would not have believed—despite the reverence for war that was everywhere—that she stood beside a man who, a decade and a half later, would return from the ravages of civil war transformed into a haggard-eyed American Ulysses.

As happened to Ulysses, the cycle of violence followed George home from war. Unlike Ulysses, he had to answer for murder. He was tried in the newspapers and twice before a jury of peers. The enduring themes found in Homer's *Odyssey*—manly honor, fate, and mankind's long journey home—resonated throughout the trials, but with uniquely American reverberations.

This book is about those reverberations and more. George was born into a society that only four decades earlier had been radically transformed by the cultural and political sea changes of American independence. As he grew from boy to man, in the 1830s and 1840s, a market revolution, early industrialization, and aggressive western expansion further transformed nearly every aspect of life.[2] The American Civil War was both a product of these transformations and a turbulent force for change. When George mustered out of service, America was a confusing echo chamber of hopes, changes and fears.

Already contested notions like human agency, friendship, and sanity would be debated in George's trial. Nothing was more contested, though, than the meaning of home and the duties a man and woman had to it. In the decades preceding the war, America's famously unsettled society had sentimentalized home—and the mothers within it—the more that men were absent. During the Civil War, Americans, whose families were traumatized and reconfigured by the conflict, further idealized home, even as they could never return to what it once had been. George was a sentimental father and husband who, like millions, exchanged his bedroom for a war tent. Five years later he returned to his cherished household, long after Mary had begun pleading with him to quit the war. He struggled with his homecoming and then killed a man in the name of protecting his home—a space that had become foreign to him.

Though he would be lionized as the defender of family and home, he had spent (and would spend) much of his life with other men, far from his family. In the following pages we encounter him in jail, away at school, killing on battlefields, at the office, performing rituals in a lodge, mingling in hotel lobbies, and chasing success on the frontier. What the newspapers called "a domestic tragedy" was, at core, a tale about American family strained by war and worldly ambition.

★

THE STORY OF GEORGE COLE invites us to probe some of America's foundational ideals—perhaps especially the most cherished ones. The architects of the United States depicted freedom and equality as the birthright given to humans by nature.[3] For Thomas Jefferson, the nation's purpose was to secure for men the freedom to pursue happiness. Abraham Lincoln would call this pursuit the "race of life." America is a promise—as awe-inspiring as it has been poorly kept—to make humans masters of their own destinies. No matter how halting and uneven its road to freedom has been, America *is* a story of progress.

The portrait of George Cole's America, however, summons us to consider the moral problem of freedom itself, especially when such expanding freedoms are tethered to individual happiness in a competitive realm. Is the story of freedom and equality—America's greatest gifts to humanity—by necessity the story of metastasizing individualism? Is the "pursuit of happiness" tied historically to ambition and the enlargement of the self at the expense of others? How has the supposed freedom to make one's own destiny shaped the way humans measure themselves and those around them? Do widening freedoms in modern societies—where one's status is supposedly determined by merit—spawn fretting about one's place in the world? Do they invite nursing of grudges about rigged systems? Do they promote seeing others through the lens of competition over community?

For well over a decade, I immersed myself in the world of a man whose troubled life raises these questions about American society. I have *worried* about the meaning of America and its most deadly war.[4] The surviving fragments from George's life do not fit nicely into some tidy historical thesis. No lived experience does. I have tried to let some of the rawness of experience simply be. Still, the fragments left from his existence, at least as I have laid them out, give form to a story about the national creed of self-making, and what many mean by "the American Dream."

I have scoured personal archives, newspapers, military records, and auctions for any source related directly to George. Still, for large portions of his life, the otherwise unremarkable man entirely vanishes from view. In the pages that follow, I often explore George's America through the experiences of his wife, his Black soldiers, fellow officers, and others. In the story I tell, George is something like the eye of a storm—the unstable, sometimes invisible center of a larger force swirling about him.

This force—of desperate self-making amid expanding freedoms—is so pervasive in the sources that it is at times astonishing. I want to be clear, though, that George's story is much too narrow to represent how "average" veterans experienced the Civil War and life after it. For many Union soldiers, the war brought intense pride, lifelong fraternity, and purpose. For Northerners, suffering and loss were infused with what they believed to be transcendent truths found in religion, patriotism, the sacrifice of oneself for community, and antislavery.[5]

The prevalence of sincere stories that lent meaning to such national loss surely caused many soldiers and families to endure torment in silence. George was not typical. But he was far from alone in his desperation to succeed in life. He was one of countless soldiers from Lincoln's massive army who were fated to wrestle with mental and physical wounds, and to spend the remainder of their lives searching for their place in a brutally competitive America. I believe his struggle, no matter how strange, tells us much about America in the Civil War era. His story speaks to the moral problem of freedom. So long as freedom is that mechanism that sorts out the deserving from the undeserving, and measures humans through merit in the so-called race of life, it is one of the greatest moral challenges of America and the modern world it has shaped.

A NOTE ON THE SOURCES

Newspaper accounts and court records have been invaluable to my research. They revealed some of the nature of Mary and Hiscock's secretive relations; they captured details of the core drama. But they rarely rippled outward beyond the murder and the weeks leading up to it. My attempt to tell George's story would have been impossible without the war's unprecedented expansion of the army and its vast—if less than reliable—recordkeeping apparatus. Terse regimental records, courts-martial (military trials), and pension documents have been vital in uncovering aspects of the war that can only be described as brutal, godless confusion.

Most of what I know about George's intimate suffering and wild visions is only knowable because of private letters, which were written during the war, from his jail cell, and in his vexed life following his exoneration. They were preserved by descendants of George's older brother and US senator Cornelius Cole. Successful men like Senator Cole bequeathed fortunes, as well as dry attics and other secure spaces, to family (often women) who ensured the preservation of letters, journals, and keepsakes. Today, vestiges of George's private struggles are pressed into manila folders in archives at the University of California, Los Angeles, swallowed up and scattered within some eighty boxes of documents that mostly relate to Cornelius's political and business legacy. Thanks to the work of descendants to preserve the charmed life of his brother, I was able to write about George's struggle to become "somebody" in America.

NOTA BENE

Readers might take interest in the extended notes that I have made available on a companion website: StrangeAndTragicWounds.com. There I drill deeper into various aspects of the story, venture further down into interesting caverns, and discuss problems with some of the sources. It is there that one will find more analysis of relevant scholarship and of George's society. There one can find a bibliography and additional images, including reproductions of some of the primary sources.

The symbol ‡ appears in the end-of-book notes to indicate whenever more can be found on the website.

For the sake of economy, all sources have been reduced to acronyms; bibliographic information for them is provided in "Key to Sources Cited."

PART I

BRED *in the* BONE

That Will Show in the Flesh which is Bred in the Bone;
From this Law in Nature, Escape there is None.

—CORNELIUS COLE, George's older brother

CHAPTER ONE

AMERICA, REPUBLIC
without GRACE

CHILDHOOD IS THE STORY that adults wear out their lives trying to resolve. Little is known about prisoner George Cole's youth. His parents marked him at birth with the young nation's revered past. It was the start of a peculiarly American tale.

★

HIS MOTHER, Rachel Townsend Cole, would have first suspected she was pregnant with him in the surrounding weeks, or days, when Americans learned of the deaths of John Adams and Thomas Jefferson. A seemingly supernatural event choreographed by God, both Founders had died on the Fourth of July, on the fiftieth anniversary of America's Declaration of Independence.

Rachel had already given birth to eight children. She likely suspected that something was different. If not, on March 26, 1827, through labor pangs she learned that she had been carrying twins. She and her husband, David, drew from the American Revolution's military pantheon for names. The first boy they named George Washington. The other they called Joseph Warren, after the major general who engaged in the first battles at Lexington and Concord, and who was one of the first martyrs of the revolution.

Less than a month later, George's infant brother died. There is no record of why. The family buried him in a cemetery near the farm. Baby Joseph's namesake had famously been killed at Bunker Hill in the first throes of the revolution. The Cole family couldn't have missed the parallels. Washington—or "Wash," as they often called George—had survived the all-too-early death of his brother, Joseph Warren.[1]

The naming of children merely hinted at the ways the revolution continued to shape daily life. The American Revolution was like the sun after it has set; apparently gone, its incomparable, borrowed energy continued to animate life everywhere in the republic. What was seemingly gone was everywhere.[2]

The military triumph of American patriots had cleared the way for a world-changing experiment that elevated man's role in the unfolding drama of the cosmos. Emboldened by Enlightenment optimism in human capacity, the Founders engineered a government (and, by extension, a society) that promised citizens the freedom to pursue happiness, in which one would reap rewards according to merit. This was a principal purpose of government. James Madison, the architect of America's constitution, said that the first object of government was to protect the "different and unequal faculties" of its people—their unequal talents—that naturally yield inequality in wealth and property. America existed, in other words, to ensure that inequalities in wealth and power were the results of unequal capacities, not unequal chances.[3]

In the two generations between the revolution and George Cole's childhood, ordinary Americans came to believe that they had constructed, or were constructing, a society ordered by merit. The Christianity they digested at the table and from the pews made the ordering seem divinely inspired. They saw themselves as part of a perpetually unfolding tale of progress in which children, through their own merits, worked tirelessly to reap the fruits of their labors and surpass the limitations of their parents.

Never, in any place in the world, had so many ordinary folks believed, and lived as if, they managed their own destinies. And perhaps, never had ambition so regularly gnawed away at so many, especially among the descendants of Puritans who migrated to frontiers such as upstate and western New York.[4]

Less than two years before George's birth, New York State finished constructing the Erie Canal, a 350-mile artificial river that connected the Hudson River to Lake Erie, seeming proof that Americans really could make their own fate. By the time young George began walking, tributary canals connected the Erie Canal to Seneca and Cayuga Lakes. The budding society he was born into was soon transformed by the brisk exchange of crops, lumber, clothing, furniture, and all manner of finished goods to and from New York City and beyond. The first railroads soon followed, bringing more goods to farming families, opening up commercial opportunities, and arousing ambitions for a people who had already laid claim to some two-thirds of what would eventually become the contiguous United States.[5] On lands brutally stolen from Indians, American children grew hungry for a prosperity their parents had never known.

ORDINARY SCHOOLING FED THE HUNGER. George's brother Cornelius described their district schooling as more useful than ornamental. The studies comprised what "Mr. Lincoln called the three R's: reading, 'riting, and 'rithmatic."[6] George carried books on his three-mile walks to and from school. He kept a copy of one book, *Latin Grammar*, in his pocket so he could sneak passages as he tended to his family's crops.

He graduated from district school to Lima Seminary, a preparatory academy founded by Methodists. Professor Alverson, who taught mathematics there, declared that George learned the most rapidly of any student he ever knew.[7] His journey from district school to academy was a crowded path.[8] George, many of his siblings, and Luther Harris Hiscock were part of a generation who cut their teeth during the "age of academies." Between the revolution and the Civil War, Americans erected thousands of academies. Hundreds of thousands of parents, many from farming communities, sent their children—often away to board—to learn under the tutelage of schoolmasters. Unlike Latin schools for the privileged, these academies admitted any child whose parents could scrape together the funds.[9] There were likely more than six thousand such American academies by 1850. They sprang up disproportionately in New York State, especially in the upstate farming lands.[10]

Some of the children from the Cole family attended the Ovid Academy. For economy's sake, Cornelius boarded there during the weekdays. As the next-youngest son, George almost certainly did too. It was seven miles from their farm. The academy had strict curfews and codes of behavior; over one hundred students lived under the watch of faculty trained in New England colleges.[11] Academies across the republic prepared children for the marketplace by encouraging close friendships, or partnerships, as well as competitive factions among young peers. Rivalries abounded between antebellum academies; students learned that they were in competition with one another. Their peers were potential friends or opponents.[12]

The academies prided themselves on a practical pedagogy, often "fitting" students for college and professional careers. As early as 1819, critics noted the disturbing departure from the classics and an increasing emphasis on business success. One critic in a British magazine complained that the education was tailored to "the counter and the counting-room." As far as that object went, he scoffed, "there is no striking defect in them; it not being a difficult matter to teach a lad to count his fingers and take care of his dollars."[13]

The privileged Charles Francis Adams Jr. (who had commanded Black troops and served near Cole in the war) would come to despise the fact that his father had not sent him away to the kind of boarding schools attended by the Cole children. "I should have been compelled to rough it with other boys," Adams wrote. He resented the refining, emasculating education that his elite parents insisted on, instead wishing he had been taught to wrestle and compete and been "rubbed" into shape. He wished that he had been trained in the ways his and Cole's contemporaries had been, to grab for more, and that he had been better prepared for competitive manhood and counting winnings.[14]

IN 1847, George began attending Wesleyan, a Methodist university in Middletown, Connecticut, nearly three hundred miles east of his home by Seneca Lake. The bonds of family soon pulled him back. In his second year, his older sister Emeline—"how dear to me"—grew seriously ill. Her sickness and eventual death appear to have led to George's own failing health. His condition grew so grave that he had to return to live under his parents' roof, where he shed nearly fifty pounds.

In a letter to a pious schoolmate, an emaciated George complained about his separation from his buddies. His sight was failing. His tone suggested that even if he could read, he would need to return to college to find inspiring books. His parents, too, bordered on death from grief. He yearned to get back to school and to escape "the status quo."

"I have seen my own bright hopes and anticipation recede from my grasp," he wrote, "and I know not how distant the time may be when I may again live, for this dull monotonous existence cannot be called by that name."[15] His home became a place of sickness and mourning, where loved ones edged their way toward their tombs. He loved his family. But, in this letter at least, he came to feel for his folks' home as one might for a graveyard—sober respect tinged with a sense that it was no place for the living to long remain.

After the family doctor informed him that he would not return to Wesleyan that year, George wrote to ask his friend to sell his school possessions—his table, mirror, washstand, and two chairs—and forward him the money. He asked to be remembered by a schoolmate, Thomas Gould, but then corrected himself midparagraph when he recalled that Gould had recently died of typhus fever. "But his spirit is now as near to me as you. Poor Gould, How I was shocked to hear of his death, but 'pallida mors acquo &c,'" he wrote, drawing from the Roman poet Horace and his Latin ode observing that "pale death knocks at the doors of all alike."[16] George could talk about death to his college peers in ways that he probably could not with his father and mother.

He longed to return to college, where it would be his "turn to shine some day." He claimed that he took joy in his classmates' current prosperity and that he yearned to grasp their hands again. It was common for young men of George's generation to form intimate, romantic attachments to male friends. It was a useful brotherly love between aspiring young men. They needed hands to clasp that could guide them through a fast-changing world that their fathers had little experience navigating.[17]

His tender letters and longing to grasp hands were the product of a new kind of society; it was how young men found their way, with less dependence on fathers, through the maze of American opportunity and risk. Vertical relations, between fathers and sons, no longer held as much value as horizontal bonds between friends. Male intimacy between chums emboldened American sons to follow their ambitions away from their parents' farms.[18]

★

AT WESLEYAN, George learned that not only was man generally good but, when infused with faith, so were his worldly ambitions. This thinking had long been preached in America's Protestant churches. During the two centuries from the birth of the American colonies to the birth of George Cole, a changing Christianity fundamentally transformed how Americans viewed the nature of man. The stern teachings of Calvinism, in which God saved only those whom he selected, gave way to a view of a God too kind and loving to condemn kind and loving humans to hell. God's power to save was diminished, man's elevated. When the first Puritan settlers arrived in America in the 1630s, salvation was obtained through miraculous grace; by George's day, salvation was largely a matter of merit.[19]

This kind of religious thinking, so prominent in America's era of revivals (which spread wildly in the days of George's youth), swept over much of the nation, but especially in northern towns and cities like those that dotted the canals in upstate New York.[20] This change in outlook—and the gradual grinding down of the sharp edges of Calvinist teachings—gutted the once mysterious, passive miracle of grace, transforming it into a process of self-mastery where humans controlled their own fate.[21]

American churches spread a new self-mastery gospel. And no church spread like that of the Methodists. George's family was one of the many who settled in western lands, drifted from their Calvinist moorings, and began attending church with the

Methodists.[22] By the time George was an adolescent, Methodists had more members than the combined total of fellow Presbyterians, Congregationalists, Lutherans, Episcopalians, and other Reformed churches. Only Baptists came close. In the first decades following independence, Methodism especially attracted salt-of-the-earth believers. Methodist pews originally teemed with lowly laborers, subsistence farmers, women, free Black people, enslaved people, and young folks without roots. But by the time George had left for war, Methodism had become the gospel of success.

As Methodists became a people of refined taste, they blazed the trail that the rest of America's evangelicals would soon travel. More than any other denomination, they seized on tools of the market to spread the good word. They fanned out across the nation, down countless turnpikes and back roads, to peddle the gospel. They formed complex networks of circuits, stations, districts, and general conferences. They published religious newspapers with unrivaled reach. They formed the first denominational publishing house.

The Methodist message (and the means of spreading it) drew from and advanced early capitalism. From the beginning, Methodists preached a gospel of self-improvement and industry to countless American plain folk who, though they may have distrusted well-heeled bankers, plantation owners, and urban elites, had internalized the connection between rising in the world and virtuous striving. Their gospel of striving was particularly alive at Wesleyan, where George learned to see his dear parents' home as a place for falling behind or dying.[23]

Since its founding by Methodists in 1831, Wesleyan steadily attracted small cohorts of aspiring young men from all over the country, most heavily from New York. Methodists could no longer be accurately ridiculed, as they had been in the young nation, for their folksy preaching and crude education. When the Cole brothers attended Wesleyan, Methodist leaders could boast of some nineteen Methodist colleges and universities, nearly seventy academies, and two theological seminaries.

In an era when college presidents had powerful sway over the minds of undergraduates, the first Wesleyan president, Willbur Fisk, espoused a more practical and "useful education." Fisk built an institution that sought to make "the pupil a man of enterprise and activity." For a man to reach his highest potential, Fisk taught, he "must be put upon his own resources, and must understand, [that] if he is ever any thing, he must make himself; and that he has within himself all the means for his own advancement."[24]

By the time George arrived at Wesleyan, the school had built a reputation for converting farmers' sons into ministers, teachers, and lawyers. Business, though, had dominated the hearts of the students. During the school's first half century, alumni wound up in trade and business more than any other vocation. Even students who stuck with farming would return home to their plots with more technical understanding of agriculture and increased market savvy.[25]

During George's stint at Wesleyan, President Stephen Olin, an ordained Methodist minister, presented himself as a surrogate father who molded his sons into successful men.[26] Students dressed in locally made uniforms consisting of black stockings, tall black hats, and stiff white collars. They couldn't call buddies from windows, carry canes into rooms, or play cards. They had to be in chapel for prayer by five forty-five in the morning.[27]

Olin used religion to fan the flames of worldly ambition. In one speech to George's fellow students, he argued that to deny America one's talents would be "nothing less than treason." The nation needed to be led by "educated, vigorous, laborious, enterprising men." He observed a "vulcanic energy" across the nation that drove scientific enterprise, manufacturing, and infrastructure improvements like railroads, turnpikes, and canals. The young generation, he warned, would face eternal shame if it did not harness the "full tide" of improvement.[28]

George's generation could not afford to simply pass on the torch as it had burned before. They had to bring "new light, and vivacity, and momentum" that would quicken and multiply the energies of all worthy enterprises. Olin insisted, of course, that the young men redouble their moral commitment to God. The market had to be turned into a tool for Christ. The church could "usher in the millennium" only if it could first channel the world's advancements toward the Kingdom.[29]

For the large-framed minister—who was known for weeping and extending his long, trembling arms from the pulpit as if reaching for the lapels of his students—this was no mere rhetorical exercise. For a society awash with vain ambition, confidence men, alcohol, quackery, and demagoguery, only religion and education possessed "the true panacea." Only with the aid of the rugged cross and schoolbooks would young men choose holy duties over the "incitements to selfishness and ambition which throng the avenues to professional life."[30]

His core message held the tension of an overtightened bow. He warned against the siren song of the world—and then sang that song to promote Christianity. Faith would chasten them but would never "dim" their worldly aspirations. Biblical truths lent clarity to enterprising men. The "business of life is simplified" by Christ's gospel. Those fools who rejected God's guiding light fell behind. Lacking clear convictions, unconverted men dithered and faltered, sure to lose energy because of the "insufficiency of worldly motives."[31]

In case he wasn't clear enough in his hours-long lecture, the president of Wesleyan promised the young men that Christians would "advance in the race." If they doubted that God was in all their "schemes" or that heaven's blessing was not behind some venture, they would second-guess themselves. Doubt destroyed effort. Piety would sustain them while godless men flitted from one half-hearted ambition to the next. Only in the devoted life could they locate the "secret of all eminent success." Christ, Wesleyan students were assured, would purify and reward worldly ambition.[32]

George's college president had wanted his pupils to consider entering the ministry or perhaps become teachers. But his own words betrayed his knowledge about where most of them were bound. Despite much pleading about the urgent need for repentance and allowing the word of God to take root in the soul, his teachings revealed fear that his students could not resist the pull of the world.

At the time George was immersed in this Wesleyan culture, commercial pursuits for wealth were widely celebrated in the North—if sometimes denounced—as the measure of a man's talent and the great equalizing force in America. The "trading spirit" and "anxious spirit of gain," as one worried Yankee preacher called them, had taken possession of Americans everywhere. At Wesleyan, George had lived in a hive of religiously infused striving. He longed to be around fellow strivers. But his mental breakdown, and the death of his sister Emeline, had gotten in the way. He had feared falling behind his classmates and getting stuck in the sphere of his parents. He was a Methodist boy who had taken his school lessons to heart.[33]

CHAPTER 2

to SEE OURSELVES *as* OTHERS SEE US

WHILE GEORGE WAS AT COLLEGE, then sick at home, the nation expanded by more than a million square miles through war and treaty. The volcanic energies that the Wesleyan president hoped to pair with Christianity were channeled into military conflict with Mexico from 1846 to 1848.

Though George and a few of his brothers were of fighting age and drawn to military life, none of them volunteered for the Mexican War.[1] Some of them, though, raced soon after to the lands wrested from Mexico. In 1849 two of his older brothers, Cornelius and Elijah, recruited a party to cross the continent in pursuit of gold in California's foothills. Cornelius, who had recently graduated from Wesleyan, had begun studying law under the tutelage of William Henry Seward (who would later serve as Abraham Lincoln's secretary of state), and he longed to take his legal training and aspirations to the Pacific coast. The Cole boys brought their plans to their father. He studied their maps of the lands freshly stripped from Mexico and gave his blessing.[2]

George stayed behind. He may have still been suffering from his illness. Maybe he had nobler ambitions. It was said that he came to believe that medicine was his calling while under the care of the village physician and that his brush with death turned him to the compassionate and respected art of healing. In the Coles' village, according to Cornelius, physicians held more prestige than ministers.[3]

★

AFTER HIS OLDER BROTHERS lit out for the West, George began his studies at a medical college in Geneva, New York. In 1851 he started practicing medicine in the village of Trumansburg—in the town of Ulysses, only ten miles from his boyhood farm, where Mary Barto, the stepdaughter of a local judge, won his attention.[4] There is no surviving image of Mary. She was noted for her "unusual attractions of person and mind," and for a body "robust and athletic." She knew how "to make herself agreeable in company."[5]

Her family had been some of the first White people to settle in the Finger Lakes region after American soldiers had driven out Iroquois Indians. If George and Mary had not already known each other, their kin had crossed paths many times. Within a half year, a minister married them in her parents' home parlor.[6]

The newlyweds moved to nearby Havana in 1852 or 1853, when the hamlet was ripe with optimism. The Finger Lakes village was positioned along the Chemung Canal, which fed into the mouth of Seneca Lake just to the north, across which goods were ferried to and from the Erie Canal. Havana had been built on the ashes of the Iroquois settlement first destroyed by an expedition of American revolutionary soldiers; it boasted its own bank and plank sidewalks that were expanding along the fronts of stores. Brick and stone had begun replacing wood. An Episcopalian church was constructed in 1853, a sure sign that "respectable" Christians had a presence in the village. A few years before, a village newspaper bragged that Havana played a notable part in the "onward progress" of the country, with its "crowd of customers trafficing within the stores," the "endless" lumber and produce consumed by locals, and, most of all, the "unquestionable solvency of nearly all the business men."[7]

George was drawn by this promise of commercial "onward progress" in Havana. He bought out a pharmacy and bookstore located right between Havana's parallel canal and railroad line.[8] (His attorneys would later claim that he abandoned medicine because of his "peculiarly" sensitive temperament. They said that, after several seasons, he couldn't bear it when his patients succumbed to sickness and death.) His store stocked a motley inventory of cures and goods for self-improvement and refinement: putty and paint to repair furniture and brighten drab walls; cream for blotchy skin; ornate lamps; scripture and sentimental novels; writing slates for students; trusses for hernias; perfume; and diaries.

He purchased several advertisements in the local *Havana Journal* to alert his neighbors where they could find medicines, oils, lamps, "School Books! School Books!!," pills that would treat anything from asthma to "worms of all kinds," and other cures.[9] His store was one among thousands that sprang up in towns and villages during the first half of the nineteenth century that, along with traveling salesmen, provided mass-market goods for ordinary people who were determined to improve their lives. The objects flowing from New York City, Rochester, Elmira, London, Boston, and artisan shops across upstate New York and central Pennsylvania allowed his neighbors to show others (and themselves) what they were making of life's opportunities.[10]

Material possessions were the mark of one's character and diligence, applied from behind the plow, workbench, or desk. In a fluid society without titles of nobility, material possessions were proof of one's earned standing. George's shop sold the props of merit, the treasured objects that, like relics displayed in a Catholic church, made the gospel of American success palpable and believable.[11]

Props increasingly crowded the stage, such as satin damask sofas, grandfather clocks, daguerreotypes set in gilded frames, diamond-tufted cushions, oval marble tables, and piano fortes. Gradually, increased wealth from expanding markets drew more toilers into the performance. George's store was stocked with hundreds of things that, like touchstones, seemed to verify the personal worth of a customer and, in so doing, validated the glittering claim of America. Ordinary people were not destined to remain within the material and financial restraints felt by their parents.[12]

★

BOOKS, like the ones George stocked in his bookstore (or the many he later had delivered to his cell), were a common touchstone for aspiring Americans. They were an essential luxury needed to improve the self.[13] George's parents had owned books. Cornelius remembered that a bible and a few books were found in every farmhouse in the village. But when family members had desired more, they borrowed copies from the district library system, which had been adopted by New York State when George was a young boy.[14]

George opened his bookstore betting that families had come to see books as private property and less as communal sources of knowledge. He needed customers who believed that they needed to read (or appear to read) the books they displayed in their homes. During the first half of the nineteenth century, the growing ownership of bookcases in towns and villages—something rare in the previous century—meant expanding personal libraries. A private library displayed in a parlor bookcase was becoming one of the clearest marks of refined tastes and self-improvement. Booksellers' advertisements in

Havana's papers were surrounded by publicity for gewgaws, ornamental lamps, beautifully tinted wall paint, and diaphanous window shades. Together, the things and the books distinguished the aspiring farmer from the plodder who was contented to remain in the material and intellectual ruts of his father. They were testaments to a carefully managed life.

George's store stocked "cheap publications" but also advertised higher-quality books, especially gift books, which were popular annual publications. Gift books often had embossed or varnished covers and contained moral tales, sentimental poetry, and gorgeous prints from steel or copper engravings on the finest paper. Such fine books were meant to be displayed where guests could see them. One's library was designed to be gazed on as much as read.[15]

IN EARLY 1853, George converted the space above his bookstore into a place where locals could document their improving condition. He built a daguerrean gallery, a studio for making daguerreotypes, one of the earliest forms of photography. Within the span of a single morning, his customers could pose before the camera and then cup in their palms an image of their bettered selves. There was a lot of money to be made from providing this miraculous experience. In the 1840s, some three million such likenesses were created each year by Americans who tried, often again and again, to capture something elusive in themselves.[16]

George took to the craft just after its heyday, starting up against stiff competition from other local daguerrean photographers, especially William Brown, who plied the trade in Elmira, nineteen miles south. Brown ran his own advertisement, conspicuously placed just below George's in a local newspaper, that claimed he had five years of experience. He apparently did brisk business but saw smaller galleries like George's as a threat. Before Brown began advertising in the same paper and same column, he modified his Elmira advertisement, adding these words: "TRUTH IS MIGHTY and WILL PREVAIL." He made new assurances. He claimed that he had won prizes for his work from artists and judges who had pronounced it the "best ever seen in Elmira, and equal to any taken in the large cities."[17]

New to the business, and up against a fierce competitor, George attested to customers that he had just purchased "German instruments" along with all the latest improvements in New York City. He had also furnished his gallery "without reference to expense." He was saying what any daguerrean had to say. His improvements in the gallery would allow him to capture the elegant improvements of his customers.[18]

Both George's and Brown's galleries were constructed above bookstores. Customers leafed through books on the ground floor while sitters above posed in natural light that shone through a roof window diffused with blue filters.[19] Photographers attempted to make likenesses seem like other genteel works of art. Brown boasted that his guests would be pleased by his "walls adorned" with fine art, sketches of famous Americans like Henry Clay and Daniel Webster, and daguerreotypes of Jenny Lind (a beloved Swedish opera singer), William Graham (a former secretary of the navy), and Millard Fillmore, whose three-year presidency had recently come to an end. Like the painted portraits of dukes and duchesses or the likenesses of political giants, ordinary people's images deserved to be gazed on. Framed by gilded or intricately carved wood, their likenesses belonged on the walls or bookcases of decorated parlors.

George's advertisement stood out from those of his competitors. It was more philosophical and somber. At the top, he quoted a line from Robert Burns, the Scottish "ploughman poet," who wrote in the tongue of Lowland Scots. The line comes from a poem about wanting to see oneself as others do: "Oh, wad some power the giftie gie us, to see oursels as others see us" (Oh, would some power give us the gift to see ourselves as others do). By quoting Burns, he signaled to readers his own elevated tastes. And by telling readers that Burns was an

> **NEW DAGUERREIAN GALLERY.**
>
> "Oh, wad some power the giftie gie us, To see oursels as others see us."
>
> So wrote the eminent poet, Robert Burns.
>
> AN OPPORTUNITY is now offered to carry out the poets suggestion. The subscriber, Dr. George W. Cole, would respectfully idform the public, that they are now opening a permanent Daguerrean Gallery, is the Canal Buildings, over the Drug Store, furnished without reference to expense, and conducted in such a manner as to make it an agreeable and pleasant place of resort and every way worthy the attention of the public.
>
> Mr. C. Would also state, that he has just returned from the city, with an improved set of German Instruments, together with all the late improvements, which will need but to be seen and tested to be appreciated.
>
> The value of these keepsakes are not appreciated until we are deprived of the society of those we esteem. How many have lost a Father Mother, or a darling child without a shadow t recall their features. After the separation some little tcy or trifling article of apparel is often k pt, cherished for years as a token of remembrance— How much more valued would be a well executed Daguerreotype of the loved and lost. Are you a parent ! what wo'd you not give for a likeness when a child, it would show the effects of time, and recall many pleasant recollections. This opportunity you can now afford to your children, and should they be snatched from your embrace by the cold hand of death, your possession of their Daguerreotype, if taken by a good artist, would afford sweet consolation.
>
> If the present opportunity is improved, you may at some future period, have reason to feel grateful for these gentle hints from Dr. G. W. Cole, Daguerrean, who can always be found at his Rooms, where the citizens of Havana, and surrounding country, are respectfully invited to call.
>
> April 16, 1853.   1tf

George Cole placed this advertisement for his gallery in a small-town newspaper teeming with ads for cures, health products, furniture, clothing, and books—the objects of refinement that so many of his American peers used to measure personal worth and success. More than any other technology, photography gave his contemporaries a sense of controlling their identity and the perceptions of others. *Courtesy of Thomas Tryniski, owner of the website Fulton History, www.fultonhistory.com*

"eminent" poet, he revealed that he was not merely selling refinement to the refined but trying to attract less polished, aspiring individuals into his gallery of miracles.

George understood that photography promised to resolve the irksome mystery of how one was perceived by others. A fixed image offered confidence, even mental rest, for aspiring people trying to find their place in a nation in flux. Through a set of controlled rituals, customers struck a pose, revealed their finest attire, and often held a book or another possession in their hands as they attempted to capture themselves as they longed to be seen. Unlike the mirror, which could only hold such an illusion for a moment, and which no other person could see at the exact same angle, the photograph promised to permanently capture how one wished to be seen while also addressing the confusion of how one was seen through the eyes of others. The likeness gave the illusion that one could somehow control a multiplicity of perceptions in a society of moving people. This was desperately needed magic for the problem of American ambition. The miracle of the daguerreotype was that it seemed to transform unstable images of the self into a permanent manifestation of personhood. George may have been a hack at the craft, but he understood what he was selling.[20]

HIS LOVE for reading and writing poetry was evident in his first advertisements. So was some of his deepest pain. About a third of the ad dwells on death and the loss of loved ones. "How many have lost a Father, Mother, or a darling child without a shadow to recall their features?" he asked. It was something he could speak to honestly, from experience with patients who had been found dead in the morning to having lost his sister and his infant twin brother before the availability of photographic likenesses.

His camera would reduce the sting of death for parents with young children especially. "Should [your babes] be snatched from your embrace by the cold hand of death, your possession of their Daguerreotype, if taken by a good artist, would afford sweet consolation." He printed these "gentle hints" around the same time that, within the walls of his own home, he and his young family had been fending off the hand of death.

In the spring of 1853 Mary gave birth to their first child, Fanny. Soon, both mother and baby contracted a severe case of malaria. In Havana, a swampy, muddy town, mosquitoes were a pestilence. Facing the prospect of burying his own wife and child, and knowing that many in town contracted the same deadly ague, George moved his family back to Trumansburg, where Mary's folks lived. He continued his business for a while, but circumstances soon forced him to sell his interests.[21]

By 1855, Mary was well enough to conceive and carry to term their second daughter, Alice. The next year the Coles moved again. This time they turned to farming in the western end of George's childhood village. He had witnessed the many farmers who had made a prosperous life by sending grain, wool, clover seed, salt beef, apples, honey, and wax along the lake to the Cayuga-Seneca Canal and then to the Erie Canal.[22]

Medicine, his book- and drugstore, and the photography gallery had not worked out for him as he had hoped. Neither was farming kind to him. Times had changed. The expanding markets, made possible by rails and canals, had transformed farming in his childhood village. By midcentury, local farmers had primarily planted the cash wheat crops of White Flint and Old Red Chaff. Yet competing farms to the west, especially the prairies, were driving wheat profits down. Maybe George believed he could improve on the farming he had learned from his father or become a new breed of farmer, one who embraced the agricultural science taught at Wesleyan. This new science was widely celebrated and promised to be taught in newly chartered agricultural colleges in upstate New York.[23]

Whatever George's struggles had been with the shifting world of farming, by various accounts, Mary grew unhappy with life on the farm. She may have wished to escape the solitude of rural life and young motherhood. As his friends would tell it, George gave up the farm in response to Mary's longing to socialize and to be in the company of refined folks. They said she was "much accustomed to society" and that she grew miserable with her retirement to the country.[24] It was a story about unfulfilled aspirations that everybody knew—and was likely true.

The desire to leave the world of planting was a common symptom of a wife's worldly ambitions. The dread of country life is echoed again and again in sentimental fiction of the era, in which young heroines rise from hayseed obscurity and shine in the city or bustling town. In these stories, the journey often begins in the country cottage. But the heroine is destined to be discovered by refined people. Americans read over and over how, after some heroine's simple virtues come to light, she is thrust into a dazzling world where she gains deserved attention. The stories would have meant many things to the many readers, but they revealed a shared hope that worthy women would be plucked from their limited spheres behind cottage doors and exalted to high society.[25]

When Mary's stepfather died in 1857, she inherited enough money to at last seek her place in the city. George followed her there. They hoped a city of strangers would see them as they dearly wanted to be seen. That anxious desire to take part in the world, increasingly felt by women, further drove a wedge between them. George's struggles to make something of himself had been tied to his wife's own awakened ambitions.

CHAPTER 3

the FALSE DAWN *of* SENECA FALLS

MARY BARTO WAS NOT YET SIXTEEN WHEN, in 1848, the Seneca Falls Convention on women's rights—the first of its kind in the world—took place less than thirty miles from her village. She was still three years from wooing George when Elizabeth Cady Stanton, Lucretia Mott, and some three hundred others gathered in a brick Methodist church known for opening its doors to social reformers. The convention sent ripples into the Barto home, where conversations about women's rights would have invited suspicion, if not alarm, at least among its male members.[1]

The convention's participants resolved that women were men's equals and that foolish women should be kept from publishing declarations to the contrary. Many of the attendees signed their names to the "Declaration of Sentiments," a manifesto for women's rights patterned on the Declaration of Independence and its denunciation of King George III. In the Seneca Falls declaration, the transgressions of King George became the sins of every George—the "repeated injuries and usurpations on the part of man toward woman." Man had kept woman back from public life. He had barred her from using her full talents and from equal avenues toward "wealth and distinction." He stunted her ambition and robbed her of its fruits.

Most of all, the declaration decried the fact that when a woman married, she was deemed "civilly dead" in the eyes of the law. Much more than a rally for women's vote (an issue that caused deep division at the convention), Seneca Falls was about the unrealized self. Much of the focus was on the half selfhood that women experienced in wedlock. Marriage was women's central problem.

★

WOMEN'S RIGHTS REFORMERS depicted coverture—the legal fiction that in marriage a husband *covered* his wife's legal and social identity—as the single greatest obstacle to women's happiness. Decades after Seneca Falls, advocates like Stanton would paint coverture as a hulking Goliath that came tumbling down with the passage of the Married Women's Property Acts, the first of which passed in New York in 1848.[2]

But most of the political players who brought about the passage of the property acts, one might say, were more concerned with protecting every down-on-his-luck George than they were with the rights of any Mary. A major impetus behind the property acts was that by forming a legal boundary between a husband's and wife's estate, the man and his dependents would be partly protected from devastating business failure and debt. The cultural power of coverture was hardly stopped by reforms in women's property rights.[3]

For Mary and many other New York women, coverture did not disappear with the property acts. Legislators did not free them from coverture or make them masters of their own money and property.[4] New York judges instead nullified the various acts by continuing to view cases through the lens of coverture; they often placed great burdens of proof on wives to demonstrate separate estates.[5] Regardless of what judges did, ordinary wives and husbands mostly lived their lives as if little had changed. Most wives did not bring separate estates to their marriages, did not partition familial possessions, and did not support themselves with their own wages. Couples tended to view intermingled assets as primarily the husband's. Wives who did have separate estates often signed them over to their husbands in times of financial desperation—something that Mary would later do for George, or would promise to do, before the war.[6]

Mary's story was one about American women's expanded property rights and how legislation only partly delivered women to the shores of selfhood. Like Mary, countless other women—often in contention with their husbands, mothers, fathers, brothers, and judges—swam against the currents and undertow of law and the enduring habits of family.

MARY HAD AN ACTUAL GEORGE TO contend with, and two Henrys besides. In November 1848—only seven months after New York passed the Married Women's Property Act of 1848—her aging father, Henry Barto Sr., made out his will. He intended to leave Mary and Henry Barto Jr., his son from his first marriage, a significant inheritance.[7] Minus a modest amount left for his widow and extended family, the rest was to be split evenly between Mary and Henry Jr.[8]

It is not clear whether her father had simply assumed that Mary's estate would naturally become her future husband's as tradition dictated or whether, instead, her father wished to pass his money to her alone, to be kept as an estate separate from her future husband, as recent legislation promised he could.[9]

When Henry Sr. died, nearly a decade later, in February 1857, Mary had been married to George for over six years. They lived on their farm, in George's boyhood village of Lodi, with two young daughters. Despite the property acts of 1848 and 1849, Mary would watch her supposed rights dissolve into traditional family practices enforced by the community, particularly its male members.

The devil was in the details of routine paperwork and the will's distribution. As the executor of his father's estate, Henry Jr., her stepbrother, provided a simple list of those named in the will. Even though their father's will had made no mention of Mary's future husband, George's name was written into the first petition. After listing Frances (Mary's widowed mother) and himself, her brother wrote, "Mary B. Cole^{wife of Geo. W. Cole} residing in the town of Lodi, Seneca County U.S., both of full age." Henry Jr. had added "wife of Geo. W. Cole" in the tight space above Mary's name, maybe for clarification, or simply because of the tradition of identifying a married woman through her husband's surname. In the most humdrum details of the first petition, her selfhood was fastened to George's.

In the official notification six days later, the county judge required those named in the original will—in which, again, George was not named—to appear before him in his office in Ithaca. The notification was addressed to the relevant parties in a slightly different way, listing all the heirs, starting with the mother, followed by "George W Cole & Mary B Cole his wife residing in the town of Lodi in Seneca County N.Y."

The official notice transformed George into one of the will's intended recipients, while Mary became "his wife," an appendage to him. Eleven days later, in sworn testimony, Henry Jr. said that he had personally delivered the notification to "Frances Barto[,] George W. Cole and Mary B. Cole," "the persons" named in the will.

Henry Jr. knew better than anybody that George had not been in the will. Regardless of recent laws passed, the inheritance was doomed to be confused as her husband's. This was not some calculated legal sleight of hand but instead appears to be the result of husbands, clerks, and judges (and perhaps wives) talking and thinking as they were accustomed to do.

Mary's legal right to receive an inheritance began evaporating in the tedium of administrative paperwork. Her brother and the magistrate wrote in the traditional language of coverture. Regardless of what had been guaranteed by the recent property acts, George became part of the will's legal distribution, and she became a mere part of him. The inheritance introduced deep strains into their marriage. It is not clear how much of their marital discord traced back to the confusion in the will's distribution. The confusion likely had something to do with why Mary first sought legal help from Luther Harris Hiscock.[10]

THE WINDFALL OF MONEY brought new hopes and great strife. After the murder, the prisoner's defenders began telling stories of George having wanted to return to plowing in his boyhood village, only to feel pressure from his wife to leave the farm for urban life. She was a lonely young mother with a taste for refinement. "At her instigation," they claimed, George sold the farm and moved his family to Syracuse. It was she—the story went—who goaded her humble farming husband into pursuing worldly mobility.[11]

In truth they both had desires to make more of themselves. And they likely both desired urban middle-class life. The family of four moved to Syracuse, the largest city in the region save Rochester. Soon after their move, George bought out half the shares of a lumber business and opened up another bookstore, apparently with some of what was supposed to be Mary's money.[12] The Coles soon met Hiscock, a married attorney roughly their age.

Hiscock could boast the well-bragged path of self-made manhood, from farm to city, and from books to political power. After he attended an academy, he taught and was elected superintendent of schools. He began studying law, was admitted to the bar in 1851, and had begun to gravitate toward antislavery politics. He was likely involved with the Underground Railroad in upstate New York, something that must have made him attractive to the Coles, who shared similar antislavery sympathies. He then ran—as a Democrat—for the office of surrogate of Onondaga County, challenging the incumbent, "Colonel" Minard (a dubious military title that came from his service in the Fifty-First militia). Minard's supporters painted Hiscock as an inexperienced upstart who had dangerous sympathies for abolition. A "true patriot," they wrote, would vote for Colonel Minard and leave "Hiscock to be taken care of by runaway negroes and their admirers."[13]

His admirers voted Hiscock to victory. He set up his office in Syracuse and as county surrogate made final decisions regarding estates and wills, overseeing the authentication of and challenges to inheritances. He soon became one of the most experienced men in the city regarding women's estates. By the end of his four-year term, he had shifted the balance of his legal practice to Syracuse.[14]

According to George's private letters, Mary's stepbrother, Henry Jr., tried to get his hands on her money too. There is no wonder why she would have been drawn to Hiscock's experience in managing women's estates, especially given the expectations by men around her that her money should help them in their worldly pursuits. Hiscock became the Cole family attorney. They fast became friends, even if George felt wary from the start.

★

THEN THE WAR CAME. When President Abraham Lincoln called for volunteers in the spring of 1861, Hiscock was too thick in private grief to take up arms. Only several weeks before the firing upon Fort Sumter, his wife, Lucy, had died after a grueling battle with tuberculosis. A city paper reported that though her sickness had dragged on, the blow had fallen on Hiscock with a "crushing weight." He was left to raise two children in a world plunging toward war. He didn't enlist.[15]

George rushed into the fray, casting aside whatever successes or connections he had established during his three years in Syracuse. He started the war with promise—as a captain in the Twelfth New York Volunteer Infantry, a regiment of foot soldiers drawn from Syracuse and central New York.

In early May 1861, in unseasonably raw cold, his regiment marched before civilians in Syracuse. Women of the city pinned patriotic rosettes on the breast of every soldier, over nine hundred of them. They then handed each warrior a copy of the New Testament. Many sobbed as they exchanged small gifts and "articles of comfort."[16]

Rev. Sherman Canfield—the pastor who, right after the murder, would visit prisoner Cole and Mary in jail and plead with the veteran to resist killing himself—delivered a sermon to an emotional crowd. He promised that the patriotism of the moment was not out of line with the teachings of meek Jesus. The minister reminded the crowd how George Washington "daily prayed to the God of battles." The war that lay ahead was like the one fought by the generation of 1776. The Union, he said, was the great beacon of hope for the world and was worth protecting.

GEORGE AND HIS COMRADES marched off under the banner of a God who—many believed—expected men to make something of themselves. He was off to kill Confederates because American empire in the West had brought to a head the decades-long conflict over slavery. At root, rebels and Yankees had incompatible visions of how men could best make themselves.

Slave masters and future Confederates had contended that slavery alone guaranteed a rough equality among White men and an equal chance for them to rise. In the most perverse logic, slavery somehow promised equality. Lincoln, and Republicans like George who shared his vision, saw it another way. In the first months of the war, Lincoln framed the conflict as a cosmic struggle over men's right to rise. It was a war between a slave-based society that cruelly condemned some to uncompensated toil and a free-labor system that guaranteed all men "an unfettered start" and a chance to prove themselves in "the race of life." (Near the war's end, Lincoln assured battle-worn troops various times that they had fought so that the poorest of boys could rise, like he had done, from obscure poverty to the White House. That kind of government—an "inestimable jewel"—warranted the sacrifice of blood.)[17] Before the first shots of war, some in Lincoln's party had already begun framing the emancipation of enslaved people as necessary for Black Americans to prove how they measured up against other men. Frederick Douglass called the war the "Golden Moment" for Black men to demonstrate their worthiness of liberty. They would at last earn their freedom by proving themselves on battlefields to be worthy of it.[18]

It was a war for ambition and mobility as much as it was for any other cause. A war won by Union soldiers promised to erase the artificial line that divided Americans into free and enslaved men—and replace it with one that separated all Americans into those who, by their own making, advance and those who fall behind.[19]

★

ALONG WITH COUNTLESS WOMEN, Mary would learn how war redrew lines between wives and husbands. It cut asunder households, leaving spouses to deal with the exposed nerve endings of separated family. The unexamined daily habits of marriage—the routines, the common pleasures, the fragile compromises—would need to be renegotiated. More darkly, war could strain marriages with disabilities, looming death, sexual impotence, opium and alcohol addiction, shortages of labor on the farm, venereal disease, and the traumatizing secrets of soldiers.[20]

The nation's cries for wartime sacrifice drowned out the call for women's rights. Conventions trumpeting wives' demands seemed selfish amid reports of the death of husbands and sons. The teetering fate of four million enslaved souls and the work of binding wounds took precedence over the cause for women's selfhood.[21]

Still, the war would require wives to take charge of household finances and negotiate business matters. Mary engaged in a flurry of real estate transactions during the war, many without George on the deed.[22] With her new freedoms came acute loneliness. Various accounts say that the sexual encounters between her and Hiscock started when she fell into deep depression. She couldn't endure it when George, badly wounded and unwilling to quit the war, dangled over death. As the story went, she believed she was going to die from anxiety and called on Hiscock to get her will in order. War would break her.

Judging by her few surviving letters, Mary was by nature a worried woman. But she persisted in getting what she wanted, often in a self-deprecating way that diminished her selfhood. There is no evidence that she engaged much in women's rights or its battle against coverture. From the ordinary procedure of her obtaining her inheritance as a young mother, to applying for a widow's pension later in life, to Hiscock locking her into his arms in the hour she needed him to formalize her will, Mary's statutory rights were, in the end, defined by men—executor, clerk, lawyer, judge, pension agent, brother, father, husband, insistent lover, perhaps rapist. For Mary, and many others, the promises of Seneca Falls were mockingly remote.

For George, the great promise of war mocked him from the start.

PART II

DELUSIONS *of* MANHOOD

Delusions of Children are of one kind,
of manhood another.

—CORNELIUS COLE, *Memoirs*

CHAPTER 4

FOG *of* WAR

IN THE TEDIOUS DAYS SPENT awaiting his trial, the prisoner had ample time to wonder what the ravenous public would learn about his soldiering days. He had done so many brave things. Yet, like every veteran, he had been part of things he could not fully explain to civilians. And he had secrets.

GEORGE COLE'S WAR BEGAN WITH SCANDAL. In July 1861, he led his company into a conflict that set in motion the first major land battle of the war. It was the first of many black eyes for the Union army. He was a captain in the Twelfth New York, under the divisional command of General Daniel Tyler, a wealthy manufacturer who obsessed over the fame that awaited him if, in the first hours of the war, he captured Richmond. Though he was instructed to probe the enemy's flank, and forbidden to engage, he ordered men down a bank toward a Virginia creek called Bull Run, where the enemy lay in wait. George's company was one of the units sent into the death trap at Blackburn Ford.

Salvos from the opposite bank brought confusion, then panic. Men from the Twelfth ran. Tyler blamed the New Yorkers for cowardice and disorder. He published a report that named two companies that stood their ground—neither of them George's. Some reports had described George as an exceptional officer among incompetent peers. George wrote to his family that he was one of the few who stood bravely. A prominent reporter from the *New York Times* had witnessed it. He was sure of it. If only—George had wished throughout the war—somebody would vouch for his bravery. Some soldiers blamed the regiment's colonel for ordering them to retreat. Others claimed he had abandoned his men. A report exonerated the colonel and found that soldiers had become confused over similar uniforms and shouts they wrongly believed came from officers.[1]

George's identity as a warrior was entangled with the reputation of his regiment and his commanding officers—or, really, the stories that newspapers and reports told about them. Soldiers lucky enough to fight in the right army under the right general took enormous pride in their organizations. After battles, they longed to read about how "they"—that is, the identity soldiers borrowed from their regiment—were depicted in print.[2]

George longed for a new identity. Anonymous soldiers from the tainted Twelfth New York had written letters to newspapers grousing about the lack of discipline in camp, the ratty uniforms, the second-rate firepower, and the discontent among the ranks. He wrote to his superior, the chief of cavalry, that his company felt "very much demoralized & we believe we can be of much more service" in the cavalry. He asked to be transferred with some of his men to the Third New York Cavalry.[3]

His colonel signed his name to a short letter—penned by George—that encouraged the transfer.[4] The appeal was successful. His company was absorbed into the Third New York Cavalry in September.[5] This would have profound, unintended consequences for him.

Nineteenth-century Americans shared a romantic vision of the mounted trooper lifted on a stallion above the infantry's dirt. Union cavalrymen did tend to see more action than foot soldiers, but as troopers (mounted men) soon found out, it was often not the kind that garnered attention in the newspapers. Cavalrymen rarely fought in pitched battles but instead made quick assaults on narrow targets, destroyed property, and, in general, molested the enemy with minor skirmishes. The transfer that George and his comrades had wanted so dearly placed them outside many of the grand battles that would generate headlines over the course of the war.[6]

After the transfer, he bought an identification disc from the regimental sutler. Soldiers soon realized that the conflict would be more lethal than Americans had anticipated. Clearly, the US government was not prepared to reclaim and identify slain soldiers. Identification discs, dangling against men's breasts or pinned to their uniform, were proof of their deepest fears. A soldier's head might be blown off by a cannonball; his cadaver might be left on a battlefield to bloat and rot into a heap of sinews and maggots. The disc George bought was an investment in what might have been the last trace of his identity.

His disc was a bronze coin with a profile of George Washington on one side. Soldiers had holes drilled at the top so the disc could be worn as a necklace or pendant. On one side, Washington's head was encircled by thirty-four stars along the perimeter, representing the unruptured bonds of states before secession; at the bottom, stars converged at the word "Union."

The backside of the coin assured George that his selfhood—worthy of photographing and mounting on walls—would not be entirely lost in the fog of war or dissolved in mass death. The discs were purchased wholesale from die sinkers in New York City, then peddled by traveling salesmen to sutlers who pounded personal details into the prefabricated blanks—a soldier's name or a "2" at the end of a precast "186_." Seemingly personalized, the mass-produced discs were the product of enterprising Yankees who capitalized on the tension felt keenly by soldiers. American soldiers had come to believe in their right

50 DELUSIONS OF MANHOOD

Like many soldiers who dreaded dying and becoming an unrecognizable cadaver, George Cole bought an identification disc emblazoned with the profile of George Washington on the obverse (*above*), with a mass-produced, yet personalized, reverse (*below*), where his name would have been stamped with metal punches. *Reproduced with permission of the American Numismatic Society*

to die as individuals; yet they were part of a modern war and the modern nation's claim on its faceless millions.[7]

IN APRIL 1862, the second spring of the war, George's cavalry regiment was transferred into the Department of North Carolina. It was a promising change. Forces in the Department of North Carolina, under General Ambrose Burnside, had recently captured the river town of New Bern and other strategic points along the North Carolina seaboard. Thanks to these victories, the Union blockaded major rivers like the Neuse, Tar, and Roanoke, cutting off supplies to the interior of the state.

George would witness few heroics in North Carolina (at least not the kind that his lawyers could later draw on to mesmerize jurymen). After his unit's arrival, the Department of North Carolina would fail to significantly enlarge any of the Union footholds. Soldiers looking for military glory grew restless. Instead of major campaigns, George's Third New York Cavalry took part in a series of unremarkable engagements and raids on small towns in the interior. One of George's fellow officers spoke for many when he wrote he could not find any merit in "being shot or captured" in "one of these miserable little skirmishes where neither side could possibly gain any thing worth a single life." Dying in a skirmish was a "very different thing from falling in battle" in Virginia or the "great battles of the West." Scrape-ups with snipers and ambushers were "boy's play in comparison."[8]

George's regiment had been brought to New Bern for an important reason. They were asked to stamp out guerrillas who raided and brought terror to Union men in eastern North Carolina. Rebel guerrillas—called partisan rangers—were growing in strength and boldness.[9] Guerrilla bands terrified Yankees, often sneaking about in civilian garb, ready to shoot a Union man in the back. They set Union soldiers on edge by making persistent, small-scale attacks on places that were supposed to have been under Union control. Their snipers skulked in brush and trees to pick off Yankee pickets and scouting parties. They had informants and messengers, many of them women. They struck fear in the hearts of cavalry scouting parties and made Southern unionists in the area pay in blood for their treachery.[10] It was in this climate of paranoia and vengeance that George's life was instantly altered.

★

IN JULY 1862, Confederate guerrillas ambushed some of the troopers in George's company. Two of his soldiers were mutilated. In this whirlwind of brutality and vengefulness—exactly when was controversial—in one of the many, nameless skirmishes, Captain Cole spurred his horse across a field in pursuit of one of the guerrillas. Just as he raised his saber to strike, his horse was shot from under him. (Some believed that his horse stumbled in a ditch. Nobody seems to have been sure. It was dusk, getting darker by the minute.)[11]

His twelve-hundred-pound black stallion came crashing down into the weeds. His friends would say that it nearly "mashed" his body in two. In a violent flutter, the beast rolled lengthwise over George's body. The cantle (the saddle's back rim) dug and rolled into his pelvis. The pommel (the protuberant front end of the saddle) crushed his chest and partly popped through his sternum, leaving a two-and-a-half-inch indentation and purplish-black contusions that lasted several months. Like a rolling pin, with deadly pressure, the horse's back crushed his groin and ruptured his "suspensory ligaments," squeezing part of his lower bowels and the mucus membrane out of his rectum.

He was "picked up for dead," he recalled, by his comrades, who tied him upright to another horse. Knocked out of his senses, panicking for air, he bumped along in a blood-soaked saddle for two days until he collapsed in his camp.

He healed slowly. The debilitating attacks returned frequently and he had periods when he could defecate but once every two weeks. After some of his most painful evacuations, he would hemorrhage nearly a pint of blood into a jar and then, with his fingers, stuff the sagging guts back beyond his partially paralyzed sphincter. In the worst moments, his bowels protruded some five to six inches from his anus.[12]

What had happened was confusing from the start. War records suggested that during the accident his revolver fired a ball into his right thigh. George's army medical records inexplicably said nothing about the actual fall. He recuperated in a field hospital. For how long is uncertain. Soon after, his tenderfoot private and personal orderly, Edwin R. Fox, nursed him for nearly a month as he lay "in confinement." Fox followed his commander's instructions on how to treat the wounds, administering injections to stimulate bowel movement, cleaning the profusions of blood, and waiting on his captain like a surrogate nurse. In late July, George returned home to Syracuse. He walked with the aid of a cane for a season. He then returned to the field with Mary, who trekked back and forth between her daughters at home and her husband at the front. In November she came to nurse George and remained for the winter.

His protruding bowels eventually sloughed off and contracted. He somehow kept his wounds relatively secret in army and family circles. Many of his subsequent comrades knew he had been hurt but not exactly how. Until the end of the war, he would tend to most of his daily duties; but at night he was often "driven out of bed" for fear of suffocation as he panicked for air. His moaning and his coming and going disturbed the sleep of comrades.

Whatever it was that had happened in the field with his horse, it led to his slow ruin and had something to do with his path to his jail cell. He grew more and more peculiar. He took less care of himself in grooming and dress. His comrades would later recall that he began to suffer from delusions, and grew less patient in his pursuit of success, and more ambitious and grasping. He was aware that something was wrong with him. He would sometimes wish openly that he had been killed. And in the harrowing months after the fall, he detected that his marriage was in deep peril.[13]

★

SOMEHOW, HE STAYED IN THE WAR. Some sense of duty, or force, goaded him on. He remained in his bed during the next few raids, in which his comrades looted and brought destruction to every town they entered.[14] In one raid, they destroyed furniture, caved in fireplaces, and brought cattle to the second floor of a hotel outside Williamston, slaughtered the beasts, and left the carnage to rot. The destructive expedition sprang some thirty Unionists from a Confederate jail. And as happened in many raids in the region, hundreds of enslaved people—exploiting the fact that their masters were in hiding or on the run—formed a caravan of refugees that trailed the soldiers back to New Bern and eventually to the swelling refugee camps behind Union lines.

Through much of autumn, Mary nursed George's wounds. Then, in December 1862, he doggedly returned to his saddle and helped lead his demoralized men in the Kinston Raid, also called Foster's Raid. Formerly enslaved laborers from refugee camps felled and cleared pine trees blocking the roads that the Third New York Cavalry would gallop, in advance of some eleven thousand soldiers. The Union forces were ordered to burn the Wilmington and Weldon Railroad bridge, disrupting supplies to Robert E. Lee's soldiers in Virginia. The raids would also cut off rebels' supply lines of food from farmlands in the Carolina interior, as well as medical and military goods smuggled through Union blockades along the coast.

At the battle in Kinston, he led a charge against the enemy that at last won him a modicum of fame and hardened his Third New York's reputation for ruthlessness. They torched houses and left wounded Confederates dying on the sandy grounds. When one rebel, Thomas Gibson, tried to surrender, a soldier from the Third New York shoved his gun against Gibson's temple and executed him point blank. A rank-and-file foot soldier from another New York regiment wrote his father that the Third "never" took prisoners if they could help it. On the raid, he said, "when [the cavalry] got after any rebs they would put the muzzle of their carbines behind their ear and blow their brains out. They are a perfect set of tigers, and the rebs are afraid to death of them." They brandished all kinds of weapons, he said. "They are bully boys from N.Y."[15]

Vengeance came with more wrenching losses. After preventing guerrillas from burning a bridge, the retreating rebels fired two six-pounder howitzers at their attackers. One of the projectiles hit George's private, John Costello, smashing his head to pieces. Just outside Kinston, fleeing rebs doused the Neuse River bridge with turpentine and set it on fire. As the Union soldiers scrambled to extinguish the flames, a nearby musket discharged in the heat, instantly killing Colonel Charles Gray, from the Ninety-Sixth New York Volunteers. Ninety-one other Yankees were killed during the raid, with just under five hundred wounded.

Before the perilous return to base, a "negro" informed George that just hours before, the rebs had hastily abandoned armaments in a nearby fort that they left under the guard of a single soldier. George stormed the fort and captured a pair of thirty-two-pound iron artillery pieces, brass pieces, and other guns and weapons. One of the artillery guns had been lost by the Union at Bull Run. On top of this, George's company captured eight rebel prisoners. With these "trophies" and the corpse of Colonel Gray in his care, George returned to New Bern.

Though his body was a wreck, his military fortunes appeared as bright as ever. He and his company were singled out by department commanders for gallantry and bravery. On the last day of 1862, he obtained a promotion to major. His achievements were recognized in his hometown newspaper—though nearly six months later—in a brief account about the size of a postage stamp, entitled "A Gallant Officer." The report was based on another report from New Bern that spoke of George as "the hero of the cavalry fight of Kinston."[16] Safe behind lines in New Bern, he would have time that winter to further heal and to imagine what an injured man with ambition still might make of himself.[17]

CHAPTER 5

GEORGE WASHINGTON, TOWN DESTROYER

IN APRIL 1863, George Cole returned home on a twenty-day furlough. When it was nearly over, his doctor in Syracuse certified that the soldier needed more time to recover from his chest wounds. He got an extension. It wasn't enough. His injuries lingered, and there were other reasons for delaying his return to the battlefront. His widowed mother was at death's door. Heavyhearted and sick, he returned to the war.[1] The nation needed him to carry out more destructive raids.

Within a few weeks he learned of his mother's death. It was at her feet that he had first glimpsed the connections between destructive war and progress, between intimate pain and happiness. It was under her care that he first hefted the historical weight of his name and learned its connection to American empire. She died in the Cole family home, on a patch of land resonating with violent patriotism that had once dirtied young George's heels.

IN 1779, during the American Revolution, General George Washington had ordered General John Sullivan to exterminate Iroquois villages in upstate New York, especially around the Finger Lakes, where, decades later, the Coles would establish their farm. Goaded forward by grisly, largely true tales of Indian

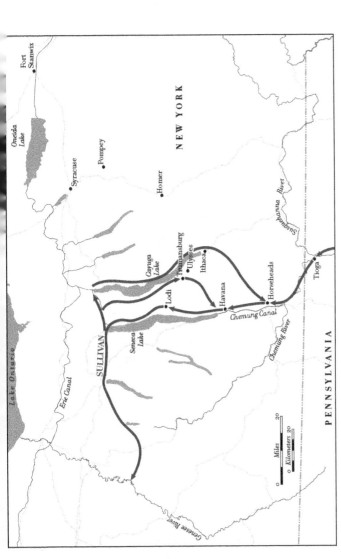

This map of the Finger Lakes region in the mid-nineteenth century has been overlaid with the path of John Sullivan's destruction during the American Revolution, which eradicated large portions of Indigenous people from the region. The line of destruction, mostly south to north, freed White speculators to survey the lands and map it into square grids. No line mattered more, perhaps, than the east-to-west course of the Erie Canal, which transformed the Iroquois heartland into a region of farming settler families with growing ambitions and an appetite for things. Notice Havana, where George started his photography gallery, next to the Chemung Canal. Lodi, Trumansburg (Ulysses), and Pompey are the birthplaces of George, Mary Cole, and Luther Harris Hiscock, respectively. The Stanwix Hotel took its name from the famed Fort Stanwix of the revolution. *Drawn by Mapping Specialists*

attacks on White settlements, Sullivan's soldiers torched every Indian village in their path. As they did, they were smitten by the rich soil that yielded succulent melons and corn. They described the place in letters and journals as if it were the American Eden. Natural beauty overcame them. They ached to possess it.[2]

By the time the US Constitution was ratified, surveyors—some of them Sullivan's men—had already begun mapping out roughly one and a half million acres, converting them into a grid of right-angle plots that made up the "New Military Tract," originally intended for soldiers. The geometric precision converted the Iroquois lands into assets easily mapped out on paper and then peddled by bankers and jobbers to aspiring families in cities and towns to the east.

It would have been a lot for a young mind to digest, if indeed George learned of it, that in 1790, the Seneca warrior Cornplanter told George Washington of the pain the president's name brought to those who heard it. He reminded him of the 1768 Treaty of Stanwix, which had promised that White people would not trespass a line on the map that had long since been erased by the wagon wheels and feet of settlers and soldiers. "Father," said Cornplanter, "when your army entered the country of the Six Nations, we called you the town destroyer; and to this day, when that name [George Washington] is heard, our women look behind them and turn pale; our children cling close to the necks of their mothers."[3]

Around 1800, George Cole's grandparents left New Jersey for the stolen, mapped-out Eden. They were part of a flood of migrants, including some of Sullivan's former soldiers, who rushed into western New York. As they saw it, they came to improve their lives on orderly plots organized from bountiful lands once wasted on Indians.

The land around the Finger Lakes revealed its brutal past, especially to curious children who often found charred corn, arrowheads, wampum, and pipes that had been turned up by plowshares. Relics of snuffed-out Seneca communities cropped up along their paths to district school and academies. At least one destroyed Indian village lay close to the Cole farm, tucked beside a craggy hill. In the children's favorite nooks along the lakeshore, they found traces of Seneca homes. An old Iroquois woman wrapped in a blanket repeatedly appeared at the Coles' farmhouse door to sell the family her beads and baskets. It isn't clear whether the family bought her wares, or ever let her in—or if the boy named after Town Destroyer ever locked eyes with her.[4]

The Cole children learned that General Sullivan's trail of destruction ran straight through their parents' farm. Neighborhood children gathered in the treeless corridor to act out the expedition. They rehearsed the drama of slitting the throats of their horses, just as Sullivan's men had been ordered to do after finishing their scorched-earth expedition. At least once, some of the Cole children visited a village to the south called Horseheads, where the slain beasts had been left to rot down to heaps of bleached bones.[5]

★

But George Washington Cole was a motherless man now and the brutal work of Yankee empire awaited him. The war was, in large part, a struggle between two incompatible visions of America's expansion into western lands—and whether it would be an extension of Yankeedom or that of the slave-driving South. Though the actions of George and his men were often cruel, he could tell himself—as Washington's men had done—that he was clearing the way for the happiness and prosperity and progress.

In July he was ordered to lead a cavalry battalion up the Tar River Valley some seventy miles to strike at the towns of

Greenville, Tarboro, and Rocky Mount. The mission aimed to exploit the thinly defended interior of the state, as more and more rebels had been transferred from North Carolina to crucial theaters in Virginia and the West.[6]

Rebel papers documented the destruction of what would come to be called Potter's Raid. One rebel correspondent singled out George's regiment as "a band of thieves and robbers." In the raid's lurid details, rebels found proof of Yankee viciousness and the suffering of God's elect people. One Southern newspaper emphasized that even the officers stole and plundered.[7] They "completely gutted" the town of Greenville, where they also freed twenty-five Black prisoners. In Tarboro, raiders smashed their way through a Masonic lodge, stealing the "fine regalia," jewels, gavel, and sacred emblems. They torched water tanks, warehouses, the town hall, and a jail. Reports claimed that George's fellow raiders pilfered as many horses and mules as they could handle, slaughtering the rest.[8]

George and company remained in one town long enough to prevent citizens from salvaging their burning bridge.[9] In Tarboro, he ensured the destruction of huge quantities of cotton and a stockpile of medical supplies desperately needed in Confederate hospitals.[10]

George was living up to his name. The North Carolina raids were especially brutal to women. Yankees targeted the daily necessities of life; they burned flour, torched every cotton gin in their path, including a cotton mill that employed 150 "white girls." Early in Potter's Raid, Union soldiers captured the Confederate official in charge of distributing relief funds to families. They took his horse and relieved him of $6,300 that had been designated for the neediest kin of soldiers in Craven County. Upon hearing news of Potter's Raid, one Confederate colonel cynically predicted that the Yankees would surely make Tarboro their "first point of attack, or rather destruction, for there was nothing to attack but women and children."[11]

His suspicions proved true. The raiders charged into homes around midnight, turned families out of their beds, and left "many a lady & her helpless little children" to sleep in the woods. George's regiment ransacked parlors, turned over furniture, and snatched earrings, breastpins, and watches from their frightened victims' persons. Papers noted how raiders tugged wedding bands from a resistant woman's fingers and stole "petty trinkets," children's clothing, and loads of liquor.[12]

Even raids on industrial targets punished households. Besides torching thousands of barrels of flour, they destroyed Tarboro's cotton factory, which produced the yarn that locals needed to make clothing. All over the Confederacy, particularly in blockaded regions, impoverished women confronted a shortage of cloth. When George and his men destroyed yarn, cotton, textile mills, or a Confederate woman's garments, it was a way to make rebel soldiers' wives and mothers atone for secession.[13]

In another raid that took place two weeks before Potter's Raid, a witness fumed that on the Sabbath a "vandal horde of negroes and Yankees," led by escaped enslaved people, stormed into two small towns just southwest of Kinston. Besides stripping jewelry from persons, ripping up bed clothing, stealing away with enslaved people, and cutting down shade trees, the plunderers forced themselves into the home of an attorney to destroy his wife's wardrobe.[14] In Tarboro, raiders ripped or burned garments—Sunday dresses, petticoats—in front of mothers and wives.[15]

Still, large quantities of women's clothing made it into the overloaded wagons. Black soldiers accompanying the Union forces might have ensured that there was as much stealing as destroying. It isn't clear. These men would have been sensitive to how badly clothing was needed by wives and mothers in refugee camps. Male refugees often inherited ratty war uniforms to wear while they did intense manual labor for the army.

In this depiction, Black servants, perhaps soldiers, wash the clothing of officers. While they do the traditional work of women, a female refugee sits and watches. While many female refugees did vital work for the Union, this depiction suggests the widespread depreciation of their labor, and a bristling unease about their dependence. *"'Washerwomen' in the Army of the Potomac,"* Frank Leslie's Illustrated Newspaper, *December 10, 1864, 189. Courtesy of the American Antiquarian Society*

Females had to rely on northern charity and their own skills in sewing and mending in the camps. White soldiers often viewed female refugees as burdens on army resources, their destitution somehow proof of indolence and dependence.[16]

MISERY FOR SOME BROUGHT JOY for others. As Major Cole and his comrades looted and burned the countryside, refugees from slavery formed behind them, some on foot, some mounted on their masters' mules, horses, and carts. Several hundred enslaved people joined the raiders. One of the few Yankee correspondents who remained in North Carolina described the escape, saying that everywhere the Federal troops passed, they were "hailed by these persecuted people as their deliverers." When the destroyers turned back toward New Bern, the band of fugitives swelled behind.[17]

Confederates reported that some enslaved people refused to run and that others showed loyalty by helping to hide their masters or putting out fires started by raiders' torches. Masters frequently preached about the cruelty of Yankees, leaving many of the enslaved to fear the cruel world they knew less than the one they didn't. Confederate descriptions of the escaping refugees favored words like "seduced," "forced," or "carried off." Some enslaved people, indeed, were forced to flee at the end of a rifle barrel. It was not unusual for Federal soldiers in tidewater Virginia and North Carolina to conscript local Black people into the army. George himself boasted a few months after the raid in a letter to family that he knew how to "rope in darkies fast" during raids.[18]

George took the advance as the Yankees groped their way back to their camp in New Bern. With stuffed pockets and wagons loaded with plunder and refugees, the raiders pushed through the sleepless blur—which was now entering its third day—cutting through woods and sparsely traveled back roads, often in the confusion of darkness.

Many of the fleeing families could not keep pace. When rebel forces began swarming the band of raiders and refugees, George repeatedly ordered his men at the rear to shoot canister and grapeshot from mountain howitzers—cannon that cavalry units could disassemble into parts and lug on pack animals. The rebels had artillery that could hurtle shell nearly twice as far and with more precision. Outgunned, he urged the column onward.

In the early predawn darkness of July 21, the delirious troops took rest near a church. George received orders to rotate his battalion to the rear, where he would be charged with protecting the long column of refugees who had become easy prey.

The tangled back trails had stretched the swollen column of refugees into a broken line of small bands, trickling on and on in the nearly moonless night. One witness noted how he watched the last, desperate runaways scuffling along in the first light of morning, pressing on to catch the main column of Union soldiers that had passed several hours earlier.[19]

Rebels only needed to follow the column of enslaved people to locate the enemy's rear. Rebel squadrons continued to shell George's troops. Once, when his men had to stop to feed and water their horses, an enemy shell tore through the face of one of his lieutenants. Halting put his men in danger.[20]

While resting his men near a critical bridge, he received orders from his acting colonel, George W. Lewis, to "pass the negro column" and make haste to join up with the main column. It is not clear whether he was given specific orders to burn the bridge, but he passed over it and then ordered a lieutenant with two companies to remain and set it on fire.[21]

What exactly happened next is lost in war's fog. Carolina rebels closed in on the desperate exodus. In the early morning, Confederates began firing from a small brass cannon strapped to the back of a mule. The soldiers were just starting to cross the bridge. A rebel lieutenant in the Fiftieth North Carolina named J. C. Ellington would not forget what he witnessed. The cannon's fire "utterly demoralized" the refugees, Ellington wrote. Jolted by its discharge, the refugees made a "mad rush" to keep pace with their deliverers, who were "now fleeing for their lives."[22]

The scene was "indescribable." Many in the refugee cavalcade panicked, whipping madly at their horses and mules. Some tried to halt their horses and buggies. Others continued full tilt. Wagons jackknifed and spilled over amid a din of confused cries. Spooked horses dragged wrecked buggies and carts into the woods.[23]

Some of the Black soldiers who played a part in the raid sacrificed their lives to rescue the fleeing families. "One negro captain"—he wasn't a captain but may have been a noncommissioned officer—stood up in his buggy, drawn by two hard-charging gray horses, and made a suicidal charge toward three attackers. They riddled him with bullets. Some Black soldiers stayed back to defend the lagging refugees. Perhaps because they understood what a recaptured enslaved person might face, they could not condemn the runaways to the whip and noose. They became part of the sacrifice.[24]

The Carolinians chased their prey through the trees and captured "several hundred negroes." After scouring the woods, they found "several" infants and small children who had been "abandoned to their fate" in the thickets. Some frantic mothers and fathers, perhaps, had prayed that Union soldiers, or God, would rescue their children. Some of the babies may have been made into orphans only minutes before. "Many others," Ellington recalled, were "either killed or wounded in attempting to escape through the woods nearby."[25]

One Northern reporter said that a "large number" of refugees were taken as prisoners "into the hands of their former masters, doomed now certainly to a slavery worse than death itself."[26]

George reported to his superiors, with a hint of defensiveness about his tainted role as a liberator, that his men waited for "at least an hour for the negroes" to cross the bridge. And only with none approaching did the soldiers set it ablaze. A Yankee reporter made no mention of a long gap in the refugee column but instead said that the fire was lit when approaching rebels initiated another attack. George knew that many refugees—perhaps five hundred—were sacrificed as they were squeezed into a narrowing trap of two converging rivers.[27]

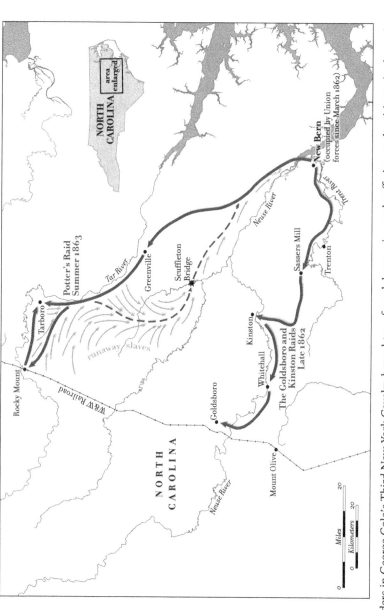

The raiders in George Cole's Third New York Cavalry brought profound destruction and suffering to the citizens in the region around the Union base in New Bern, North Carolina. It was somewhere near Scuffleton Bridge that George and his men doomed hundreds of escaping enslaved people. *Drawn by Mapping Specialists*

He wrote in his report that the abandoned refugees were "gobbled up by the rebel squadron in our rear, and unable to come up." He learned later, somehow, that some of the refugees successfully took cover in the woods, where they hid all night. About "one-third or one-half the whole number of negroes and mules were lost at this place."[28]

★

WHEN DARKNESS RETURNED, so did bargaining with the devil. North Carolina troops who had raced from Kinston intercepted the Yankee expedition one more time before it reached New Bern. Rebels burned various bridges and the Union column—so close to safety—was imperiled.[29]

According to General Edward E. Potter's own report, when the fleeing Union soldiers discovered an ambush ahead, near Otter Creek, they eluded the trap "by taking a very intricate path through a plantation."[30] Potter did not elaborate. But almost certainly, an enslaved person or one of the Black soldiers helped them navigate a private plantation and a hidden "pineywoods road" leading toward safety.[31]

Of course, rebels had motives for letting the raiders barely escape. For Confederate soldiers, whose families suffered from wartime shortages, *almost* catching raiders became its own end. Pestering the rear brought them scarce goods. According to a Tarheel witness, George's comrades at the rear began "throwing away every incumbrance" and "disgorg[ing] much plunder" in the path of their attackers. They upturned carriages and emptied some of their sacks of pilferage.[32] Strewn behind the army were clothing, "fine bed quilts," china, silverware, beasts of burden, and meat.[33] The raiders, though, limited the number of horses that fell into the hands of the feared guerrillas. Some of the men drew their blades and slit the throats of their horses.[34]

After Potter's Raid, one Southern correspondent reported that "40 other negroes mostly women and children have been captured near Greenville, that were left behind by the Abolitionists on their hasty retreat." Maybe the refugees were mostly women because local masters, anticipating the advance of the Union, had shipped enslaved men to plantations deeper within the Confederate interior. There was evidence, though, that male refugees perhaps had been strategically pressed forward by their Yankee liberators, while females became part of the expendable plunder left behind to placate the enemy.[35]

Stolen dresses were expendable too. It appears that the stealing of dresses from rebel women served several purposes. It was an act of revenge against traitorous rebel women. It promised clothing for female refugees. And, if needed, it promised to slow the approaching enemy. Confederates found "all sorts of" women's clothing tossed behind the raiders' escaping wagons.

As for the refugees who made it to New Bern, they tasted only bitter freedom, a blend of ecstasy and shame for having lost family and friends to Pharaoh's army.[36] George's terse military report hints that he felt some shame too. The truth was hard to swallow. Little of it made it into print back home. Shortly after the raid, a paper from George's hometown had reported that a train of refugees, following the Union cavalry, had fallen into the enemy's hands after "taking the wrong road."[37] Soldiers knew, though, that Black pilots rarely took the wrong road.[38] Nothing was said in the report about dooming hundreds to be recaptured or the trail of women's dresses and lifeless horses.

George had been desperate to end the hellish raid. His groin had been chafing and jouncing in the saddle for several days. Nearly half of the raiders had lost their hats from nodding off against their horses' necks. Some were so delirious

In this triumphant image, a massive column of enslaved families and Union soldiers marches into Union lines. The officer on the horse (*left* and *inset*) bears a strong resemblance to Major Cole. "*The Effects of the Proclamation, Freed Negroes Coming into Our Lines at New Bern, North Carolina,*" wood engraving, Harper's Weekly, February 21, 1863. Library of Congress, https://www.loc.gov/item/95501775/

that they passed out, dropping from their horses and into enemy hands.

Sacrificing some of the fleeing souls had saved some of George's soldiers and other endangered refugees. It ensured that the disc hanging from his neck was not needed to identify his abandoned cadaver on a back trail. He could comfort himself that his namesake, the American demigod whose image dangled against his bruised breast, had once cleared the way for farming families like his own, by ordering a destructive expedition that left Iroquois villages in ashes and spent horses drenched in blood. His experiences had taught him that suffering, and the pursuit of happiness, had some absurd, inseparable bond with one another.

CHAPTER 6

BELOW *the* BEAST

BENJAMIN FRANKLIN BUTLER, known as "Beast Butler" by his many critics, bore the name of America's Founding Father and patron saint of self-made manhood.[1] He was a calculating, thick-trunked, and cockeyed lawyer from Massachusetts who was gifted with a towering intellect and a tongue sharp enough to serve up his biting thoughts.

George detested him from the start. He saw Butler as proof that the army had failed to reward hard work and talent. Butler was the epitome of what George and others called "political generals"—men who won commissions for political reasons, not military merit.[2]

ANIMOSITY FOR GENERALS COULD RUN DEEP. War subjected millions of soldiers to the whims and decisions of a few powerful men. Soldiers could not wake, eat, or turn left at a forked road without in some way hewing to the grand strategies of the War Department and the decisions of generals who, with jowls hanging over maps, had the power to funnel young men into the grimmest or most glorious fates.

In the summer of 1863, George's "bully boy" Third New York Cavalry was transferred into what would become known as the Army of the James, a department rigged together from underused or poorly performing commands. It amounted to the defective parts of Abraham Lincoln's stumbling war machine.[3] This newly consolidated army operated directly south of the Army of the Potomac, dooming it to relative obscurity. Throughout its existence, the lesser-known Army of the James and its men lingered in the shadow of the Army of the Potomac, whose soldiers squared off with the troops under Robert E. Lee. An army of understudies, the Army of the James got second grabs at allocations of troopers, horses, supplies and glory.[4]

The Army of the James played a critical role in Grant's massive orchestration of campaigns throughout Dixie; it had a role in the siege of Petersburg and the destruction of its rail lines to Richmond, which would bring the rebel capital to its knees. Nonetheless, the Army of the James won fame for futility. Its humiliations did not cement a brotherhood of shared defeat. Instead, enmity hobbled its command from the beginning. From the highest brass to its young officers, it was beset by a striking cast of troubled, contentious men. All armies, North and South, suffered from blundering and chronic backbiting. But in the Army of the James, it became part of its identity from within and without.[5]

The friction seemed to arise from the narcissism of small differences. It was truly a legion of Yankees. A higher percentage of its units hailed from northeastern states than in any other army in the Union. It drew heavily from antislavery and men-on-the-make from towns and villages in New England and upstate New York—the cradle of the Republican Party. Its soldiers were mostly like George, Lincoln men who had worked the plow or were but one generation removed from the soil.[6]

In 1864, more than three-quarters of the officers in the Army of the Potomac had military experience or training before the war. Fewer than a third of the officers in the Army of the James could boast such experience or training. It was the kind of army that Lincoln took great pride in, one made of self-improved amateurs. These were Yankees who represented all the crafts and professions: businessmen, shopkeepers, printers, and sons of farmers who would supposedly be judged by their raw abilities, not credentials and connections.[7]

When Butler took command of the Army of the James, he had already earned a national reputation as a brilliant antagonist of Southerners, an advocate for refugees and Black soldiers, and the embodiment of military cronyism and folly. For George, and many other critics, Butler had no business taking such a lofty command. Several officers, including George, futilely tried to have Butler removed for illegal or unethical behavior.[8]

Benjamin Butler posing in the uniform of an army major general. Few men were as committed to the civil rights of Black Americans as Butler. From the day the two met, George's ambitions and failures were entangled with and complicated by Butler's. *Library of Congress, https://www.loc.gov/resource/cwpb .04895/*

★

When Butler took command of the Army of the James, he immediately rubbed George the wrong way. In the fall of 1863, George obtained a twenty-day furlough from Butler's predecessor, General John G. Foster, to return home to Syracuse on sick leave. He was still suffering from his fall. He spent some of his furlough embroiled in a civil lawsuit brought against him by a fellow Syracusan. George claimed that the plaintiff had delayed the procedure, hoping that George would be forced back to war and, therefore, be unable to defend himself in absentia.[9]

He stayed beyond his allotted furlough in order to defend himself. When he returned nearly a week late to camp—which was now under Butler's command—he was court-martialed for absence without leave. He argued to his fellow commanders that he had been subpoenaed to testify in his own case and that his evidence "saved [him] at least $600." He claimed that he would have been "pecuniarily responsible for not appearing as a witness in the . . . court as summoned." His comrades sympathized with his plight. A civilian, after all, had sued a soldier and had tried to exploit his sense of duty. In the court-martial, a tribunal of fellow officers found George guilty—as he certainly was—but added that it was without any "criminality," advising that he be immediately returned to his command without punishment.[10]

Butler reviewed the trial proceedings and rejected the verdict, stating that "the accused cannot be guilty without criminality." He took George to task for engaging in flimsy reasoning and putting private interests before the nation's. It was, Butler stressed, personal business that kept George from the war. Even worse, the suggestion that George had caused himself to be subpoenaed as a witness in his own case, and therefore would have been liable to himself for not attending, was,

Butler wrote, "an ~~subterfuge~~ [Butler thought better of such a potent word and crossed it out] evasion not worthy of an officer and a gentleman. Who could have moved for an attachment for not attending the court but Maj. Cole and who would have been punished for non attendance but Maj. Cole by Maj. Cole[?]"[11]

Butler had credentials to justify this verbal assault. Famously, in the first hours of the war, in the middle of trying a case in a Boston court, someone had passed him a note charging him to immediately prepare a regiment from his militia brigade. He interrupted the trial in dramatic fashion, asking the judge to postpone the case.[12]

His criticism of George was personal, casting dishonor on an already jealous soldier. "The more manly course," he added to his review of the verdict, would have been for George to refuse military pay during his absence. He decided to relieve George of duty but then crossed out the harsh judgment. Perhaps not wanting to jeopardize his chances at promotion—or reveal any weaknesses to what appeared to be a merciless commander—George made no mention of his injuries in his defense.[13]

FROM THE START OF THE WAR, as George saw it, his deeds had been passed over by officers who rewarded cronies before the deserving. He had scrutinized army regulations and the inconsistent policies for seniority. He wrote letters to his commanders to ensure his rightful promotions.[14] The maze of networks and favor-seeking left him disillusioned.

In truth, since his injury, he had grown more desperate and increasingly relied on the favor-seeking he denounced. As soldiers did when they wanted a promotion that seemed to elude them, he wrote pressing letters to friends. His best shot was his brother Cornelius, recently elected to Congress. In a letter to him in late 1863, when George was just coming to terms with serving under Butler, he wrote a gem of a begging letter. He said that he didn't like to blow his own horn and that he had never before been compelled to focus on his own doings. Underlined words of anger flocked together under his hand. "I want to get out of this, where I can have the credit of what I do," he wrote, "& be robbed as I have been, no more." If given a "fair show," he promised, "I can make my mark soon."[15]

He claimed that since the first month of the war, he had never been off duty "unless wounded or sick" due to his accident in 1862. He had been a vicious foe to rebels. "I with my company took prisoners & killed more rebels than the whole number of my company, (over a man each)." He later added "with my company" after the "I" to soften his boasting.[16]

He used his letters to seed more letters, supplying Cornelius a list of men from Syracuse and claiming that "an abundance" of letters could be obtained from them. George told him to call on a certain druggist named Rogers. He hoped to get an influential letter from Thomas Davis, a congressman who was skilled in praising friends. George told his brother to find Samuel Trull, a man who had served as the doorkeeper to the assistant secretary of state.[17]

George's seed letter was a detailed record of a man's frustrated ambitions. His greatest hope, he now openly confessed, was to return home a "General." He believed this could happen by shaking loose memories that bore record of his military exploits. "If you go to Syracuse," he wrote, "ask Smith for the particulars of my rescuing with my own hands the regimental flag of the 12th [New York regiment] at Bull Run." Smith was a prominent Republican back home. He knew the particulars. "Ask Henry J. Raymond of the Times," he added, to see "if he recollects on the 18th of July 1861 that I alone in the 12th Regt rallied my company at Blackburn Ford." (Blackburn

Ford was the humiliating beginning of the war when George's regiment bolted under fire.) Raymond was the editor for the *New York Times*. "Describe my tall black appearance & swearing some & see if [Raymond] will remember it!" George clung to hope that two and a half years after Bull Run, Raymond remembered some flash of gallantry in the first hours of the war. If only a friend could just jog his memory.[18]

He was coming to despise the fact that Butler exploited the cause of freedom for his own rising ambitions. But George had done the same. After he had made it to the grade of major (thanks to his own bravery and help from Black guides), he obtained a modest promotion to inspector of cavalry at Fort Monroe around the time of Butler's arrival. Still, he made a case that he merited greater rewards. "The command of a brigade of darkeys," he wrote Cornelius, "is the height of my ambition, for I know how they fight." He wanted to be made a brigadier general, especially over the Black men he had once led to freedom.[19]

"Our regiment [Third New York Cavalry] has a good name," he boasted, "& I have made it!" His statement about what he had done "with his own hands," in a letter designed to leverage connections, was part of a nineteenth-century ritual in which self-made men bragged and begged in the same breath. Though his highest goal was to lead a brigade (which would make him a brigadier general), he asked his brother for aid in first obtaining a colonelcy. And this, he believed, was only feasible with a commission over a regiment of Black soldiers: "Now I think you know my very desires, if you can properly assist me. I'll do the fighting for both of us meanwhile, for I like soldiering. . . . The reason I said I might prefer a commission as [colonel] now in a darkey regt is that [it] would come at once & cost nothing to get it up, for you must know the loss from my business (by hasty leaving when war broke out) has left me nearly poor again, but I count it gain in self respect."

He lacked the money to raise a White regiment. He said that he feared he would not be able to leave his little girls a fortune, but he might still leave them some glory. That is, "if I only had the chance to reap what I sow."[20]

★

THE HARVEST HAD NOT BEEN JUST. He had watched men "less capable" get promotions before him. They had joined the war late and, by "pulling wires," had outstripped him. As he saw it, he immediately abandoned his business because of principles. Though principles "don't pay in public, it makes a man respect himself," he said, as though he half-believed it. To his mind, his superiors and peers had worried more about cementing deals at home than winning the war. "They don't know the first thing, but to pipelay and hang around home."[21]

Laying pipe. Pulling wires. George used terms that any antebellum American man on the make would have recognized in others but rarely applied to himself. These colloquialisms evoked images of men tugging at webs of relations, dependents, and allies to further personal interests. By manipulating connective networks, "wire pullers" used friendships to make seemingly out-of-reach forces move or bend to their will. While the term "laying pipe" supposedly originated in a shady election bargain in which plumbing jobs were traded for votes, it came to denote political corruption. It evoked an image of hidden, buried connections.[22]

Laying pipe and pulling wires were what *others* did. When friends were relied on to achieve one's rightful station, it was a triumph of merit. The selective recognition of wire-pulling was inked onto countless sheets of stationery in nineteenth-century America. George's letters followed something of a formula, the kind found in a wartime exchange between Union general-in-chief Henry W. Halleck and Brigadier General John

Schofield. Halleck recognized and complained about the deluge of special request letters. The head of the Union army, Halleck said that if Schofield could just witness a few weeks at the military headquarters, he would see "how difficult it is to resist political wire-pulling in military appointments." Halleck continued, "Every Governor, Senator, and Member of Congress has his pet generals to be provided with separate and independent commands. I am sick and tired of the political military life." Trained at West Point, Halleck felt that sending soldiers to fight under "political generals" like Butler and others "seems little better than murder."[23]

But, in a kind of ritual found in letters from self-made men, Halleck decried political pipelaying in the first paragraphs, only to lay pipe vigorously in the remaining pages. After denouncing "pet generals," in the very next portion, Halleck promised Schofield that personal pipes were being laid: "Rest assured, general, your services are appreciated, and will not be overlooked. I have already presented your name to the Department, and will again urge it on the first opportunity. There are, however, only a few vacancies to fill, and hundreds of applications backed by thousands of recommendations. Under such circumstances results are always uncertain."[24]

A restless anxiety twitched throughout George's war letters. Men of ambition like him could always hear the faint, muffled picks and spades of undeserving men like Butler and others laying pipe inches beneath their own.

CHAPTER 7

TEARS *for* UNCLE TOM

IN LATE 1863, not long after shaming George Cole for returning late to the front, Butler launched a bold, unprecedented effort to arm Black men and hasten Union victory—a plan that his allies hoped would help win him the office of the presidency in the upcoming election. The gambit opened new chances at promotion for hundreds of White soldiers. George was one of the beneficiaries.

AFTER WRITING A SERIES of heavily underlined, begging letters, George at last secured his commission to colonel. He immediately set out to recruit formerly enslaved people for his regiment. Over the close of 1863, he recruited some 1,200 refugees and freedmen for the Second United States Colored Cavalry. He found most of them among the tens of thousands of freedmen who had taken refuge in and around Portsmouth and Norfolk, Virginia, and in familiar places where he had been a raider in New Bern, North Carolina.

He did not hold the cynical view, shared by many White Northerners, that Black troops were a convenient way to spare White Yankees from rebels' bullets. A proud antislavery man, and like many fellow Republicans, he viewed Black soldiers as a fulfillment of Abraham Lincoln's vision of free men taking destiny into their own hands. He was outspoken about his hatred of slavery and claimed that his opinions had cost him respect and rewards in the White cavalry. He claimed he was robbed of a promotion by a violent copperhead who hated him "politically" (and who also happened to be named George Washington).[1]

In the surviving letters to his family, he was nearly silent about the individuals he commanded. He did not share their names. He did not meditate much, as some White officers did in letters, on the character of Black people or the supposed virtues and weaknesses of their race. His only notable description of the men came in February 1864, six weeks after he recruited the regiment. To his brother Cornelius, he penned a buoyant account of how he had walked through camp, making his way through the crowd of soldiers he had recruited from teeming refugee camps.[2]

He was immediately struck by their industry. As many soldiers under Butler did, they had recently begun their service by constructing "freedmen's villages" on the abandoned farms of Confederate notables—but mostly on the burned-out lands in and near Hampton, Virginia, that had been torched by departing rebel troops in August 1861.[3] A Philadelphia paper described the result of the fires as "nothing but a forest of bleak sided chimneys and walls of brick houses tottering and cooling in the wind."[4] Black recruits in the Army of the James reclaimed these spaces and built homes for family members, often attaching small wood shanties to towering chimneys left behind from the destruction.

Butler's "General Order No. 46," issued weeks before George began recruiting, promised each Black soldier food and shelter, as well as "a certificate of subsistence" for his family upon mustering into his regiment. The care of family was a key enticement for recruiting Black men into Butler's army. Their sacrifice for the Union, pledged Butler, would relieve the "help-

"Slabtown," a freedmen's village, built on the ruins of Hampton, Virginia. Here, George's freshly recruited Black soldiers helped erect rudimentary dwellings for refugee families. The town soon bustled with industry: gardens, shops, churches, and schools. The families of soldiers, though, relied heavily on the uneven pay of their enlisted sons or husbands. Benjamin Butler promised recruits that the government would provide their families basic rations for the duration of the men's service for the Union. *"The Freedmen's Village, Hampton, Virginia,"* woodcut engraving from a photograph, Harper's Weekly, September 30, 1865. New York Public Library Digital Collections, https://digitalcollections.nypl.org/items/510d47e2-ee39-a3d9-e040-e00a18064a99

lessness of their women and children." If the soldier disappeared, or deserted, or was found guilty in a court-martial, however, his family's subsistence could be terminated. From the moment of recruitment, their soldiering was inseparable from their roles as husbands, fathers, and sons.[5]

George would soon have to confront how deeply his recruits connected their service to care for family. He could never understand its depth. He knew they labored diligently, but not what inspired them.

He witnessed recruits building homes for families and took assurance of greater things to come. It confirmed his hope that once freed, these men would embrace industriousness. After they built cookhouses and stockades, he bragged that the enormous project had cost the government only "two kegs nails and two thousand feet roofing." These were not shirkers who sapped Union resources but future self-made men who were resolved to work for their own destinies. "Not one [Black recruit] has needed a reprimand yet," he enthused.[6]

He saw a few actions that troubled him. His soldiers lined up at a sutler's tent and, in his opinion, squandered their ten-dollar bounties (issued thanks to Butler) on handheld mirrors and buckskin riding gloves. He disapproved. Perhaps he believed that they had not yet earned the right to pose before a mirror—to stand in military accouterments, imagining how others saw them. It was, perhaps, too close to his own path to manhood. Perhaps he hoped his soldiers would save their money for land instead. He did not elaborate.[7]

He noted with some pride, though, that before they purchased fine riding gauntlets, they pressed into lines to purchase spelling books that they petitioned him and fellow officers to help them put to use. He confessed that their "tireless & persistent" efforts to learn to read "shamed" him into about six hours a day of study, which was more than enough for him.[8]

The men pleaded for daily tutoring, in addition to the rigors of drilling and manual labor. Throughout the South in the decades before the war, harsh literacy laws had forbidden the teaching of enslaved people (and in some states free Black people) to read or write. Enslaved people often risked whippings, dismemberment, or death for the chance to read—secretly turning pages in a swamp clearing or a cellar, or congregating in late-night meetings where they scoured smuggled spelling primers, bibles, and newspapers. Only about 5 percent of the enslaved population was literate before the war began.[9]

Mirrors. Clothing. And most importantly books. In their early moments of freedom, with money in their pockets, George's soldiers grasped for the things that so many of his Finger Lakes neighbors and family had used to make sense of their own expanding freedoms and changing sense of the self.

★

THERE WERE REALITIES that the soldiers could not change about themselves. Many recruits had a traumatic past recorded on their bodies. In writing about this, George was swept into a kind of reverie by their scarred backs and weathered features.[10]

He looked over the recruits, who had been stripped naked for examination, and noted how "nearly all" had "awful whip scars." He walked up to one older man with a particularly "horrible back" and asked the freedman if he was going to settle for the cruelty. Just as he did, George realized that this was the same man who had once guided George's imperiled comrades to safety during a raid in North Carolina. This older soldier, to whom George gave no name in his later recollection, had "piloted me to that battery that my company took by assault, where I earned my leaf"—the gold oak leaf on a major's shoulder straps.

As he walked among his recruits, another "burly chap" kept looking at him. Conscious of the recruit's eyes following him, George peered into his face and to his astonishment recalled a nearly dead man whom he had once rescued from a swamp. He had been a half-alive skeleton when he had suddenly appeared before George and "gave himself up." After George's men gave him something to eat, the refugee returned to the swamp and brought out "four more wretches"—the only survivors of some sixteen other runaways who had been hiding for four months. The other dozen had been mauled by dogs or gunned down.

Many other faces among his fresh recruits were vaguely familiar to him. He was certain that they had been "picked up" in past raids. "They know me but they all look the same to me," he added. It wasn't within his powers to recall the faces of the many he had brought to freedom.

Standing among his naked recruits drove his mind to vivid scenes from the past. When he stopped to read their scars or peer into their eyes, he saw flashes of his own achievements in the war and promises of future glory. Soldiers with scored backs, who weren't going to "settle" for cruelty, would surely serve under him as fierce warriors bent on revenge. "I expect trouble to restrain these men when active duty comes," he wrote. "There is bitter & vindictive feeling in nearly all."

He believed that his recruits had enlisted for retaliatory warfare and that they would deliver stunning victories for their new colonel. Their deepest desires, in other words, complemented his own. This was a delusion shared by many White officers. "I think few better [regiments] than this will prove itself to be in time. I am confident & hopeful for I know this colored cavalry will be a success," he enthused. He apologized in his letter for going on at length about his past and future connection with his recruits. "But it attaches these fellows to me," he concluded, "to know I was their usher into liberty." They were living witnesses to the most glorious scenes of his raider days. Their bodies bore the marks of evil from which he had rescued them. He was drunk with optimism. He believed in a promising future again. He was an "usher" of freedom, and military fame lay just on the horizon.[11]

BRIGHT HOPE SOON DIMMED. By the early months of 1864, in the fields of Virginia, it was clear that his soldiers would not participate in heroic battles. Instead, internal conflict erupted, with officers disciplining or humiliating the men. The men resisted. George's letters, for whatever reason, were silent about these frictions. But his White officers left traces of the trouble. Some of the young officers he picked were unfit to lead formerly enslaved men. One of the most unfortunate promotions he made had been to a smooth-cheeked boy named Robert Dollard.

In late 1863, Lieutenant Dollard had heard rumors that General Butler had approved the formation of two Black cavalry regiments.[12] Dollard got his break when Colonel Cole, "an impulsive, warm hearted and dashing" officer, came calling in camp to offer him a captaincy in his newly authorized Second Colored Cavalry.[13] For this, Dollard took a shine to his new colonel and his mentor. He revered Colonel Cole like a father.[14]

Dollard held sentimental expectations that primed him for conflict. He was from a small New England village and likely had little to no experience with Black Americans before the war.[15] He fancied that he had come to know enslaved Americans through reading Harriet Beecher Stowe's novel *Uncle Tom's Cabin*. The story had brought on a flood of emotions, especially passages such as the one in which the old loyal enslaved person Tom, who was beaten into his grave, forgave his killers as Christ had done on the cross.

Dollard had shed "bitter tears" over its pages. He, like countless Northerners, had been moved by Stowe's book. When those Northerners became soldiers, they filtered reality through Stowe's stories. Once, when George was hunting down North Carolina guerrillas and stole a first-rate bloodhound from a slave owner, he mused that he had captured one of the "negro-hunting" dogs from the pages of the novel. He prized the war trophy so much that he sent the dog north to Syracuse under the care of a Black man, probably a war refugee whom he had helped free before converting him to his personal war servant.[16]

Despite the tears, Dollard started the war in a Massachusetts regiment that terrorized freedpeople.[17] The soldiers formed a brotherhood around pranks and rituals of cruelty. The hatred was so widespread that when, later on, soldiers like Dollard accepted promotions into Butler's Black army, they were

Robert Dollard included these three images in his recollections. *Left* and *center*: wartime likenesses of George and the boyish Dollard, both in officers' jackets. *Right*: Dollard, decades after the war, sporting the mustache that George preferred. In the front matter, Dollard dedicated his book to his beloved commander: "To my old Commander in the Campaigns of 1864 and 1865, before Richmond and Petersburg, Virginia, the late General George W. Cole, a brave and generous soldier, this book is dedicated." Robert Dollard, *Recollections of the Civil War and Going West to Grow Up with the Country* (Scotland, SD: the author, 1906). Library of Congress, https://www.loc.gov/item/06045041/

ostracized by White comrades.[18] Dollard had been prepared, it seems, for the chronic abuse that would plague George's regiment.

In January 1864, within the first days after the regiment's organization, George's lieutenant colonel issued a general order: "No officer will be permitted to use under any circumstances an enlisted man as a servant nor will he be permitted to draw pay for a servant unless he had one actually employed." Forcing Black soldiers into servitude was a widespread evil. A month earlier, Butler got wind of similar abuses and forbade White officers in the Army of the James from impressing or forcing Black people, especially enlisted soldiers, to be personal servants. Instead of hiring a servant with their government allowance, officers preyed on their own men and pocketed the money.[19]

In the Union army, securing a Black servant was a symbol of power. Ordinary White soldiers came to see servants as one of the first trappings of authority. As one New Yorker griped to his parents, "each one of them [officers]" had a "Nigger servant . . . whom they generally feed out of our Rations, it is a well known fact that they are treated better than we are." The better treatment of Black servants was hardly a fact. As one Massachusetts soldier wrote home, "Every private wants & Every officer has his colored servant who he feeds scantily, clothes shabbily, works cruelly & curses soundly & his curses includes the whole race."[20]

Black servants became a verbal and physical target for White soldiers' frustrations. Jealous soldiers who had to make their own coffee or find their own firewood could take out their frustrations on the object—that is, the human—that reminded them of their own inconsequence. In 1861, Union soldiers in Virginia had led an officer's servant by a rope around his neck, dragging him about the camp at the point of a bayonet.[21]

After a fresh promotion in his Massachusetts regiment, Dollard had "captured" for himself "a big black boy about six feet tall" to carry his personal blankets and bags. The first night that the servant went to sleep in camp, resentful soldiers pelted the servant with clods of dirt. If they wouldn't dare attack their new lieutenant, they might get away with punishing the man who symbolized their lieutenant's promotion.[22]

Every Black soldier, already under the thumb of a White commander, was a potential target to be coerced into servitude. Black soldiers could not be promoted above the line that separated commissioned officers from the enlisted men, and just as importantly, White officers within Black units could never be demoted below it. The army's color line heightened the usual tensions found everywhere between rank-and-file soldiers and officers. Questions of authority, and abuse of authority, were tangled up with race.[23]

DOLLARD RECALLED that the enlisted men in George's regiment were "submissive and obedient" during the first days of training. There was, however, soon a "hitch" in the commissary department, leaving the Black soldiers short of rations "long enough to get quite hungry." When bread and coffee finally arrived, he was struck by the scene of half-starved soldiers huddled in the snowy company street devouring the victuals like famished hounds.[24]

Dollard's recollections of events were rich with detail but at times short on accuracy. Regimental bookkeepers revealed that food shortages were not the result of logistical hitches; the real cause was manifested months later when Colonel Cole issued an order to the regiment stating that he had received a complaint from the enlisted men about "scanty rations." Because not a single complaint had been issued by any of the company officers to the Regimental Commissary (where rations were distributed) or to regimental headquarters, George concluded that such scarcity was "caused by Officers eating the rations of enlisted men."[25]

The Black men whom White officers encountered were not the childlike, patient Uncle Toms of Dollard's imagination. They came from tidewater Virginia and North Carolina, where, in the recent past, commercialization had begun to transform towns and cities, and with it the way that enslaved families experienced bondage. Tidewater bondsmen often learned skilled labor through apprenticeships; they "hired their own time"—working in factories and shops and on canals, turnpikes, railroads, ships, and barges. They often hired themselves out with the consent of their masters. As a result, they shared a sense of manly independence.[26]

And because tidewater masters frequently bred enslaved men and women, and sold enslaved family members to the expanding Cotton Kingdom to the west, the soldiers shared tragic memories of loss. The men in the regiment were fathers and husbands and brothers who had witnessed family members disappear again and again.

Many saw themselves as craftsmen and protectors of their endangered kin.[27] They joined the army to ensure that their loved ones were fed and safe from harm. They enlisted in large part to make that bargain with the Federal government. Butler had promised as much. It became increasingly clear, though, that their independence and role as guardians of family would not be respected by their officers; they could do little to ease the suffering of kin back in the refugee camps.

They also often could do too little to protect themselves. Danger lurked on all sides. They had to shield themselves from abuse from their own officers, while dreading falling into the hands of savage rebels.

CHAPTER 8

a GOOD DEAL *of* TROUBLE

ON MARCH 9, 1864, three months after their enlistment, George Cole's soldiers clashed in Suffolk, Virginia, with rebel troops serving under the notorious brigadier general Matthew W. Ransom. The rebels had gathered a few miles outside the city, bent on murdering Black men who occupied it. Ransom's men mostly hailed from nearby towns in eastern North Carolina, not too distant from the region that George and his comrades terrorized in 1862 and 1863.

The rebels appear to have singled out George's regiment. When the Confederates first entered the city, exhausted from having marched through deep sand, they sprang to life after one rebel officer yelled, "Run boys, run, and we will catch the G[od] d[amne]d niggers yet!" Confederate women along the way stood at their doors, praying and crying, some waving handkerchiefs and calling out to "kill the negroes." Some rebel citizens ladled out water for their thirsty liberators. Somebody shouted that they had sighted Black men in uniform. The rebels gave chase and scattered the Black cavalrymen with artillery fire. Eventually, the Confederates surrounded two of George's Black squadrons.

Ransom's men offered them no quarter. One atrocity—though there seem to have been more—was described in detail by rebel witnesses. About ten of George's soldiers—including, perhaps, one White officer—took cover in a small house, and from inside it took aim and fired at their attackers. The Confederates encircled the structure and set fire to it. A rebel witness boasted to a Southern newspaper that when the flames and smoke forced one of the soldiers to leap from a window, "a dozen bayonets pierced his body; another [soldier], and another followed, and shared the same fate." Of the roughly dozen men who had been trapped in the burning house, all met the same end save three who, with "manly resolution," were "burnt to cinders." Ransom's men, seething at the mere sight of formerly enslaved men in blue uniforms, refused to bury the bodies.[1]

In their reports, George and his fellow officers wrote enthusiastically, saying nothing of the cold-blooded executions except that some soldiers had been killed or were missing in the swamp. These reports caused General Benjamin Butler to write that he was "perfectly satisfied with [his] negro cavalry." Yankee officers claimed that the Black soldiers had fought with courage and coolness, repulsing an enemy many times their size. George's cavalry had "whipped" the rebels. No surviving Union report said anything about the atrocity. Butler, who was at Fort Monroe some distance off, apparently never learned of it. A newspaper from George's city of Syracuse even dedicated a paragraph to the battle, with not a whiff about atrocities, only saying that George's men had lost twenty soldiers.[2]

A MONTH LATER, the horrors of Suffolk were eclipsed by the massacre at Fort Pillow, Tennessee. On April 12, rebel soldiers under Nathan Bedford Forrest (future founder of the Ku Klux Klan) overtook the fort and murdered White and Black soldiers who had tried to surrender. Northern papers supplied Yankees with tales of Union soldiers buried alive, tents of wounded men set on fire, and Black men who were bayoneted as they pleaded on their knees for mercy. Outcry throughout the North led to a congressional investigation by the Joint Committee on the Conduct of the War, which quickly produced a widely read report that largely corroborated the grim stories printed everywhere in Northern newspapers.[3]

With the two-week-old Fort Pillow controversy swirling about and the killings at Suffolk still haunting George's soldiers, rebels struck again—some of them from General Ransom's brigade. Under the command of Brigadier General Robert F. Hoke, and with the help of a Confederate ironclad ship that crept down the Roanoke River, rebels fell upon and slaughtered several hundred innocents in Plymouth, North Carolina, an enclave along the Eastern Seaboard that attracted refugee families and pro-Union White people, including deserters. Many of the rebel killers hailed from North Carolina and might have been itching to wave the black flag in retribution for the raids that had brought suffering to their families. As with Fort Pillow and Suffolk, Plymouth's grisly details were murky.

What is clear is that a great atrocity was committed. The testimonies of various witnesses and participants who wrote letters immediately afterward (and years later) paint a sickening scene. Separate witnesses wrote, with no apparent connection to one another, that upon laying siege to the town and obtaining surrender from the outnumbered Union forces, rebels chased down, cornered, beat, and shot a frantic group of fleeing Black soldiers, male and female refugees of all ages, and "Buffaloes" (White Southern soldiers who joined the Union military).

At the time, few knew for certain what happened in Plymouth and its surrounding swamps. Exaggeration, pacts of silence, muted voices from illiterate refugees, and especially the silence of the slain made it impossible to say how many were bayoneted while pleading in the mire or stripped naked and executed in a firing line. It may have been fewer than fifty. It may have been several hundred.[4]

The best clarity that Americans could hope to find came thanks to the intervention of Butler. It came three months later. With the help of his aides, he extracted damning eyewitness testimony from a Black soldier named Samuel Johnson, described as an orderly sergeant in George's regiment. The affidavit was recorded somewhere "in the field." In it, Johnson told the story of how he had accompanied his White officer, Lieutenant George W. French, to recruit soldiers in Plymouth for Colonel Cole's regiment. The killers sprang upon the town. "Upon capture of Plymouth," the affidavit stated, "all the negroes found in blue uniform, or with any outward marks of a Union soldier upon him, was killed."[5]

The testimony painted a picture of an unusually lucky Samuel Johnson who hid in the shadows to witness a raft of atrocities in multiple places. He saw men hanged in the woods. Others were stripped naked and shot on the bank of the river. "Still others were killed by having their brains beaten out by the butt end of the muskets in the hands of the rebels." Rebels tied ropes around the necks of some of their victims and dragged them through the streets.

Johnson reported that he escaped execution by swapping out his uniform for some civilian clothes he found. He passed himself off as a local, found work raising some of the sunken Union boats from the Roanoke riverbed, and skipped around from place to place until he was forced to be a servant for a Confederate officer in Richmond.

Rebels and skeptics immediately called into question Johnson's testimony. They said he was a "bad affidavit man." Their suspicion, though, stopped short of the likely truth that Johnson did not exist. There is no record of a Samuel Johnson serving in George's regiment. He was likely an invention of

Butler's imagination, a product of his moral commitments and righteous indignation, and of his political machinations.[6]

It was a lie for the best of reasons. Something dreadful had happened at Plymouth. The phony affidavit promised to amplify the events of Fort Pillow and expose Abraham Lincoln's reluctance to take revenge on the reported atrocities committed against Black troops. Butler likely reasoned that a little fiction would expose the true lurid nature of rebels and change the war. Given the massacre of so many witnesses, Butler likely concluded that a forged account was the quickest path to truth and righteous revenge. Even more, a fictional, detailed account could push Northerners to demand a harder war and keep alive Butler's chances at challenging Lincoln in the coming presidential election, a mere seven months away.

Even with the shocking affidavit, however, the killings at Suffolk and Plymouth did not draw the widespread ire that resulted from Fort Pillow. The repeated reports of atrocities, though, surely ate at the nerves of George, his wife, officers, hunted Black men, and the families of the soldiers. Union men had been put on notice. Lieutenant George W. French—the White officer with "Samuel Johnson"—had truly been captured at Plymouth, imprisoned, and never heard from again. (His mother wrote desperate letters in vain to military officials.) Rebels threatened to return captured Black soldiers to slavery or to execute them on the spot. Captured White officers, they warned, would have hell to pay. After Mary Cole learned of the atrocities awaiting Black troops and officers like her husband, she grew nearly suicidal from the anxiety. The murky scenes of Suffolk, and then Plymouth, spread untold suffering.[7]

★

GEORGE COLE'S SOLDIERS BURIED the stabbed and charred bodies of their comrades at Suffolk. Then they returned to camp, where they had to negotiate tensions with White commanders. Camp was no refuge.

Violence in George's regiment often loomed when whiskey could be had. It was had often. Though George had initially refused to approve whiskey orders, the men experienced little shortage of alcohol. Within four months of the regiment's formation, George (who was morally opposed to drinking) had already relented to his junior officers' weakness for the cup. "Officers of this Regiment," he wrote in an order, "who feel the necessity of getting drunk will notify the Adjutant and he will designate a suitable time, but not on march or move."[8] In his regimental orders, he sometimes sounded like a father with depleting powers. His orders said more about his weakness as a commander than they did about established order.

And so, with their wounded colonel's reluctant permission, the officers drank too much, too often. The bonding ritual of drinking took the edge off pain, depression, guilt, and anxiety about death. It drowned out the longing for home. It also magnified tensions and invited vendettas into the open.[9] It brought communion and, just as often, racial enmity. Butler understood this when he wrote that drunken officers were "the curse" of Black soldiers in the Army of the James.[10]

During a May operation along the Chickahominy River, soldiers claimed that Robert Dollard stole their rations of whiskey. Instead of dividing it into portions for them on fatigue, he kept it in his own canteen for personal use. (One soldier testified that he remembered another one of Dollard's "boys" hauling the canteens on a march.) Dollard claimed drinking whiskey and quinine kept his malarial fever in check. It was a respectable alibi for any soldier who had served in the tidewater regions of Virginia and North Carolina.[11]

Drinking could not cure his hatred for proud Black soldiers. On a dusky May evening, still looking for his Uncle Tom, he swaggered up to a supply depot and insisted that the Black sergeant, Richardson Watson, who was from another company, allow him to use two Black sentinels to help carry ammunition. Watson refused, said that "his men" were not under Dollard's charge, and reminded the captain that sentinels could not leave their posts.[12]

Outraged, Dollard belched a jumbled curse about "not giving a damn" about any "black niggers" and stated that he didn't care if the regiment got its ammunition, though the rebels were just up the river. He surged toward one of the guards who was "just walking up and down his post," slapped him with an open fist, and began kicking him amid a storm of profanity.[13]

Black soldiers recalled the episode of drunken rage with clarity. But the brotherhood of junior officers—save one—protected Dollard with silence when he was brought to his court-martial. Dollard rightly testified that he was just doing what others did and had done.[14]

When Captain William Perrin, another one of George's young officers, found himself accused of similar bouts of drunkenness, his confession revealed how closely connected inebriation was with physical abuse. Like Dollard, Perrin wound up in a court-martial. He had been charged with drunkenness and forging orders to obtain more whiskey. The trial technically had nothing to do with the treatment of Black soldiers. Throughout the trial, though, Perrin and other witnesses repeatedly and vaguely referred to "complaints" and "trouble" in the regiment. At the close, Perrin asked to make a final statement, which he ended by defending himself from something for which he had not been officially accused. About the so-called complaints mentioned by others, Perrin told officers from other commands, "Perhaps you are aware that there has been a good deal of trouble among the officers and men of the Colored Cavalry. But I can say for my men and myself, that I have never struck a man a blow in earnest for eight months. And so far as that matter about complaints applies it does not apply to Company 'G.'"[15]

Compared with the violence everywhere else, he let it be known, his company had been a model of harmony. If he had struck a soldier on the face, or jabbed him in the gut, or kneed him in the testicles, it had not been done "in earnest." In George's regiment, and likely throughout the United States Colored Troops, the common sins of officers known as "complaints" in the ranks were code for chronic White-on-Black violence.

★

THESE COMPLAINTS WERE DOOMED to end in tragedy. Sylvester Ray, a soldier recruited by George himself in North Carolina, refused his pay in the summer of 1864. Black soldiers smoldered in anger to learn that, due to federal policy, they would make roughly half of what their White counterparts made; they were paid ten dollars instead of thirteen, minus three dollars to pay for their uniforms. Proximity to kin in the nearby refugee camp heightened the tensions in the Second Colored Cavalry. News from family members about hunger or unmet needs was a day's walk away. Every cent less was an assault on family. "Boys we are being robbed," Ray bellowed, then threatened officers—"so help me, Jesus"—that the rest of the soldiers would refuse to sign as well. When an officer commanded Ray to fall out of the ranks so that he could be taken to confinement, the pistol-hot soldier screamed, "I won't fall out, where's my gun[?], I'll shoot you, damn you, or any one who puts a hand on me[!]"[16]

That warning, that he would shoot anyone who laid hands on him, echoed over and over in the regiment. Nothing inflamed the men's tempers as much as when White officers tried to tie them up personally or command others to do so. By the regiment's first summer, a violent ritual emerged in which Black soldiers sharply resisted whenever White officers attempted to bind them with rope. The rituals became so common that on Independence Day in 1864, George issued an order directed at his abusive officers:

> From this date all Officers of this Regiment guilty of Striking, kicking, or tying up for punishment or personally abusing enlisted men will be severely punished. Guilty men may be punished in a legitimate manner by Court martial or shot for insubordination at once.[17]

This poorly worded order, of only forty-four words, would ruin the life of at least two men in the regiment.

After first forbidding officers from terrorizing enlisted men, the order confusingly added that "guilty men" could be killed on the spot. Colonel Cole failed to clarify who the "guilty men" were. Read one way—perhaps against the grain—it meant that officers guilty of abuse would be tried and punished, and perhaps even summarily shot, for abusing an enlisted man. The order suggested that abusers like Dollard might soon get their comeuppance. Read another way, the order said that "guilty men"—whom officers had wrongly abused—should either be court-martialed or, if deemed uncontrollable, killed on the spot.

Only weeks after the order's issue, violence returned. Dollard was at the center again. After the war, he told a dubious version of the story in which his Black officers had been willing, like armed Uncle Toms, to blaze away at unruly comrades in order to protect their commander (him).[18] But the regimental records reveal something else. Several Black soldiers testified that in July, Washington King, a Black sergeant, gathered boards in the summer rain for an anticipated move to another camp. John Jones, a White second lieutenant (the lowest rung of White commissioned officers), commanded King to give up the boards. "These are our boards, we hauled them out of the swamp," protested King. Fighting over firewood was a sure sign that soldiers had languished in an area too long and had scavenged every scrap of wood within a large radius. "Let [the wood] alone or I'll tie you," snapped Jones. He then ordered King to his quarters three times, and when King ignored the warnings, Jones commanded a Black orderly sergeant named Henry Williams to tie King up. Predictably, Williams refused, insisting he would only take such an order from Captain Dollard.[19]

Dollard galloped headlong into this chaos and dismounted his horse, ready to stamp out the insubordination. Some of the soldiers concluded that he had been off drinking again. Others had begun planning to arm themselves for the coming trouble, perhaps to make good on Colonel Cole's recent order. Dollard lined up the company with a waving gun, rushing them out of their tents before they grabbed their own arms. Once they were in line, he laid into Sergeant King, who—perhaps in a half taunt, or perhaps looking to test the meaning of George's order—allegedly told Dollard, "If you think I've done wrong, tie me up."

"I'll blow your brains out," Dollard barked.

"Well sir, if you think it is right you can blow them out," King replied.

Dollard repeated Lieutenant Jones's original orders by again commanding Sergeant Williams to tie up King. Williams refused as he did before, responding that King had not done anything to warrant the humiliation. He had simply protected his firewood from a greedy officer. Dollard growled that he would "rather kill a God damned nigger than a rebel" and that if he had known earlier as much as he did now, he would have run them "all into the rebel lines long ago!"

He raised his loaded pistol to King's throat and—after a short moment—pulled the trigger. As several Black witnesses attested, they heard the cap go off, but no discharge followed. Perhaps rain that day had dampened the caps or cartridges. Or maybe the Black witnesses were wrong about the gun being loaded. Whatever the case, Dollard was swept up by rage. He wanted to kill King, his un–Uncle Tom.

Dollard made a desperate exit. He went to George's tent, where the detained King swore that he overheard him admitting to George that the gun was loaded and that he could not tell why it had failed to fire. This suggests that Dollard, at least, believed that George's order gave an officer the license to murder a soldier for insubordination. In the resulting court-martial, Dollard testified that his Colt revolver frequently went off at half cock and that he didn't mean to pull the trigger. (Why an officer in the cavalry would settle for a handgun that went off at half cock, which he wore on his belt, was an issue left unexamined.) As with the other accusations against Dollard, his fellow officers banded together to ensure acquittal.

Colonel Cole leveled charges against Dollard, which suggests that George intended his order to protect his Black soldiers, not to enable them to be impulsively murdered. Butler then brought Dollard to Fort Monroe and, in the privacy of his headquarters, tried to browbeat him into a full confession. Butler knew how rare it was to get White officers to turn on their own. When he read the charges back to Dollard and the latter insisted on having a legitimate military trial, the commander snapped and threatened to stiffen Dollard's punishment should he be found guilty.

Upon learning of Butler's threats, George "earnestly protested" Dollard's treatment from the despised commander. George came to believe that this "was the cause of Butler's hatred" toward him.[20]

Though George had charged Dollard and originally testified to the soldier's drunkenness, he strangely softened his court testimony. He said that Dollard was one of the best officers in uniform. Perhaps it was a way for George to get back at Butler, who wanted Dollard harshly dealt with. George's awkward testimony, which seemed to clear Dollard of serious wrongdoing, sounded like the words of a colonel who desperately wanted to be admired by his young officers. This apparently humiliated Butler.[21]

Before the officers in the court exonerated Dollard, Corporal Allen Pierce gave his testimony. (Pierce was the supposedly loyal Black sergeant who, in Dollard's postwar tales, was willing to kill another Black soldier before attacking his own commander.) Pierce testified that his captain had "popped a cap at Sergeant King" because, among other things, Dollard "was a little intoxicated."[22] He could not swear to having heard everything that Dollard said; he did, though, recall his commander saying enough to strongly suggest guilt: "I'll kill one of you—if you don't mind; I'll kill you, you damn black nigger." If Pierce had truly once felt "intense loyalty"—as Dollard claimed later—he, at least once, mustered the courage to speak truth to evil in a room filled with White officers.

Racial hostilities continued to seethe. The forty-four-word order, a botched effort to stop the violence, only made tragedy certain. By late summer, George's world was cratering. His regiment, and his strained marriage, had reached the point of no return.

CHAPTER 9

NO RETURN

During the course of the war, George Cole applied for and obtained various furloughs to return home, especially after his fall from his horse.[1] More often, Mary came to him. During the first three years of the war, she kept her marriage together by crisscrossing the borders between home and the battlefront, sometimes with their two daughters in tow. She was there at the front from January to April 1864, somewhere not far from the early standoffs between George's officers and the enlisted men. She was staying somewhere nearby when his soldiers were burned and bayoneted in Suffolk. Because of these horrors, she returned home in late April 1864 in a downward melancholic spiral. Some newspapers later claimed that while at the front she had tried to kill herself.[2]

Soon after her return to Syracuse, George wrote to his brother, Cornelius, asking him to notify Mary of an impending halt on mail and to warn her not to assume the worst from silence. He didn't want her to feel "uneasy." She had reason to be. The year before, the Confederate government had announced that captured Union officers would be "put to death or otherwise punished." With the cold-blooded murders at Suffolk, it was all that she could bear. When she arrived back home, the papers were filled with reports of the wholesale massacre at Fort Pillow.[3]

Mary wrote back to her brother-in-law to thank him for keeping her informed; she lived in dread. George had been right to worry that she was on edge.[4] It was a great relief when she finally received "a few lines" from George. But because a soldier could have been killed and buried during the time it took to deliver his latest and last letter, she never could get enough mail to stave off the dread. "You can imagine," she wrote, "with what anxiety I devour the papers hoping to hear where they are and what doing." Somehow, up to that point, her husband had escaped his enemies "almost miraculously."[5]

She doubted such miracles could continue. She had already suffered as much as she had "thought possible" before he accepted a promotion in the Black regiment. His association with Black soldiers, she knew, would bring peril. Since the rebels murdered "indiscriminately in cold blood" and no notice was taken by "our government," she wrote, George's life "seems to hang by a thread."

"If he goes through this safely and is not promoted," she warned, "he must either resign or I shall die. I can't endure such wearing anxiety." For this reason, she too was desperate for George to get a promotion to general. Another rung up the ladder of command would further remove him from the path of bullets and the execution that might befall him upon capture. He had promised her that he would soon apply for a leave. She wanted him to resign his command immediately and return home. "He will not look on the dark side," she wrote, "but says he is going through the war."

She feared that George had aims to avenge the atrocities committed on his men and had decided to take "the matter into his own hands at the first opportunity." He had disturbing plans, she worried, to slay his way to justice. He was not alone in his lust for retribution. The next month, during Benjamin Butler's campaign to take Petersburg, in which George's Second

Colored Cavalry played some part, it was widely reported that Black soldiers "took no prisoners" as they overwhelmed Confederate forts and works. They yelled "Fort Pillow" as they executed helpless rebels.[6]

Warmer days promised more action for George, which only brought her more dread. He did not resign as Mary hoped he would. She continued in Syracuse under a blue haze and, by the summer of 1864, their marriage was at a crossroads. Over the next year, her husband did not return to Syracuse as he became embroiled in Butler's operations in Virginia. Nor did Mary return to the front for some seven or eight months, the remainder of 1864, probably the longest period that the two were apart during the war.

The warm months of 1864 would be the darkest of days at home and in the field. It was at this time, in Mary's daily unease and loneliness, that Luther Harris Hiscock began his aggressive pursuit of her. As she verged toward ruin, so did some of the men in George's regiment.

GEORGE'S YOUTHFUL PROTÉGÉ EDWIN R. FOX was like a railcar moving inexorably toward buckled tracks. Fox and George had fought together since the first year of the war, in the Third New York Cavalry. When George was crushed by his horse, it was Fox who had nursed him until Mary arrived. Nearly fifteen years George's junior, he had served as his orderly before George recruited him as a line officer for the United States Colored Cavalry.[7]

Fox and his comrades began their command over Black men with a warning, probably from George himself. According to Fox, they were "ordered to treat the men with kindness and punish them lightly." But as Fox put it, he "soon learned the mistake in that." His trouble began in a place called Bunches of Walnuts, Virginia, roughly twenty miles south of Norfolk, where a large portion of the men had been recruited from refugee camps. The soldiers first showed signs of mutiny on the subject of inferior pay, no doubt emboldened by Sylvester Ray's threat to shoot officers.[8]

Fox tried to persuade the men to do their duty despite the insulting pay. "It made them worse, if anything," he recalled. Preaching and reasoning only fomented unrest. During one confrontation, he dragooned a soldier up to a tree and ordered him tied. He avoided personally tying up the man by giving orders for it to be done. Then, repeating the regimental ritual, the other Black soldier refused to tie up "one of his own color." Fox ordered another soldier to do it. He refused as well.

Fox darted to his tent to retrieve his gun. With hard authority in his hands, he repeated his orders. Finally, at the end of a muzzle, the soldiers tied up their comrade.

It was an empty victory. His gun could not resolve the root problem, which was the abuse of power exerted on proud men who resisted it. In May he confronted a trooper who refused to mount his horse. The soldier responded with profanity and bravado, dismissing Fox's orders to climb into the saddle. And so, given that he had established armed threats as the basis of authority, Fox pulled his pistol on the trooper and threatened to kill him. The soldier dared Fox to "shoot and be God damned."

Fox's bluff had been called. He froze and shrank in defeat, explaining later that he "didn't like to shoot a man who was looking right into the muzzle of [his] pistol." From that day forward, when he ordered his men to do something they especially despised, he was faced with the conundrum of grabbing for his pistol, each time with less effectiveness.

Morale was low for officers and privates alike. George's troops had moved inland to support the grueling siege of Richmond and Petersburg and had been forced again to surrender their horses—to White troopers who took priority. The dismounted soldiers mostly did guard duty, dug what was an unimaginable chain of earthworks, supplied the army with food, transported bodies, formed picket lines along the front, and occasionally took part in small, ineffectual movements. The injustice of unequal pay continued to hang over them. The violent (often inebriated) tirades and "troubles," and the "hitches" in rations, were coming to a head.

In this climate, on August 2, 1864, Fox laid into Henry Edwards, a Black rank-and-file soldier. Edwards had escaped slavery from a region in North Carolina just north of the towns that had been devastated by George's Third New York Cavalry. He probably made his way to New Bern during one of the many raids of 1862 and 1863. He was twenty-one years old when he enlisted on Christmas Eve in 1863. He was likely recruited by George himself. The mustering record described him as "yellow" with black eyes.[9]

Fox assigned Edwards to guard duty. Edwards took to his bed instead, claiming he was too sick. It was an early August afternoon, at a place called Cedar Level, some twenty miles south of Richmond. A Black sergeant recalled that Edwards pretended he was asleep when Fox found him in his tent. Fox claimed that he had seen Edwards up and about earlier in the day. Some believed Edwards to be one of the many men with declining health; others thought him to be malingering. Nobody could be sure in a regiment of malnourished men.[10]

Fox ordered him to be taken from his bed to the guardhouse, to which the soldier responded that the man who took him there would be a "son of a bitch." When the soldier continued to mumble, Fox took three steps in his direction and threatened to kick his teeth down his throat. Fox wisely cooled a little, backed off, and departed. Shortly after, he summoned Edwards back to the officers' quarters, a short distance from the company tents. He ordered Edwards to lug a large wooden rail on his back and walk a beat through the company street as others took dinner. Edwards reportedly hauled the beam for an hour and a half along the tent-lined street. He was no meek Jesus. On his Via Dolorosa, Edwards liberally cursed his superiors as he stumbled along the dirt road.[11]

As the officers ate, Captain Silliman Ives suggested that Fox make an example of Edwards by bucking and gagging him. When Fox returned from supper, he found the soldier resting on the beam, which he had cast to the ground. Enraged, Fox ordered him to pick it up again and continue along the street. Edwards refused, adding, "I think I've carried it a good while."[12]

Another officer claimed that when comparing Fox's troubled company with others in George's regiment, he considered the state of discipline "quite good." More than one soldier claimed that, up until this fallout, Fox and Edwards had been friendly toward each other. Edwards, in fact, had "always stuck up for Lieut. Fox," and vice versa. A witness recalled them getting along as if Edwards "thought a great deal" of Fox.[13]

A public challenge from one of his more loyal subordinates made Fox's waning authority obvious to all. When Edwards again refused to lift the beam onto his back, Fox scurried to his tent to grab the last remnant of authority he had left. And as he knew, even that authority would soon become a mockery if he did not pull the trigger. Below all of this lay George's order—written some weeks before—that seemed to give an officer license to shoot an insubordinate soldier "at once."

By the time Fox returned, Edwards had grabbed the beam in hope of placating his enraged commander. But Fox had already lost his cool and was looking to finally win the war of wills. After ordering a resistant Edwards to pick up the beam, Fox heaved it into the air so wildly that he almost struck himself with the spinning rail.

(About this time, a witness to the conflict, Sergeant Samuel Brown—who had had a similar standoff with Fox just that spring—turned from the gathering crowd and walked off toward camp. He saw two guards coming down from the guardhouse, and together they quietly ducked into the orderly's tent.)[14]

Fox ordered his Black officers to have Edwards "bucked and gagged."[15] Edwards insisted that he had done nothing wrong and therefore deserved no such punishment. When Edwards saw Fox approaching with rope in hand, he challenged him: "You can't tie me, you have not force enough to do it." This taunt only made Fox more determined. Another officer convinced the raging Fox to let some of the Black troopers bind Edwards instead; even though he risked looking like a coward, Fox relented. He ordered two Black guards and a corporal to tie up Edwards, who continued to protest. One of the guards, Owen Dennis, grabbed Edwards by the jacket and told him "not to be so fractious." He pleaded for him to obey orders and insisted that "a little bit of suffering would not kill him."[16]

Edwards eventually offered his naked wrists to the Black men, saying, "You shall tie me any way the Lieutenant wants me tied, but the Lieutenant shan't tie." After Dennis tethered the right arm, Edwards offered his left to be tied by the Black corporal. He was sending a clear message about who could tie up a Black soldier and who could not.[17]

But to Fox's tastes, the soldiers had tied Edwards's right arm too loosely. So he ordered the right hand cinched by the corporal, who straightway objected, saying that he would "not allow" the ropes to hurt Edwards's wrists.

Fox insisted on cinching the ropes himself.

"I want to tie you," he said.

"You shan't tie me," quipped Edwards.

In this moment Fox chose to cross the line, seemingly baited by Edwards's daring him to do so. In attempting to tighten the cords on Edwards, Fox could be considered—in the logic of George's order—one of the "guilty men" who deserved a court-martial or immediate execution.[18]

(At about this time, Sergeant Brown, who had cut away a few moments before, emerged from the orderly's tent and joined the crowd again, apparently along with the two guards, who were armed.)

Fox stood amid the gathering crowd, raised his gun in the air, and hollered to Edwards, "I give you fair warning in the presence of all here, and if you won't obey the order I shall shoot you." He brought his gun to the level and declared that he would give Edwards three chances to submit.

"Very composed," according to accounts, Edwards again said that he would let others tie him, but Fox never. As one Black comrade recounted, Edwards simply "would not let any white man tie him."

"Will you let me tie you?" Fox asked.

"No, but the others can," responded Edwards, with arms still wrenched behind his back. "I am already tied," he added.

When Fox asked a second time, Edwards begged to have a word.

"Lieutenant will you allow me the privilege of speaking three words?"

Fox consented. "I will."

Staring down his officer, Edwards warned, "It is your time now and it is my time hereafter. My carbine never tells a lie."[19]

The soldiers all knew what this meant. A Black comrade later summed up Edwards's threat by saying that "if [Fox] shot him he better shoot him good, for in battle [Edwards] would shoot him." It was a murderous threat. Fox knew it. As he recalled hearing it, Edwards had threatened to "blow [his] God damned brains out."[20]

"You are talking nonsense; you don't know what you say," Fox replied, apparently rattled by the boldness.

"I know what I say," Edwards flexed.

Needing to prove he was unfazed by the soldier's unflinching bravery, the lieutenant then asked the third, and final, time. Some soldiers heard him cock the gun's hammer while he took aim only feet away from Edwards's black eyes. Sensing imminent danger, Edwards turned his face and contorted his body by twisting it away from Fox, still gesturing to his comrades that they could refasten the ropes.

As Edwards turned, Fox blew out his brains from just behind the ear. He did not have to look the soldier in the eye when he pulled the trigger. One of the soldiers standing at Edwards's side wrenched away and, as he did, heard Edwards's body fall to the earth. With his face in the dirt, lying on his left side, Edwards let out "one long" parting groan. His body lay beneath the boughs of two plum trees.

Fox backed away. For about two minutes—or for what seemed like two minutes—nobody spoke.[21]

Another officer grabbed Fox to rush him off to George's tent—similar to how Robert Dollard had been whisked away a few weeks earlier. As the murderer departed, the camp—tucked in a grove of fruit trees—began breaking into a scene of confused distress. The silence was replaced by "considerable howling and crying." As he mounted his horse, Fox could hear Edwards's comrades "crying" and "halooing" from their tents. He escaped before the loudest wailing. One White officer who heard the cries of sorrow admitted that he found it "rather hard" to describe the sounds.[22]

Fox personally heard no threats against his life as he fled the scene. But one of the first men to speak threatened that if somebody shot "one of his own color," the killer would never live to tell of it.[23]

Later in the evening, hunkered down and under arrest in George's quarters, Fox got word that the men had "kicked up considerable disturbances and threatened to kill all the white men" around the camp. George had lost control of his regimental soldiers—the same men whom, eight months earlier, he dreamed would bring him and themselves glory.

★

IN THE LAST DAYS OF AUGUST, at the close of his court-martial, Fox told fellow officers, "I considered myself doing my duty." His peers agreed and acquitted him of murder.

General Butler sent a report of the trial to President Abraham Lincoln and the War Department, arguing that while Fox had clearly killed Edwards, he could not justly be convicted of the specified charges. The homicide "had not that malicious intent which would justify a verdict of murder." He concluded that Fox had been confused by a poorly composed military order and that the tragic killing could be traced to George's words. As Butler saw things, the clause about "guilty men" getting "shot at once" had confused Fox.[24]

Fox was not alone in his interpretation of the order. Nobody seems to have tried to stop him, other than to advise him to perfectly follow the order to the letter. First Lieutenant Benjamin Swarthout, who witnessed the murder and at one time held the loaded gun while Fox made his first attempt to retie Edwards, had cautioned Fox to order a corporal and two guards—all Black men—to do the tying. By insisting that only Black hands did the binding, Swarthout tried to keep Fox in line with the order.[25]

The company captain also admitted that he told Fox, in some sort of shorthand, that if Fox "was going to punish" Edwards, he should "do it up right." George's regimental officers had read the order closely, mining the text for technicalities.[26]

The enlisted men mined it too. Edwards made it clear that Fox could not personally abuse him or tie him up, though his actions and words taunted him to try it. Perhaps Edwards had known that if Fox crossed the line, some of the Black comrades had decided to kill the officer. First Lieutenant Swarthout testified that when the Black guards "came with their carbines" during the standoff, he ordered them to lay their guns in a tent. Those guards apparently were joined by Sergeant Brown, who had also been ordered to put away his gun.

Strangely, during Fox's trial, Brown told the jury of White officers that the three Black soldiers ducked into the orderly's tent and "looked at" a little book. Brown did not elaborate. It could have been a book of hymns. Or a bible. It is most probable that the men hid away to consult the book of regimental orders and to interpret one last time the potent, confusing words of their colonel.[27]

Butler approved the jurors' exoneration but declared Fox to be "unfit" to be an officer over Black troops. On September 13, he dismissed Fox from the army.[28] Fox would not stay away for long. After what he had seen and done, he would always belong to a brotherhood formed in the madness of war.

CHAPTER 10

the RESURRECTIONISTS

ONLY THREE MONTHS INTO HIS COLONELCY, George Cole set his eyes on another promotion. He scoured army regulations like sacred texts, locating hidden details that might prove him deserving. He tried to capitalize on the confusion that resulted from the ever-changing organization of army units.[1]

He clung to the hope that he would return home with the title "General" to put before his "George Washington." Over the summer of 1864, when violence churned his regiment, he nursed suspicions that he had been thwarted by the machinations of fellow commissioned officers. He complained to his brother, "I shall not be commanded by my juniors & inferiors much longer." He feared that he was paying for his unwillingness to scrape and bow. "I am the equal to any man I know of & not much given to begging or fawning." He held out hope that he could be promoted by merit alone.[2]

A promotion over a Black brigade would make him a general. Two days later he wrote, "The position belongs to me, even by rank, had I not earned it over and over."[3] Benjamin Butler had submitted a list to the secretary of war recommending three of George's fellow colonels be breveted to the rank of brigadier general in light of their "gallant and meritorious" action in a charge at Spring Hill (Virginia, not the more famous battle of the same name in Tennessee).[4] When the brevets were approved, George vented that "others who have laid off at home and in rear, are distancing me in promotion & grown wealthy on government spoils." He insisted that he had a clear conscience. "<u>I have done my duty</u>," he said. He supplied a short list of recently minted generals, saying he couldn't fathom their names being preserved by history when they had been at home "making money while I was fighting the hardest two years of the war."[5]

★

MEANWHILE, his commanding officer entertained even taller ambitions. Butler dreamed of taking Richmond. He and his confidants believed that capturing it would ensure his path to the presidency in the approaching national election. He openly and absurdly blamed his bungled attempt on Richmond in early 1864 on Abraham Lincoln's weakness in executing criminal Union soldiers. When Ulysses S. Grant attempted to take Richmond in May, Butler began his portion of the coordinated offensive—the Bermuda Hundred campaign—with a poor understanding of fundamental tactics, especially timing and purpose. He even disregarded warnings given him by seasoned navy officials who cautioned him that ships with fifteen-foot drafts could not navigate a river with ten-foot shoals.[6]

He was widely ridiculed when his men in the Army of the James, including many in George's regiment, were tasked with cutting off the Richmond-Petersburg railroad to help Grant defeat Robert E. Lee up north near Richmond. After crossing the James River, Butler established a beachhead at Bermuda Hundred but then shrank before rebel forces half in size. He took shelter in a cul-de-sac of land formed by two hairpin bends in the James River. With the river bend to their backs, the same geography that provided safety also allowed rebels to keep many of his forces confined. As Grant famously put it, "[Butler's] army . . . was as completely shut off from further operations directly against Richmond as if it had been in a bottle, strongly corked." He had "hermetically sealed" his own army from the grand plans of Richmond.[7]

After his strategies were frustrated, Butler immediately began purging his highest officers whom he felt had sabotaged his generalship. They had doubted his strategies and undermined his authority. He also sent a letter to Lincoln asking to be promoted to major general in the Regular Army. Instead, the War Department began siphoning away his troops. Sarah Butler, his wife, and others close to him believed that he was targeted because he was outshining Grant and Lincoln. Sarah's ambitions often matched her husband's.[8]

★

THE BOUTS OF VIOLENCE AND PROTEST in George's regiment happened within the larger context of Butler's increasingly quixotic designs. In the late summer of 1864, Butler persuaded Grant to approve a plan for digging a five-hundred-foot canal across the Dutch Gap—a narrow neck of land between the ribbonlike looping of the James River. Grant deemed the canal project fantastical but allowed Butler to engage in it, perhaps only because it would keep him off the battlefield. Butler believed that if they dug out some 167,000 cubic yards of earth and then dynamited the earthen bulkheads holding the river back, the canal would immediately allow Union vessels to bypass Confederate shelling and torpedoes and make their way to a doomed Richmond.

In early September, George's Second Colored Cavalry moved its headquarters north of the James River to a place called Deep Bottom. There the men dug and maintained trenches, formed picket lines, and transferred to and from

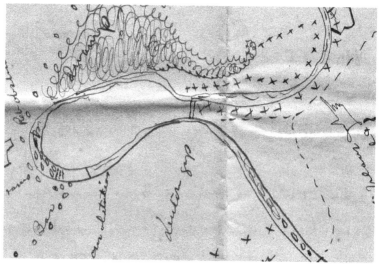

In a letter to his brother, George sketched this detailed map of Dutch Gap, where his Black soldiers were forced to work on Butler's quixotic and deadly canal project. George included his camp at Deep Bottom (top right corner) and the extensive picket lines of Union soldiers (x's) and rebels (o's) that regularly picked one another off as the days wore on. By this time George was furious that his regiment was going to be converted into infantry. He was also livid that his superiors ignored his plan (marked on the drawing) of laying torpedoes in the river to destroy rebel ships. Just south of this place is where Butler's troops were infamously "bottled up."
George W. Cole to Cornelius Cole, January 30, 1865, UCLA Library Special Collections

Dutch Gap. Divided up and dismounted, the cavalrymen lost whatever regimental integrity they had.[9]

During the project, Thomas Morris Chester, the war's only Black correspondent for a major newspaper, the *Philadelphia Press*, spent much of his time around Black soldiers in the Army of the James. He consistently wrote in buoyant tones regarding the achievements of Black soldiers. But he could not remain silent about the abuses at Dutch Gap. The "wrongs" suffered by Black soldiers and laborers in the Army of the James, he wrote, "if ventilated," would expose a "disgraceful depth of depravity, practiced by dishonest men, in the name of the Government."[10]

Black soldiers were there to dig Butler's vision into reality. They toiled alongside hired Black laborers, some White soldiers—who were enticed with increased pay—and some rebel prisoners. They drudged in what looked and felt like a mass grave, nearly thirty feet deep, as enemy shells shook the earth around them. Many of the men dug shelters into the face of the dirt canal where they could climb in to temporarily escape the threat of death.[11] Chester fumed that the soldiers were "continually exposed" to the bombardment. Black laborers were repeatedly removed from the project during heavier fire from the enemy. But because facing death was the lot of a soldier, the troops were forced to dig on.[12]

To keep them from running from Dutch Gap—as they had recently run from bondage—Union officers restrained the paid refugees like prisoners. The ranking engineer, Major Benjamin Ludlow, "amuse[d] himself by tying up these redeemed freemen" between the bouts of rebel fire. Chester wrote that they were "not only plundered and robbed, but are kicked and cuffed by those who have robbed them of their hard earnings." Abused and fleeced, they were then transferred to other parts of the department by army officers and contractors who were confident that the ex-enslaved peoples' "ignorance would be a guard against discovery."[13]

Chester cynically (and correctly) predicted that Ludlow's "successful" handling of his half-enslaved workers would lead to an absurd promotion to brigadier general over Black troops. (In his angry letters about false merit, George singled out Ludlow, whose climb to the coveted rank of general was particularly painful to witness.) Such a promotion, Chester continued, "would be exceedingly unfortunate, and unjust to those who are making so many willing sacrifices for the perpetuation

In this drawing of the canal at Dutch Gap, the masses of Black soldiers and laborers huddle and scrape away at the remaining bulkhead as two men are blown back (*center*) by a rebel shell. *William Waud, drawing from "Yankee Improvements in Front of Petersburg,"* Harper's Weekly, *November 5, 1864, 712–13. Library of Congress, https://www.loc.gov/resource/cph.3a16267/*

of the Union." It was as if Chester had been reading George's disillusioned letters.

Chester may have heard it, after all, from the mouth of George, whom he singled out for praise later in the report. He wrote that George, "more than any one else," was able to lure over rebels from the enemy's thinning picket line. Chester learned that George had lingering injuries. "The gallant Colonel," he wrote to his readers, "is now suffering from the effects of a wound which he received some time ago."[14]

George, he believed, was destined to play a heroic role in the upcoming days or weeks. "As soon as [Cole] is able to mount his favorite charger, it is generally supposed that he will open up a way" for the desperate rebels to flee into Union lines. "There is no braver soldier in the service," Chester added. "No one enjoys to a greater degree the respect of his officers or the affection of his men."[15]

This praise came less than two months after Fox murdered Edwards. Chester had only been a correspondent for a few weeks. He was a free Black man from the North who had been raised in an abolitionist home and college educated at a young age. He had recruited soldiers for two Black Massachusetts regiments. And he was smitten by the narrative of a glorious and inevitable military triumph of the Union and the destruction of slavery.

As a result, his sketches were filled with shiny bayonets and rock-ribbed Black soldiers marching to battle. His reports showed glimpses of mistreatment but were largely blind to the systemic racial tensions in front of him in Lincoln's army. He was unable, or unwilling, to see how those most committed to antislavery were sometimes implicated in the abuses of Black soldiers. He lauded Butler, casting no blame on him for scheming the canal project into being or for promising to have it completed in ten days—something that doomed the men to be driven mercilessly.

Chester rightly wrote that Butler "by no means justifies or allows any man, black or white, to be treated in an unwarrantable manner." He guaranteed his readers that the Army of the James would soon take Richmond and "fully vindicate the reputation of Gen. Butler as a martial leader." Smitten by Butler's boldness in defending the interests of refugees and Black soldiers, he was oblivious to the widespread "complaints" in the Army of the James.[16]

WHEN COLDER WEATHER SLOWED A WAR that seemed to have nearly run its course, the War Department took steps to consolidate Black units. Butler had asked Grant months before to transfer an additional eight Black regiments into the Army of the James. In this way, he argued, Black soldiers would be placed under the care of a conscientious commander who would promote orderliness within the ranks and buoy their morale. Grant rejected the idea.[17]

In late November, Butler raised his sights ever higher, requesting a massive overhaul of the armies in Virginia. He requested that the entire complement of Black infantry be transferred from the Army of the Potomac to the Army of the James, creating what would be a daring experiment. This time Grant approved. Black soldiers from the Army of the James and the Army of the Potomac were formed into the all-Black Twenty-Fifth Corps, earmarked to serve alongside the all-White Twenty-Fourth Corps, both under Butler's command. Butler could brag that in all of US military history, the boldest experiment with Black soldiers—the only of its kind—took place in his Army of the James.[18]

Grant eventually warmed to consolidating Black troops, partly because doing so addressed anxieties, widespread among Whites, over what to do with armed and trained Black men once the war ended. He appointed officers who would neutralize the racial schemes of Butler. General Godfrey Weitzel took command over the all-Black Twenty-Fifth Corps, though Weitzel was no friend to Black soldiers. Two years earlier in Louisiana, he had resisted taking them under his command. His despised Black troops, though, won him fame when they bravely fought in the Union capture of Port Hudson and obtained control of the Mississippi River. With seemingly little of the war left, commanding them promised to win him a second general's star.[19]

Butler's other corps commander, Edward O. C. Ord, like Weitzel, had demonstrated rancor toward Black soldiers, along with their families in refugee camps.[20] (After the close of the war, Ord—who saw refugees as parasites—wanted to solve the clothing shortage for refugees by making clothing out of old tents.) Within days of organizing the corps, Butler rebuked these commanders for cowriting a letter of complaint and accused them of plotting to undermine his authority. Whatever Grant's motives, his appointments brought friction to Butler's schemes and kept his visions of grandeur in check.[21]

By the close of 1864, Butler stood knee-deep in the grave of his military career, digging out the last spadefuls. He hatched a desperate plan to float a condemned vessel loaded with three hundred tons of gunpowder and detonate it as it drifted toward Fort Fisher, a key—and seemingly impregnable—North Carolina coastal holding. Although the plan was initially dismissed as quixotic, one of Butler's schoolmates convinced military brass to mull it over. Though skeptical, Grant eventually agreed to the plan. But he did not tap Butler to do it. Instead, he appointed General Weitzel to lead troops in pace with the powder ship and an accompanying naval fleet. But because Fort Fisher fell within Butler's geographic command, he suppressed the order and, at the last minute, installed himself as the expedition's ranking commander. Grant had heard the night before that Butler would be accompanying the expedition but incorrectly assumed he was only going along to witness his wild scheme.

Butler and the other commander, Admiral David Dixon Porter, despised each other so much that they had to communicate through intermediaries. Because of confusion, or lust for glory, Butler embarked with his men ahead of the naval portion, including Porter, who was supposed to take the lead. After a series of miscues, and several days, Porter's fleet caught up with Butler. Porter convinced him to move his ships farther from the fort. The condemned boat was floated near the fort. It had been filled in various sections with open-topped powder kegs and Gomez fuses timed to explode in unison; instead, when the moment came, they detonated at different times and did little more than rudely wake sleeping rebels inside the fort. (Butler would argue, with some persuasion, that the navy detonated it prematurely so that his forces would not be part of the glory.) Even worse, Butler took the boats so far out of range that, after the underwhelming explosion, his troops arrived too late to take advantage of the chaos.

On Christmas Day, when Butler's men finally went ashore, they captured a number of underage rebel soldiers before digging in for a siege. He watched anxiously from his tugboat; when General Weitzel, the officer who was supposed to be in charge, informed Butler that the fortress had incurred no damage and would soon receive reinforcements, Butler sank into a defeatist funk. As if he had no fight left once his dream of pyrotechnical warfare sank with the obliterated ship, he ordered an immediate withdrawal, pulling back men who had risked their lives to establish a beachhead. Because of his panic and an unusually stormy shoreline, many of his men were left stranded on the beach.

Butler painted his withdrawal as having saved his men from tragic bloodletting, and soon tried to spin the fiasco as a well-laid plan doomed by conspiring forces. The raging storms had foiled his plan, he argued. He had been the victim of grandstanding by naval officers. But War Department memos, newspaper coverage, and letters from soldiers roundly denounced him for yet another embarrassment to the Union. George reported that his "boys" who went on the expedition were enraged. They told George that had they not been stopped by Butler, they could "easily have captured it."[22]

By the close of 1864, George had lost all patience with Butler's damnable schemes. Somehow, his commander managed to pull off one last fizzle, even as his rivals were lowering his military career into the grave. On New Year's Day 1865, Butler called together political notables and curious onlookers to witness what he hailed as one of the greatest military engineering feats in the annals of war. While he had been leading the Fort Fisher debacle, soldiers finished digging out the canal at Dutch Gap.

Butler originally estimated that the project would be finished in ten days. Roughly four months behind schedule, a crowd of onlookers and journalists gathered to witness his final, and much delayed, act. The explosives detonated as planned. Tons of earth shot into the sky. Most of it came crashing back into the void, damming the river all over again. George was outraged; writing as if he had witnessed it himself, he fumed to his brother that the "Dutch Gap fizzled yesterday, didn't get out a pound of earth, smoked some." He called it a "great abortion" and wrote, "Montes parturient nascitur ridiculus mus," a Latin line from Horace that translates as, "A mountain goes into labor and gives birth to a ridiculous mouse." Grandiose schemes produced so little. "Genl Butler's stupid powder ship & Dutch Gap," he wrote, "have cost Uncle Sam many a million."[23]

All but loyal, hard-war Republicans denounced Butler as a bumbler and coward who abandoned his own men. The crew from Porter's flagship made Butler a mock leather medal with "in commemoration of his heroic conduct" written on one side and a pair of legs in the act of running on the other.[24]

At last, Grant had a clear case for Butler's removal. He convinced Edwin Stanton, the secretary of war, and Lincoln to release the "unsafe commander." Butler believed his removal had been spearheaded by a cabal of West Pointers who could no longer tolerate a citizen soldier outranking them. (In this he was generally right, though he would not own his mistakes.) In his mind, too few had appreciated how deeply he was committed to Black soldiers and their path to liberty. In a parting speech to his troops, he heaped praise on them. They had honored the uniforms on their backs in their fight for freedom and had "illustrated the best qualities of manhood," which even their masters could not deny. Someday, Butler said, he and his soldiers would proudly say together, "I too, was of the Army of the James."

In Lincoln's first executive order of 1865, he axed his longtime potential rival and sometime political helpmate. Butler returned to Lowell, Massachusetts, to lick his wounds.[25]

Grant designated Major General Ord to take command of the Army of the James. Ord immediately tried to stop Butler's final act of propaganda by asking Grant for permission to suppress the dissemination of seven hundred copies of Butler's farewell speech to his soldiers. In the pamphlet, Butler defended his cautious record, claiming the "wasted blood of my men does not stain my garments"—clearly a jab at Grant and those who, over the bloodiest summer of the war, had sacrificed Union boys according to what a grieving Lincoln called the "awful arithmetic." Grant ordered Ord not to interfere; he knew that Butler could not keep officers and the American public from asking questions about his long list of military failures. Soon after Butler's sacking, Admiral Porter and a more compliant general attacked Fort Fisher again, this time successfully conquering it—something that Butler had already begun arguing could never be done.[26]

From the high echelons of the army down to enlisted men, Butler's manhood was ridiculed. In a letter to Grant, Porter quipped, "I hold it to be a good rule never to send a boy on a man's errand." In a letter to Porter, William T. Sherman rubbed in the salt: "The best part of the taking of Fort Fisher was the killing of Butler. He has had no blood on his skirts and judging from the past, it will be long before his blood stains anything." The bogus general had finally been buried. Denouncing Butler's final speech as a "bombastic order designed as a fling at Grant," Sherman promised that even Butler's greatest source of power could not redeem him anymore. Grant had "quietly and completely" laid Butler "low forever," seethed Sherman. "Even the nigger cannot resurrect him."[27]

IT HAD BEEN EXCRUCIATING for George to watch. But he too, at the close of the war, clung to the hope of his own resurrection from Black soldiers. During Butler's dramatic tumble, George began to behave desperately; he believed that he had been buried by others—buried in the newspapers, buried by the intrigue of his superiors and peers. One of his rivals, Colonel Jephtha Garrard, had been making a "furious effort" for promotion by sending one of his junior officers, who could lie "like Judas," to drum up support in Washington, DC. (Garrard was related to the despised Ludlow who tied up laborers at Dutch Gap.)[28]

In his own furious efforts, George had recently stooped to sending letters to Butler asking him to pass along accounts of his (George's) merits to the appropriate authorities. He hounded Butler to send a letter directly to Stanton. Butler assured George that he had. Weak from waiting, George sought confirmation from Stanton, who replied that he hadn't received it. After some investigation, George came to believe that Butler had sent it and that the letter had been suppressed by a rival, the recently promoted General Ludlow or some other political general, with the intent to "oust" him.[29]

George then sent a sharp letter of resignation to the Army of the James headquarters, complaining that junior officers had "jumped" him again. They had been given command over a brigade that he had mostly raised with his own efforts. "It would I believe be a violation of my self respect to remain in my present position," he wrote before tendering his resignation. "I know I can do better elsewhere," he concluded. The letter, though, was intercepted by Brigadier General Edward Wild, a one-armed radical abolitionist and arguably the fiercest antislavery man in Federal uniform. Wild temporarily quieted George's rage, convincing him that dismissal would destroy his postwar reputation.[30]

George agreed to remain in uniform. Less than a week later, he wrote his brother again, bemoaning the promotion of Ludlow, the abuser of Black laborers at Dutch Gap, to full brigadier general. He had grown "tired of the 'you tickle me & I'll tickle you' sort of business." He had become weary of—and increasingly complicit in—a system where men traded on intimacy.[31]

He grew more desperate, clinging to any rumor about his rivals. He came to believe that the recently promoted Ludlow was a cousin of Butler's. (He wasn't. But Ludlow had other key cousins.) He concluded that the recent promotion of Alonso Draper to brevet brigadier general had more to do with Draper's ability to get Butler political votes back in Lowell, Massachusetts.[32] He confessed anxiety about finding steady work after the war; he discussed with his junior officers the prospect of soldiering in Mexico against the French imperial army.[33] He hoped to drum up another investigation of Butler for wartime corruption.[34]

He denounced the Army of the James as a "sink hole of military corruption."[35] Yet, until the very end (and even from his cell after the murder), he sought his commander's favor. Soon after Butler had been sacked by Grant, George sent him one more letter asking for a recommendation. From his home in Lowell, Butler assured him—"My Dear Colonel Cole"—that he had forwarded a report through the usual channels in which he named George for meritorious services and "urged" for his promotion. He said that he also sent a letter to the War Department. "I trust you will yet receive the promotion which is due you." If George wished to press the matter, Butler offered to compose with his own hand a certificate of services that George had "justly and nobly earned." He ended the letter with something he must have known would eat at George—as it would any soldier frustrated about the lack of correlation between merit and promotion: "Alas! Services are not always the test of rewards—yours truly, Benj Butler."[36]

★

THAT WINTER, Mary Cole returned to the front with her daughters in tow. They took a room in a hotel in Portsmouth, across the Elizabeth River from Norfolk. George's men had recently been transferred there after being pulled from the trenches outside Richmond.

One night, perhaps in March 1865, George traveled about seven miles to be with his family. He spent the night with Mary and most of the following day with his daughters. During their hotel visit, he wrote a letter to Cornelius Cole. War was on his brain. His men had finally finished a long winter of redigging Butler's canal. Action had begun again. He wrote of how his outposts had been skirmishing with the rebs nearly every day. Just the day before, he had taken 150 of his men through Suffolk and captured a rebel sheriff and two captains. As they passed through, he visited the place where rebels just a year earlier had committed atrocities on his regiment. He saw the burned house where his men had been smoked out and run through with bayonets. He studied the side of a road where the bodies had been dumped together in a mass grave.

Mary waited somewhere in the hotel room as he wrote about how he and his men had retraced their steps in the battle. He mused how he had defeated forces greater than his own, basking for a moment in how he hadn't needed "West Point" tactics but with his "volunteer manner" had outsmarted the rebels. He still held out hope that the vengefulness of his soldiers would bring themselves and their commander glory. "My men are crazy to get at them and as soon as a chance occurs you will hear from us certain."[37]

He shuddered at rumors making their rounds that Butler was being considered for secretary of state. He worried that in replacing Butler, Grant would dig up more "fossils" instead of promoting fresh talent. "My family are all well," he abruptly wrote, almost as an afterthought. "Mary wishes me to say she does not know when she shall go home." He was busy with war and could see his "folks but seldom." He hoped to soon bring them into camp.

Briefly mentioning his family seems to have reminded him that he was going to need employment after the war. He had recently scoured the papers, cutting out announcements of government posts and sending them to Cornelius. He especially wanted a post in the Treasury Department in Savannah, supervising the cotton trade (the thing that had supposedly corrupted Butler). "Write me the political prospects," he closed, "as I have little chance to learn [of] any[,] outside as I am."

He signed his name to the letter. Then Mary took hold of it and filled the empty space on the final page. She wrote a few lines to Cornelius's wife, Olive. It was a message to Mary's distracted husband as much as it was for her sister-in-law. "Unless I can be nearer my husband think I may as well go home," she wrote. She was in a "miserable hotel" several miles from her husband's camp, and "but for the children" she would have already departed for Syracuse. The girls enjoyed their time, "although they see their Father so little."

Mary compared herself to Wilkins Micawber, a bumbling, ever-hopeful character in Charles Dickens's *David Copperfield*. Like Wilkins, she said, she was waiting around for "something to turn up."[38] Her postscript was clear. She wanted George to fully return to his family. Though tempted to leave, she continued with him for some time.

Meanwhile, Butler the civilian was hatching a plan for his own resurrection. He believed he alone had the credentials to lead tens of thousands of Black soldiers, after the war, to South America to dig a canal across the Colombian isthmus.[39] He had not given up on what he could do for freedmen, nor what they could do for him.

Butler had originally hoped that his all-Black corps would make it easier for a conscientious commander (like himself) to protect the soldiers from abuse. But after his ignominious exit from the army, the Twenty-Fifth Corps would serve as the organizational means by which thousands of Black soldiers would be kept from going home.

While Mary waited, and Butler and George spun plans, unrest spread among Butler's experimental corps. The men's health was deteriorating, and they were desperate to return to their families. Butler's Twenty-Fifth had become a powder keg, and George's dearest hopes were tied to it. Duty to family supplied the spark.

CHAPTER 11

MUTINY

SICKNESS WAS IN THEIR LIMBS AND SKIN. It was observable in their eyes and mouths. By the last winter of the war, the bodies of Black soldiers began showing disturbing signs of institutional neglect and abuse. Much of it had to do with diet and bacterial illness. Some feverish soldiers relieved themselves near their crowded huts and tents and along the earthworks. Their cramped spaces became breeding grounds for disease.[1]

In early 1865, a medical officer in the Army of the James grew alarmed by widespread illness. He blamed it on the recruiting process, accusing careless agents of ignoring disability and symptoms of disease to fill draft quotas. General Edward Wild, who had talked George Cole out of resigning, believed that the sudden change in the soldiers' diet caused a "derangement" of their bodies. In bondage, they had more regular, if meager, portions of fish, greens, cornmeal, and yams; in their limited hours of rest they kept gardens and hunted. The army replaced such portions with erratic and sometimes repulsive rations. Added to that, Wild noted, already unhealthy recruits, sick from damp and cold conditions, were often forbidden from building personal fires. Even when fires were permitted, wood was scarce around Richmond and Petersburg, where soldiers had stripped the land of firewood for miles. Hungry soldiers worked long hours on fatigue duty, only to climb into dark, damp, and cold huts.[2]

While General Benjamin Butler was orchestrating his own military collapse, many soldiers in the Twenty-Fifth Corps grew despondent and could be found listlessly lying about in wet clothes.[3] A fellow colonel in the corps, Charles Francis Adams Jr., seems to have been referring to this when he caustically wrote to his father that a "sick nigger" at once "gives up and lies down to die, the personification of humanity reduced to a wet rag. He cannot fight for life like a white man."[4]

Adams blamed it on their lack of will. Many surgeons viewed the sickness of Black soldiers in similarly distorted ways. They gave self-fulfilling prognoses where sick Black soldiers, because they were supposedly prone to succumb to disease, received shoddy care and were denied costly medicines. Decline and death confirmed bias. Black soldiers died from circular reasoning.[5]

When the weather warmed in 1865 and damp tents dried under the sun's lengthened arc, health conditions grew worse. Fresh vegetables were rare. With loose teeth, the men chewed wormy hardtack and salt beef from sick cattle. They washed down their scanty rations with foul water from bacteria-ridden sloughs and "the washings of old, filthy campgrounds."[6]

If some surgeons and medical cadets showed genuine concern, many lacked appropriate training. Some had only treated cattle before the war. In George's regiment, a veterinarian and a stonecutter rose to the position of head surgeon.[7] The unqualified surgeons in the Black corps began diagnosing the spreading sickness as rheumatism, unaware that many men were exhibiting advanced symptoms of scurvy.[8]

As scurvy spread through the camps—along with wild rumors of what the government planned to do with Black soldiers after the war—officers received orders to tighten the screws. Military wisdom held that discipline boosted morale in the ranks. With picketing and guard duty no longer a war necessity, those soldiers who hadn't been laid low spent their days in what seemed like meaningless military drudgery. Officers were required to wear their chevrons; jackets had to be worn in the humid heat; boots were to be blackened, beards trimmed, clothes brushed, and brass polished. Three drills were to be held daily. Many White officers wanted out. They submitted their resignation papers while common soldiers had no option but to wait out the rumors. Some troopers flouted the regulations, discarding their clothes and walking through camp unclad. Ill tempers and sick bodies were everywhere.

Colonel Cole said nothing (at least in his surviving letters) about the declining health of his soldiers. He had his eye on the prize and was probably too consumed with his own failing body. He was unaware that his wilting soldiers had begun plotting an uprising.[9]

IN EARLY APRIL 1865, when Richmond at last fell, Black troops in the Twenty-Fifth Corps stood just outside the capital. They were among the first Union soldiers to enter. But not without controversy. Some reported that at the last moment, Black troops were halted so that White soldiers could take the advance.[10]

George and his soldiers took no part in the historic drama. Two weeks prior, the Second Colored Cavalry had been dispatched from the outskirts of Richmond to Norfolk for provost guard duty. The banishment of his regiment from the nation's gaze foreshadowed the fate of many Black units. The euphoria of fallen Richmond quickly turned to acrimony. Rumors and accusations spread that Black soldiers had run amok in the burning city. There were some credible reports, even of rape, but much of it added up to the wild tales of White locals seized by fury and paranoia. To defray tensions and to rid White soldiers of the insult of sharing the stage with Black troops, commanders sent the troops to places like the outskirts of Petersburg to guard the South Side Railroad. Others were dispersed along the James River, to wait and anxiously wonder about their fate.[11]

After Butler's exit, the reins of the Twenty-Fifth Corps were handed to men who made no effort to hide their repugnance toward Black soldiers and their families. George detected some of the bile but underestimated its presence at the top and its pervasiveness below. One abolition general, William Birney, said that Butler's replacement, General Edward O. C. Ord, "spelt 'negro' with two G's." Ord's orthographic sins—that is, using the slur "nigger" instead of "negro"—were as prevalent in key parts of the command as dice and drink in the camps.[12]

George's men had known the war was over when, in early May, they were transferred with other Black regiments near City Point, Virginia, a bustling port on the James that had served as Ulysses S. Grant's headquarters. Only George's superiors knew why.[13]

ON JUNE 4, George received orders to prepare and take command over an all-Black brigade. He was to "embark rapidly" on ships bound for the borderlands of Texas and Mexico and do so as *acting* brigadier general. He was finally a general, though not exactly.[14]

George believed that his brigade was needed along the border of Mexico to stop the spread of French-backed monarchists in Mexico, led by Maximilian. Some of the soldiers at first held out hope for glory, believing they were destined to make history and to deal the final blow to rebel holdouts in Texas under Kirby Smith.[15] When news reached Virginia of

Smith's surrender, hope gave way to dread. Many determined that they would be returned to slavery and made to pick cotton to pay off war debts. One officer recalled that once the troopers heard camp rumors that they would ship off for Texas with no clear military objective, a "marked change came over them and they became sullen and disobedient." A correspondent for the *Philadelphia Inquirer* reported that the officers paid "no attention" to the mutterings, regarding them as "grumblings peculiar to the African race."[16]

In roughly a week, George readied the brigade to be transported by riverboats to steamships anchored in Hampton Roads, the sea harbor at the mouths of the Elizabeth and James Rivers. Other Black brigades had recently embarked from there. Many experienced mutinies. In what one correspondent called "an outbreak or two," various soldiers had planned to take possession of the ships and cut their officers' throats. The mutinous attempts were quickly put down.[17]

George's newly formed brigade—cavalry soldiers who had been converted into infantry units—had been provided new Sharps breech-loading carbines, bullets, shiny sabers, and the accouterments of foot soldiers. Thousands of rounds of ammunition and guns exchanged hands from one regiment to the next before the men embarked.[18]

On at least two of the smaller boats that made their way downriver, George's soldiers began voicing threats. On one boat, they fired their carbines from the lower deck as alarmed officers watched from above. When an officer, Frederick Browne, scrambled down to their deck, with his revolver drawn, he was met with a "dozen" carbines pointing at his head and breast. The men warned him that he might be able to kill one of them, but not all. Unnerved, Browne slunk back to his fellow officers.[19]

Late in the evening, with rain clouds hanging in the approaching night, the draft boats reached the anchored steamship, the *Meteor*. Officers began forcing the sullen soldiers aboard. From one of the riverboats, *Whildin*, three companies grudgingly climbed up into the *Meteor*. The fourth and last company refused. Aboard the larger ship, disgruntled soldiers traded stories with other companies who had also threatened mutiny on their way down the river. Violence erupted again. When the various troops came together, recalled an officer, "they just went wild."

The holdouts on the smaller boat unslung their guns and capped them. Others drew their sabers. This further emboldened the soldiers watching from the *Meteor*. Men began yelling that they would not be shipped to Texas. Officers tried to force them into the hold until the soldiers drew their arms and fired into the air, refusing to step below. Others apparently tried to break into the steamer's storage, where the chief quartermaster had stowed away 250 rounds of ammunition for each departing soldier.

Armed men ranged about the ship, swearing they would shoot any man who touched the crank to weigh anchor. One private screamed, "I'll sooner have my throat cut than leave this harbor!" They threatened to imprison or murder the officers and commandeer the ship. They had the skills to make good on their threats. As enslaved men from the Chesapeake, some had hired themselves out as deckhands at the Norfolk and Portsmouth docks.[20]

Officers on the riverboat steamed desperately toward the wharf with the pack of mutinous men aboard. William Carter, a black cavalryman, continued to discharge his weapon, defying his lieutenant's orders to cease fire. Through the drizzling rain, Carter caught sight of approaching White troops onshore and took aim at some officers who were watching from mounted horses. He exclaimed, "What is those damned white officers coming down here for, they can't scare me. We can whip them easy enough!" Carter squeezed the trigger but missed his targets—among them a colonel and a general.[21]

Once on land, an officer rushed to get help from the Third Pennsylvania Artillery, whose major ordered a small command onto the *Whildin* to quell the mutiny. With the mutineers subdued, the boat steamed back to the ship, where the men on it threatened to fire on the boat if it continued its approach. The *Whildin* turned back again to the wharf, awaited by White soldiers who had formed a long gauntlet with muskets loaded and fixed bayonets. This time the officers forced the mutinous soldiers onto the wharf two and three at a time and then placed them under guard behind the military fort.

The *Philadelphia Inquirer* reported that women "thronged" the wharf and that they had come from refugee camps near Fort Monroe, such as Hampton and Slabtown. The soldiers were allowed, for some reason, to meet the crowd of wives and mothers, "nearly all" of whom had brought pies and baked goods for the soldiers. Whatever else happened during this meeting, the reporter did not say.[22]

What transpired over the next several hours aboard the *Meteor* is uncertain. In the early morning, after what must have been a night on edge for the officers aboard, the ship was steered toward the wharf. This brought elation to some of the soldiers who assumed that their resistance had been successful and that they were returning to Virginia soil for good.

The soldiers, like the others before, were marched off the ship and along the shore, past White troops who stood with raised guns and cannons. As the *Philadelphia Inquirer* put it, "The thought of resistance would have been the inspiration of madness." As they stacked their weapons on the wharf, they were visibly overcome with anguish. "Every sable face," wrote the correspondent, "was distorted with pain" as they unbuckled their accouterments. "Some ground their teeth in silent mortification, and tears rolled down" their cheeks as they realized they might not see their kin again.[23]

★

MEANWHILE, Major Robert Dollard, who had taken temporary command over George's Second Colored Cavalry, had a similar crisis on his hands. When his boats arrived at Hampton Roads, the designated ship, *H.S. Hagar*, was still taking coal across the harbor at Portsmouth, a town that sits across the Elizabeth River from Norfolk.

Dollard ordered the smaller boats to Portsmouth, where he allowed the soldiers to disembark. He would come to regret this as many of the men raced to Norfolk, seeking their long-overdue military pay. Accounts conflict over whether they got their money. It appears that some did and then spent it on women and liquor. Many surely wanted it for their families in the nearby camps. Apparently, some commissioned officers got paid while some (or most) enlisted men did not. "This created some dissatisfaction," Dollard wrote in superb understatement.[24]

Rumors echoed that Black soldiers would be re-enslaved to pick cotton. Some claimed that once the ship got out to sea, officers would raise "a five years flag" that would doom the soldiers to five years of servitude. Fearing revolt, Dollard ordered guards to monitor the soldiers. As happened across the water, a growing crowd of women gathered on the dock. (Like Browne in his own account, Dollard did not say a thing about the presence of women and family.) When it was time to board the ship in late afternoon, the men refused. After prodding from Dollard, some drew their guns and fired them off while yelling defiantly. Soldiers in the band were particularly resistant.[25]

There were only 13 officers on hand to stymie the 767 angry soldiers, each of whom had been issued twenty rounds of ammunition.[26] Dollard backed down from his orders and was wise enough to call a meeting with his Black sergeants. They told him about the five-years flag rumor. Showing more wisdom than he had in previous crises, he swore on his life to his sergeants that the government would not sell them into slavery and that their stint in Texas would be short. He then ordered them to return to their comrades and dispel the myths. The plan partly worked. About half the men grudgingly boarded the ship.

George reported that Dollard lost his nerve, locked himself away in the ship's cabin, and called his officers to join him. The night came and went with no resolution. At dawn, Dollard sought help from General Charles Graham, the ranking commander at Portsmouth. Graham offered the assistance of Portsmouth's provost marshal, who could deploy 130 men to force the recalcitrant soldiers onto the ship. Dollard rejected the offer, saying he would need all of the iron and bronze of the Thirteenth New York Heavy Artillery stationed nearby to crush the resistance. He knew that his next move would have to overwhelm his men.[27]

He was losing his last whit of patience (and would wish years later that he had used artillery fire instead of words). He submitted to a plea from a fellow Union colonel to only use persuasion. The men, though, did not find Dollard's case persuasive. Private Spencer Edwards spoke for many of his comrades when he shouted back at Dollard, "I will be God damned if I will go on board that vessel!" Seeing that Dollard had been right, the colonel formed his regiment in a line facing the ship, weapons primed. When the men aboard the ship saw their imperiled comrades below, they came rushing down the gangways onto the wharf. A massacre seemed imminent.[28]

It is not clear what happened next. Perhaps there were shots. Perhaps wives stood on the wharf begging the soldiers to relent. Almost all the men, save six, boarded the ship, though most of them kept possession of their guns. Shots were fired again as the ship left the dock. Dollard learned later that two horses and a freedwoman were wounded.[29]

★

BACK ACROSS THE JAMES RIVER, at Fort Monroe, the crestfallen and disarmed soldiers were forced onto the Texas-bound ship, which soon returned to its moorings in the waters of Hampton Roads. For a brief half hour of euphoria that morning, the men had believed that they had forced the US Army to hear their complaints. After boarding the Texas-bound ship again, they seemed dazed by their cruel shift in fortunes.

As the day wore on, some of the men shook their melancholic stupor and grew unruly. They broke into the hold and got their hands on whiskey rations. At about sunset, a "big, pock-marked mulatto" climbed atop the pilot cabin and, while shaking his fists at the officers, yelled, "You damned white-livered sons of bitches, we will throw you overboard." The lower deck rumbled with cheers and howling.[30]

Three officers cut through the crowd, "jerked" the man down from his platform, and dragged him up to the officers' quarterdeck. An Ohioan, Captain Sampson Whiteman—named as if God were a playwright—shoved his pistol into the soldier's ribs and barked at him to hold his hands up with thumbs joined. Whiteman had a mind to string the "mulatto" up by his thumbs and dangle him from the ship's rigging. When the soldier folded his arms and refused instead, Whiteman warned him three times before discharging his gun into his chest. For a long moment, the man's pockmarked face remained expressionless. Officer Browne wondered if the gun had misfired until the man's arms drooped down, exposing the profusion of red bleeding down his blouse.[31]

The mulatto fell "into a heap" at the feet of the officers. The stunned onlookers watched the murder from below, then began scavenging about, scouring the ship for axes, hand spikes, lumber—anything they could wield as weapons. They yelled, "Kill them; throw them overboard!" as they closed in toward the officers on the deck above. A Black soldier egged his comrades on, screaming, "Let us not go to Texas, let us die on the deck like men!" Amid the melee, another soldier was heard protesting, "I'll be shot before I go to Texas, to Hell with Texas, it's time for the colored men to talk and act too!"[32]

Officer Browne believed the men were acting with drunken bravado. He wrote that a mere sixteen officers formed a line on the quarterdeck, wagged their revolvers, and threatened the crowd of some seven hundred men. On this ship, the officers were the only ones with guns. And they had the tactical advantage of holding high ground, needing only to defend the narrow ladders between the decks.

Eventually, the crowd—jammed up against the ladders—lost its surging energy. Sixteen revolvers held them in check until a few rioters at the front ceased climbing toward their certain deaths. Browne, who took pride in having put down a mutiny, recalled that the men proceeded to huddle at the bow of the ship and glare at the officers "like wild beasts" from across the vessel.[33]

The officers truly saw the men as beasts. As the pockmarked man lay dying on the deck, eking out moans, the sixteen officers had the Parrott gun on the quarterdeck loaded with canister and trained its muzzle on the brooding men.

Browne and his officers ordered soldiers from the regimental band to ascend to the quarterdeck and form a line. The men blew into their horns as the ship listed back and forth on the water. For an hour, the band wailed the tunes of martial glory. The music nearly drowned out the audible remains of the mutiny—the mutterings, the cursings, and the cries to God—that reverberated from the bow. It helped the officers half forget about the creature dying at their feet. But as Browne noted, when the instruments fell silent between songs, the officers could still hear his groaning, rasping lungs. The surgeon rolled the bleeding man onto a blanket and, with little that could be done, left him to die slowly under the darkening sky.[34]

★

THE TWO SHIPS FILLED with broken-hearted men eventually joined a small flotilla of five vessels that steamed out into the Atlantic and down the coastline. The few men aboard the *Hagar* who had somehow retained their guns occasionally fired their weapons from the bow. Dollard, still on the verge of losing control, once again leaned on his Black noncommissioned officers to stem the unrest. They lined up their men and arrested any soldier who, against orders, carried a loaded weapon. Violators were forced to throw their ammunition into the sea.

Dollard also discovered and seized a huge cache of ammunition stowed away in the men's quarters. He stored the stockpile beneath his cabin and threatened that if the soldiers attempted to commandeer the ship—as had been rumored—he would use the explosives to bring the ship to the ocean's floor. In all, Dollard rounded up thirty-one accused leaders of the mutiny and shut them into a miserable "coal hole" during the three-week voyage to Texas.[35]

★

MARY COLE was stowed away on one of the five ships, at the brigade's headquarters. The two girls, Fannie and Alice, were with her. George had reported with pride that he was taking them to Texas, now that his promotion gave him "a good chance to take care of them." She had come to the war once again, no doubt, to care for him during a painful voyage. The turbulent passage by sea meant acute bouts of internal pain. More time on his back. Perhaps more bleeding into jars.[36]

She was in no state to care for him. She had physical wounds that hounded her too, ones that she had kept hidden from George.[37]

She knew firsthand how the war was an assault on family and how it strained the bonds of love. But nobody understood these things quite like the soldiers who had been forced on the ships and the kin they left on the wharves.

CHAPTER 12

FAMILY, *the* INFLAMMATORY STIMULUS

THE SCANT DESCRIPTION OF THE MUTINIES, printed first in a Philadelphia newspaper, painted a sad but sentimental farewell at the shore. Freedwomen gathered at the wharf to bid the men adieu with pastries and warm kisses. In truth, it was a harrowing scene of panic. George Cole knew this.[1]

George wrote the most insightful report of what happened. After the ringleaders had been shackled in Texas and set to be tried and sentenced for years of hard labor with ball and chain, he submitted his summary (the first part of which has been lost) to headquarters. The surviving report abruptly begins, "The majority of the 1st and 2d Regt USC[olored] C[avalry] are residents of Portsmouth & Norfolk & vicinity," he wrote. Once the men met their "families and Children (nearly 1000 as I am informed)," they refused to "leave them unprovided with money or rations." As a result, the soldiers "became excited and decidedly insubordinate."[2]

George admitted that twenty soldiers had escaped with the aid of their families. (Regimental records suggest that it had been many more.) He faulted his officers for calling in White troops to cow the men onto the ships. For one mutiny, he blamed Major Robert Dollard and his line officers for holing themselves up in the ship's cabin instead of staying onshore to prevent outrage.

As for the other mutiny, he accused Major Frederick Browne, who had commanded the First Colored Cavalry, for having gone off all night somewhere in Norfolk. Browne had left the men under the command of subordinate officers who "found it necessary" to shoot one of the men, though not fatally.[3] George's description of the violence was thin at best. It said nothing about the man who was shot and left to perish on the departing ship's deck.

George had the mutineers removed from Dollard's ship and placed in irons, and then took them into his custody. He considered arresting Dollard and Browne too but decided that doing so would only embolden the men. All of the disturbances, he believed, could have been avoided had his officers hurried the men onto the ships instead of allowing them to exchange words and embraces with loved ones: "for every man left Camp," he claimed in either deceit or striking ignorance, "as cheerfully as ever before."[4]

Whatever his blindnesses were, there is evidence that he was unusually aware of how Black soldiers saw one another and their obligations to family. He saw things many of his peers could not. His brother, Cornelius, had argued before Congress, in which he read large portions of a letter written by George, that Black soldiers manifested more sympathy toward one another, were less likely to abandon comrades on the battlefield, and saw themselves as members of kin and community more than as individuals.[5]

George wrote that the men had been "contented." The claim shielded him from the embarrassment of having lost control of his brigade within the first hours of transporting it to Texas. It helped him make the case that the mutiny resulted from the Union's heartless policies regarding refugee families, not George's inability to command men. He assured his superiors that he was not excusing the mutinous action; he just wanted headquarters to know "the cause of the excitement."

The other portion of the blame lay in the "stupidity" of his officers. They failed to shield the soldiers from "the inflammatory stimulus of free intercourse with the howling multitude." Dollard and Browne had allowed the powerful pull of family and domestic affections—the "inflammatory stimulus"—to tug at soldiers who were bound by duty to the war.[6]

In revealing the treasure of his men's hearts, he revealed his own. George had lived most of his life as if a man's duty required standing just beyond earshot of the cries of home. The whole ordeal could have been avoided, he concluded, had the soldiers been distracted from the howling.[7]

THE HOWLS WERE ECHOES OF PAST PAIN. The government, like a new heartless master, was hauling away loved ones into the void from which stolen kinsfolk did not return. The howls were cries of political protest. The United States had failed to keep its promises. In a matter of a few weeks, the soldiers' families went from hope to terror. Many soldiers had gone without pay for several months. Confederates who fled and torched their lands, and who were freshly pardoned by President Andrew Johnson, appeared in the refugee villages, demanding rent for past months or eviction. And food rations suddenly stopped. When Dollard invited the White artillery unit to crush the revolt, Private John Burkley cried, "I will not go on board that vessel." He made his case why. "When President Lincoln was alive my wife drew rations, but now [that] President Johnson has been in office[,] the Government don't furnish [her] any rations and I am going to remain and work for a living."[8]

Benjamin Butler's replacement, General Edward O. C. Ord, had long argued that rations for refugees should be stopped, but feared the North's protests if done suddenly. On June 5, the army's adjutant general called for rations to be terminated because, he argued, the bounty encouraged wives, elders, and children to "make little or no effort to help themselves." A day later, with Ord's encouragement, Brigadier General George H. Gordon ordered the Virginia Freedmen's Bureau to cut off food to the families. Gordon believed that Butler's original promise to provide Black soldiers' families with "suitable subsistence" was no longer binding. His order called the rations "pernicious."[9]

Rations were cut in many refugee communities. Before the mutiny, soldiers from the Thirty-Sixth United States Colored Troops, who were also sent to Texas and had been recruited from the same region as George's regiment, petitioned their general that "our family's are suffering at Roanoke Island, NC." The US government had failed to keep its promises. "When we were enlisted in the service," they protested, "we were promised that our wifes and family's should receive rations from government."[10]

After the mutiny, when William Turner, a Black sergeant, was asked in a court-martial why Private William Respers had refused to duck into the hold during the mutiny on the *Meteor*, he testified that Respers insisted he would not be hauled away to Texas without having been paid. Knowing that his family was destitute, Respers would "rather die than go." When asked why William Carter had resorted to shooting at White officers, another comrade responded, "I heard [Carter] talking about the woman he was leaving behind and he hated to go."[11]

George's men had been recruited with the understanding—backed by Butler's promise and the face-to-face enticements of recruiters—that in exchange for taking up arms, the army would provide rations for refugee wives, aged parents, and children who had made it to Union lines. In the tidewater region, an escaped bondsman had options as the architect of freedom for his family. He could hire himself out behind Union lines and establish a meager place of refuge for his family. When such men enlisted in Butler's forces, they did so first and last for family.[12]

For freedmen, establishing themselves as uncontested protectors of their families was the purest expression of liberty. Freedom meant that masters would no longer nullify the authority of enslaved fathers. Never again would masters punish a freedman's child in front of powerless parents; masters would no longer dictate the diet of his children; they would not determine when his wife awoke; they would not rape his sister.[13]

George's report of the mutiny, alongside the testimonies from the military trials that followed, revealed two incompatible worldviews—products of historical forces, formed roughly along racial lines. The soldiers who cried tears of rage on the pier and aboard the ships learned from their elders and enslaved communities to dissolve the self into one's circle of kin; the bonds of family and kin had buffered the brutality of slavery. Group survival mattered more than individual advancement.[14]

George and his officer peers—especially those who hailed from towns and cities—had grown into men in a society that cherished and sentimentalized the home. And they learned from boyhood that intimate obligations could be harnessed for the advancement of the self. George's home had always been a kind of sacred foothold for some grand chance in a competitive world. Home was the hub in the center of the wheel, from which men spun into action. From home they traveled to and from children's academies, district schools, college, the business office, and war.

George had a reputation as a tender family man. He was easily moved to tears over his daughters. He marked the anniversaries of his father's death and during the war hated that he couldn't be home to visit his parents' graves. Every time he faced danger in battle, a cherished phrase used by his deceased father "flashed" across his mind. When his mother died in the middle of the war, he was overcome with dread. He felt a "chilly recollection" that he and his siblings—scattered about America—no longer shared a common home to which they could return.[15]

Comrades and friends reported that George often talked tenderly of his wife. He carved her love tokens while laid out on his back, sent her locks of his hair, and wrote her poetry. And yet he had not lived steadily with his wife and girls for years. Something that he had absorbed from his life in antebellum America made it so that when he saw frantic mothers, or children who begged for food and protection, he viewed it as an "inflammatory stimulus," a pitiable distraction from the calling of manhood.[16]

★

IN JUNE AND JULY, the War Department transported over fifty thousand troops to Texas, nearly half of them from the Twenty-Fifth Corps. Some fifty ships had been packed with troops, mules, artillery, and supplies for Southeast Texas. Food was scarce on board, and soldiers grew even sicker in the dark, crowded, and poorly ventilated berths between the decks, which had been built by rushed carpenters the week before.[17] At sea, the cases of scurvy became a full-blown epidemic. In Texas, enfeebled men disembarked from the ships to discover the bleak environs of Brazos Santiago, a small barrier island in the Gulf of Mexico at the southeastern tip of the state.

Within a week, five hundred Black soldiers were deathly ill. The post hospital, the only facility in the region, had only eighty beds. Men lay everywhere unsheltered, many sprawled out in the hot sand. Some of the soldiers slipped into a listless, despondent trance. Some had their remaining teeth nearly enclosed by bloody, purple and black gums. Others suffered bloated limbs that oozed serum. Men hobbled about in the swampy heat with thighs and calves hardened like stones and half-fused ankle bones. Bodies were covered with foul ulcers.[18]

Brazos Santiago offered little vegetation beyond sawgrass and cactus. The officers appear to have not felt the urgency in their guts because they had a small stock of canned goods in their mess. The island's only supply of drinking water came from a desalination contraption that produced boiling, brackish water. When the island was most crowded—in the hottest months of the year—the scalding water was rationed out to soldiers at only a few pints per day. A Black chaplain recalled that the water condenser at most could support five thousand men; the island was crowded by double that amount. Soldiers who had the means purchased dirty water from the Rio Grande barreled and sold by Mexican opportunists for ten cents a canteen.[19] The mainland was hardly better, though it did have the river. In one regiment, several men drowned when soldiers rushed to quench their thirst, causing the bank to give way below them.[20]

Even the Sanitary Commission, known for providing Black soldiers with rations and medical care, was slow to alleviate the suffering. The nearest office in New Orleans ignored pleas for help until one of its agents witnessed the epidemic firsthand and sounded the alarm.[21] It took several months—until October and November—for the commission and the army to send sufficient antiscorbutics, like onions, pickles, beets, lime juice, and cabbage, to check the disease.

Men were going blind. Each day more cadavers, lugged from the hospitals and tents, were buried under sand. During the war, Black soldiers had been much more likely to die from disease than their White counterparts. They were twice as likely to perish from diarrhea, three times as likely to do so from tuberculosis. They died from scurvy—a disease for which a cure was well known—at ten times the rate of their White fellows. But in Texas, in the blistering summer months of 1865, the rates of scurvy soared to levels that dwarfed anything anybody had seen.[22]

Military brass had shown disregard and incompetence, especially George's superior, Godfrey Weitzel, who did not have his ships supplied with fruits or vegetables when they lay in harbor in Mobile or New Orleans. The surgeons and nurses in Texas were equally blameworthy. Some of the top-ranking surgeons, who were supposed to use funds allotted to them to purchase specific dietary foods for sick soldiers, used the money to stock up on personal supplies of whiskey, brandy, and Claret wine. They made Texas as convivial as misappropriated money could make it, while neglected soldiers gnawed on hardtack with slack teeth. Some soldiers saw it as a death sentence when they were sent for a stint in the hospital, where they might be ignored, abused, and fleeced of their belongings by nurses and stewards (some of them Black). One surgeon wrote privately to his father that the "desperate situation" was "damnable" and that he could not stand to see his men "murdered by inches."[23] A few officers who tried to expose the evil were punished.[24]

Most of the soldiers served as guards along the Rio Grande for a half year and more. They were more like thralls than soldiers, toiling for the government, laying iron railroad track and unloading vessels on the gulf and on wharves along the river. Some men ceased wearing military uniforms altogether. They were dying from what they called "bone scurvy" and "salt-water scurvy." Sometimes they just called their disease "misery."[25]

Before the men embarked for Texas, General Ulysses S. Grant had rejected Weitzel's request to bring and put to work some 1,500 employees of the US quartermaster. Grant told Weitzel to instead detail Black soldiers for any hard labor, and "if not, there are plenty of Negroes in Texas." Grant's meaning was clear. The men were sent to Texas more as "negroes" than as soldiers. After warning Weitzel to bring sufficient rations and ammunition, Grant ended his communication, saying, "You should take a fair quantity of intrenching tools."[26]

To the end of their time in Texas, soldiers in George's brigade continued to protest, saying what they had tried to say when they mutinied on the wharves and ships at Hampton Roads. At the end of 1865, men from the First Colored Cavalry (the regiment that had nearly stormed the ship) continued to protest over their families. In a letter likely intended for the secretary of war, they wrote, "Wee present to you our suffering at present Concerning our Famileys wich wee are now informed that Commisserys [the food commissary] has been Closed a gainst them as though wee were rebeling against US." The soldiers continued, "Never was wee any more treated Like slaves then wee are now in our Lives." They were bondsmen again. "Wee are said to be U S. Soldiers and behold wee are U S Slaves. . . . Wee had rather pay for our next years serviss and be turned out then to stay in and no pertecttion to our wife."[27]

The grim prophecies about enslavement in Texas, told and feared by soldiers and their families, were fulfilled by the US Army.

★

THERE IS LITTLE RECORD of what George did in Texas. Mary and the two girls stayed nearby until September. When she returned to Syracuse, Luther Harris Hiscock began calling on her again.[28]

In October, Edwin Fox turned up in Texas to "rejoin" the regiment, not as a soldier but as a dashed young man who couldn't quit war. He recalled that George was "completely prostrated." His trusted commander was more fitful and depressed than he had been before. His spells of joviality were punctuated by longer bouts of dejection—for a half day or even a few days—which rendered him at times incapable of holding a conversation. His troughs of depression were deeper. "He had no business to be out" in the war, Fox recalled, though Fox had no business being there either.[29]

George was a wounded paper general commanding thousands of sick drudges who had been torn from their families. His commander, General William Clark, perhaps out of pity, urged the War Department to award George a true generalship. At various times, George had assumed temporary command over an entire division when Clark was absent. Still, a comrade recalled that, while in Texas, George did not perform "any active duty." The request was rejected. General Grant said that he did not know enough about George's record to justify a recommendation.[30]

In the final weeks of 1865, on account of his health, he obtained a twenty-day leave of absence. Mary had a glimpse of her husband's ebbing condition, knowing that the wreck of a man would soon return for good to their home, where she kept her own terrible secrets. When he returned to Texas again, she must have dreaded the near future.

In George's final days in Texas, in February 1866, Thomas T. Davis—a US congressman from Syracuse—received an urgent message by telegraph:

> GET GENERAL COLE BREVETED MAJOR GENERAL
> IMMEDIATELY BEFORE MUSTERED OUT IF
> POSSIBLE.[31]

Davis then scribbled off a not-so-personal personal endorsement and sent it along with the telegraph to Edwin Stanton, the secretary of war. The congressman wrote vaguely to Stanton that he believed that George had been a good soldier.[32] Stanton then began pushing it through, at the very time that George began his final trek home. His regiment departed from Texas in the middle of February. Not willing to risk his life again aboard an ocean vessel, he made his way by land and river to City Point, Virginia, where he and the surviving soldiers of the Second Colored Cavalry were discharged.

The telegraph that brought George his dear title of "major general" had been composed by New York's lieutenant governor, Thomas G. Alvord, and his political protégé, Luther Harris Hiscock. George must have known that his last promotion came from wire-pulling. It isn't clear whether he knew that Hiscock, likely at Mary's urging, had his hands on the wire.[33]

He did not return with his identification disc of George Washington hanging from his neck. It had been lost somehow in Texas. He was luckier than many. It had never been needed to identify his rotting cadaver. He had survived war.[34]

PART III

ODYSSEY AFTER WAR

There is something hidden and mysterious about this case. A deep motive, actuated suddenly by a deeper real or imagined wrong sent that deadly ball whizzing into the brain of Hiscock.

—JOURNALIST FROM TROY, New York

Don't fear my manhood.

—GEORGE COLE to Olive Cole

CHAPTER 13

HOMECOMING

IN MARCH 1866, George Cole's enlisted men hobbled to a home radically changed by the war.[1] George returned to his own uncertain future. Since the war had ended, there had been a perceptible uneasiness about wayward veterans in America's northern towns and cities. Anecdotes appeared in the papers about homeless veterans, drunkenness, rioting, and ex-soldiers filling up the prisons.[2] George was one of the many veterans who could not put their lives back together.

HE COULDN'T FIND A JOB, and his changed demeanor hindered his efforts. Friends and neighbors noticed that the General laughed and conversed less. When he did talk, he often maundered on and on about the war. He was a pitiable shell of his former self.[3]

A few months after his return, he began repairing one of the houses that Mary had purchased while he was in Texas. He raised a barn and fixed up the yard so she could turn a profit on the property. He worked alongside a Black "boy" he had brought home from the army. The "boy" may have been a man he had risked his life to rescue during an ambush.[4]

The General occasionally sat silently inside the unfinished house. Two or three times a day, he wandered his yard "without occupation," recalled a neighbor. There was a "want of concentration of mind and a sadness." The General came alive, though, when he played with children, especially imaginatively in the barn. There was "a general conversation going on between them," the neighbor said. George told him that he liked children and liked to have them around. There was nothing "incoherent" about his conversations with them.[5]

The General might have found in the children a kind of admiration that he thought he deserved from adults. Maybe he felt less judged. When summer began he still had not found steady employment. He often made calls on the paper store of his comrade Frank Garrett. When Garrett inquired about George's increasing downheartedness, George confessed that he "would never get over the difficulty" he got at war and that "his wound had used him up so that he was of no more good to himself or family."[6]

Once, after Garrett struck George on the leg, George warned him of his painful bullet wound, adding that he "wished it had been higher up [so that] he would now be asleep under the sod of Virginia."[7]

★

IN JULY 1866, he caught a break when the Empire Windmill Company hired him as an assistant superintendent. The enterprise had recently been started by some of the most prominent investors in the city. George oversaw correspondence, which meant he was expected to address the concerns of customers, arrange payments, and sell windmills to local and distant clients. He had an office on the ground level, next to the boiler room, where he kept the books and paid the factory hands who labored in the second-floor woodshop.

The company boasted that the "self-regulated" windmills were one of the greatest inventions known to man. They could pump water, turn lathes, drive saws, crush ore, grind grain, and power all sorts of machines by transmitting wind power through a series of interconnected axles and gears. Behind the advertised confidence, there were signs of financial trouble. Empire Windmill regularly advertised announcements to its stockholders that it hoped to raise more capital stock. It was a cutthroat market where competitors infringed on patents and lured machinists and inventors away from one another. The young company had to borrow against George's earnings every month.[8]

According to the directors, George ran into trouble at his job when he began making "wild and visionary bargains" with clients, many from North Carolina. (He was, of course, intimately familiar with towns in the region that had its four mills destroyed.) The Empire Windmill directors called customers who owed the company money "good for nothing." In January 1867, the stockholders and directors voted to terminate George's job, withholding nearly $3,000 (a small fortune) still owed to him because, it was argued, he was responsible for the unpaid accounts.[9]

His fellow workers and some customers had noticed something was not right with him. When one of them asked the General to elaborate on a war experience, George became nervous and excited. His bloodshot eyes turned wild, widening and darting. He moved his hands "in a twitching manner." He got "excited in the details." His gestures were "violent." Others thought little of it. Compared with other veterans, perhaps, he did not seem unusually rattled. To some, the veteran seemed capable and gathered. He had the mark of a man of business; his step was "quick, energetic and decided." He seemed to be two people.[10]

Less than a month after he was fired, he told his brother Cornelius Cole in passing (and dishonestly) that he had quit the windmill. He could not "stand it" there, he wrote. He mused about writing a book about his war experiences but complained that he couldn't concentrate enough in his home. He joked that he'd be more successful authoring a book in Babel or at a lunatic asylum. He needed a "quiet" office because every time he sat to begin something, some matter—some tug from his daughters or Mary—pulled him off track.[11]

In a rare moment of disclosure about his wounds, he told his brother that he was "much troubled" by his injury from 1862. He had to lie on his back "more or less" each day so that his "parts" would resume their normal position. If not, his insides would get "misplaced." He feared he was in "danger of intussusception or strangulation of the large intestines."[12]

When he could, and probably from the flat of his back, he scoured newspapers for what he called a "place," a government appointment. Two place announcements, one for a tax collector, the other for an assessor, grabbed his attention. He underlined a key part of one notification and tore it out half cleanly; the second he hastily ripped from the newspaper, perhaps with scissors out of reach from his back. He enclosed them both within the fold of a hopeful letter to Cornelius.[13]

George felt renewed hope because Cornelius, after having lost his bid for a second term as a US representative, had just been elected to the Senate. George believed that with his own war record, and some help from his brother, he could tap into a system of political patronage that was beginning to mushroom after the war.[14]

The collectorship "place" paid nearly twice as much as the assessorship. He thought he stood a chance for it because the recent nomination of Major W. W. Mosely had just been rejected by the Senate. George wondered whether a letter from his wife's brother, a staunch Democrat, would secure a nomination from Democratic president Andrew Johnson. He also had a friend in the Treasury Department who had once promised him that he (George) could get a collec-

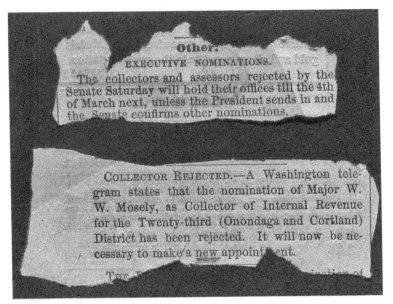

George regularly sent place announcements and stories cut from newspapers to accompany his letters. *UCLA Library Special Collections*

torship so long as the position was not occupied by another veteran. George happily reported to Cornelius that the man who currently held the collectorship was a political hack who "never was a soldier." It was his time to collect on his sacrifice for the country. "Had I better come to Washington in person?" he impatiently asked. "I want the collectorship badly."[15]

In the spring, he traveled to Washington, DC to win support. By then only the position of assessor of internal revenue was still available, his second-choice place. Fortunately, Joshua Rogers, a neighbor and friend, was there in Washington to lend a hand. Rogers had exchanged letters with the General throughout the war and knew something about his struggles. He had witnessed how, when George returned from the Rio Grande, the once "remarkably strong man" seemed used up.[16]

Rogers learned of the true extent of George's wounds just before the key meeting at the Capitol. He entered George's DC hotel room and found him stripped to his undergarments, laid out on the floor. His feet were propped up and his pantaloons pulled down so he could wrap wet towels around his groin. Rogers rushed to retrieve ice water to keep the towels cold.

Once George recovered, a day or two later, Rogers accompanied him to the Capitol, where George hoped to at last obtain the Senate's endorsement. But as George stood in the Senate Chamber—the central sphere of American male power—his injury overcame him again. He notified those nearby that he needed to leave and that he didn't think he could make it back to his hotel; they carried him to a congressional committee room, where he collapsed on a sofa and shuddered for over an hour and a half, at times groaning with hands cupped between his legs.

George didn't get the assessorship just as he hadn't the collectorship. He had foreseen his own failure in a letter; as he predicted, the local Republican Party instead gave its support to the Syracuse newspaper editor, investor, and local railroad promoter Vivus Smith. George called Smith a "trimmer," a political hack who trimmed or adjusted his sails (his stance in politics) to catch whatever wind prevailed in that hour. George was indignant, though not surprised, that Smith recently backtracked on his fierce abolitionism and had grown chummy toward Andrew Johnson and his pro-Rebel policies. Smith was no true Republican. Yet local Republicans—even some of George's supposed friends—continued to consider him a "first man."[17]

As it turned out, Joshua Rogers (who had helped George ice his groin, and whom George named as one of the friends who would likely cave and back Smith) admitted that he had gone to Washington only "partially" to help George secure a place. He was there for his own interests too. His interactions there won him a place as a detective in the revenue department.

After the Senate Chamber humiliation, back in Syracuse, the General confided to Rogers that he was losing the desire to live. He thanked his friends for the great efforts they were making on his behalf but voiced his doubts that they could amount to anything. He wondered out loud how many days he had left on earth.[18]

LATER THAT SPRING George finally got an appointment as a special agent of customs in New York City. He boarded steamers and boats at the piers, cracking down on smugglers and cheats. If he had not been doing so already, he began carrying a sidearm. The work required him to leave his wife and two daughters alone for weeks at a time. He was an absent father again but had plans to send his girls to boarding school and relocate his wife to Brooklyn.[19]

He appeared to have finally begun building a new life. But others believed he was in a downward spiral. One day an "intimate" friend, William Fink, found him sitting by himself in the lobby of the Syracuse House Hotel, a four-story edifice situated on the Erie Canal. There was an emptiness in the veteran's eyes. Fink knew dejection when he saw it. He, too, had a checkered record in business and, like George, had once failed as a hardware dealer. Though he became the treasurer at the Syracuse Savings Bank, where George's wife kept an account during the war, Fink was canned by the trustees for discrepancies in the accounts. He was accused of keeping his failing hardware business afloat by drawing funds from the bank and taking out loans with IOU notes.

Fink had noticed before how the "vacant"-faced General sometimes breezed by old acquaintances without salutation. Once Fink confronted him on the street. The General apologized, explaining that he was not well and that the injuries he received while in the army "hung over him and pressed him down." Later, at a musical concert, Fink sat directly behind George and his wife. He put his hand on the veteran's shoulder as they chatted about army operations in the war. They discussed General William Rosecrans, who had ended his brilliant war record with a humiliating defeat at Chickamauga, where he had sent a poorly worded order to his troops that opened them up for a pummeling. Fink recalled that over the conversation George grew distant.[20]

Another concerned neighbor, George Raynor, had once watched from his passing horse car as the veteran stood in front of the Globe Hotel as though lost on the street corner. Raynor remembered seeing him there on other days. He saw him once and then, upon returning an hour later, found the General anchored to the same spot, holding an abstracted pose as if lost in the streets of his own town.

On a New York City street, the veteran crossed paths with Rowland M. Hall, a fellow town destroyer from the Third New York Cavalry. "We talked of nothing but about the war," recollected Hall, who believed that George seemed coherent, not disconnected as others claimed. "I first asked him about his Texas experience," Hall remembered. George praised his Black troops and "particularly" their courage. But even as the General attempted to put his best gloss on the war, he spoke as if "something heavy" was on his mind. He was unsettled. As they exchanged stories about their time in North Carolina and his days near the Rio Grande, he had a "sad, abstracted dark look."[21]

CHAPTER 14

KILLING *for* UNION

ONE DAY IN EARLY JUNE, George returned from New York City to Syracuse, where, while walking through town, he crossed paths with his attorney and "bosom" friend, Luther Harris Hiscock. They had been closer friends before the war, but George now harbored some animosity toward him. He disapproved of how men like Hiscock seemed to have been rewarded with success for staying home from the war. If George could forgive him for that, he could not forget that Hiscock had been a board member of the Empire Windmill Company, which had never paid what it owed him.[1]

Hiscock seemed surprised to see the veteran still in Syracuse. After some small talk, or right in the middle of it, Hiscock inquired, "When are you going to New York, General?" It dawned on George that his friend inquired about his leaving town with unusual curiosity and frequency.[2]

As George remembered it, at that moment the scales fell from his eyes. His face went deadpan. He peered into the eyes of Hiscock, who, as blood rushed to his face, avoided George's gaze like a "guilty dog." The General's first suspicions had to do with money matters. He worried about Mary's own estate, which Hiscock had helped her manage.[3]

The General had other suspicions too, for at least three months, when he and Mary had participated in a fundraising bazaar. For several days they had volunteered in separate booths

A drawing of Luther Harris Hiscock, published after his death. Harper's Weekly, June 22, 1867, 388. Internet Archive, https://archive.org/details/harpersweeklyv11bonn/page/388/mode/2up

in the arcade of Syracuse's Shakespeare Theatre. Ladies in charge persuaded George to join them in a booth, dressed as an Indian chief. Mary worked in another booth a distance off, and Hiscock entered it while she was alone. Witnesses said that Hiscock appeared to be urging her "to do something." (On what that something was, the witnesses did not elaborate. Perhaps Hiscock was pleading with her to amend her will or to act on her feelings and leave her husband, or to renew their affair. Whatever it was, it was more proof that Hiscock's hold on Mary was laced with coercion.)[4]

From his own booth, George saw Mary dangling on the arm of Hiscock, who seemed to be pointing back at him, making George an "object of derision." Others noted their flirtatious friendship; some recalled the pair whispering to each other. George confronted them as they walked arm in arm. Dressed in a cap of feathers with his face painted like the vanquished Iroquois, he half kiddingly—and half not—warned them, "Take care, I am watching you."[5]

Maybe it was after this encounter that George tried to keep Mary away from Hiscock, "the only man," he later wrote, "I ever forbade her to associate with!"[6]

After their awkward meeting on the street, the General hurried home to unearth Hiscock's perfidy. Mary wasn't home, though, and he had to catch a return train to New York City before he could confront her. He approached his cousin Mary Cuyler, who had boarded with the Cole family during most of the war. He told her that he had just seen Hiscock, who seemed to be guilty of something. Thinking that George knew more than he did, she quipped, "Well, General, there has been a good deal of talk about Mrs. Cole's flirtations with Mr. Hiscock."[7]

He smiled darkly. He hadn't seen it coming. He even laughed a little as the truth settled upon him. Cuyler instantly realized that she had revealed more than George had suspected and refused to divulge more to her agitated cousin. She said that Hiscock had made frequent calls to their old house on Salina Street during the war. She said nothing about the time she saw them in a darkened room with drawn curtains. She told him that if he wanted more details, he would need to write Montgomery Pelton, the husband of Mary Cole's half sister, whose house (some said) had served as a rendezvous for Hiscock and Mary.[8]

Before returning to New York City, George hurried off a letter to Pelton: he promised Pelton confidentiality, no matter the response. "Dear Sir," he said. "There has been some rumor in Syracuse of a suspicious nature, in regard to Mary and a certain limb of the law. . . . Write me the facts fully and frankly."[9] He then traveled to New York, where waiters at his hotel found him so out of sorts that he became the target of their jokes. Within days he had Pelton's crushing reply: "There is room for the gravest suspicion."[10]

★

ON SATURDAY EVENING, the General boarded the Hudson River Railroad bound for Syracuse. A young veteran, who had once delivered a telegraph message to George before the war, took a seat next to him on the train. Missing the cues, the man tried to strike up a conversation, but the General complained that his head hurt and began scribbling his thoughts in a little book that looked like a diary. Later, the man saw George on the observation platform between the rail cars. As the train clanged toward Syracuse, George stood for half an hour staring into the dark countryside.[11]

Around six in the morning, the train reached town. He hastened to his home, a Syracuse hotel called the Jervis House, prepared to confront his wife of fifteen years. His two daughters slept on another floor above them, cared for by George's cousin. When he confronted Mary Cole, she burst into tears, promising to confess everything if he would just give her time. He did. On Sunday he sat waiting, partially dressed, in a room with shades drawn and lights put out. There, in the shadows, he listened to testimonies from several family members and friends, perhaps to verify or speed along his wife's halting confessions. Mary lay back in her bedroom as he sat in his rocking chair, listening to his guests, at times sobbing, at others scolding them for not informing him earlier. They confessed that Hiscock had been frequently seen around the Cole hearth. "I thought when I left Syracuse to go into the army," he berated his guests, "that I had left some friends at home."[12]

Mary wrote her first confession letter. George likely directed its content. In ink, in a "free bold, hand," she declared,

> Dear Husband—In answer to your inquiries I acknowledge that about the summer of 1864 L.H. Hiscock,
> having frequently called at my house on business, one
> evening in the absence of other persons, first by force

prevailed upon me to yield to his desires, and partly succeeded in his efforts at various times afterwards. From shame and fear of exposure, he obliged me to in part submit to his caresses, only desisting from his persecutions, at last, on your return.

These assaults were always made while standing. I have refrained from exposure heretofore for fear of consequences.—Mary B. Cole[13]

There it was. She had been assaulted. Hiscock persisted and "partly succeeded" through force. She finally submitted, but only in part. She was always standing during whatever it was that happened. It seemed clear that Mary had initially been raped. The odd confession only raised more questions.

On Monday morning, Mary remained undressed in bed. The General had taken no victuals since his return to Syracuse and had been up much of the night "raving" at her—probably prying into (or helping her construct) her story. He began to look bloated and red, repeatedly weeping for his "poor children." Sometime that morning, he climbed to the third floor to visit his daughter Alice, who was unwell. Both girls had stayed home from school, perhaps sickened by the turmoil they sensed in their parents. Miss Graham, a girl hired by Mary, sat in the daughters' apartment sewing new outfits for the girls. Mary tried to send the seamstress home, but Mary Cuyler reminded their mother how badly the girls wanted the outfits.[14]

That morning, George wrote a message—"Come here quickly, for Heaven's sake"—and telegraphed it to his wife's stepbrother, Henry Barto Jr., the prominent lawyer and politician (who a decade earlier had literally written George into Mary's inheritance). Barto was in Albany for New York State's soon-to-commence Constitutional Convention. He had been elected as a delegate, and as George knew, so had Hiscock, who had drafted the bill calling for the convention.[15]

Before noon, George went to the Globe Hotel, a place he had been spotted on previous days. It is not clear why. He loitered in the reading room and on the front steps. Perhaps it was here that he spun his plans. Here was his chance to exact public shame on Hiscock in the presence of men of mark. He returned home and had Cuyler pack two months' worth of shawls, dresses, and underclothing for his wife and proclaimed that he would escort her to Brooklyn, where she would take up a new residence—away from the vicious rumors and out of Hiscock's reach.[16]

Mary feared that she was "going to her death." She confided her fears to Cuyler and left her instructions on how to raise the girls.[17]

Mary Cuyler persuaded her husband, John, to accompany George to Brooklyn, hoping, perhaps, that another man might keep the General from some horrific end. Sometime that same day, George asked Mary Cuyler to mend his jacket, and as she did, she discovered an old Colt revolver in his pocket that had belonged to his fifteen-year-old daughter, Alice. (Perhaps he had given it to her during the war as a memento.) He left for the streets a second time and entered a grocery store where he was not in the habit of doing business. He asked to examine their revolvers and pistols. He looked them over and selected a breach-loading Derringer and some cartridges, asking the merchant whether they could be relied on with certainty.[18]

George and Mary had not come down for dinner in the hotel apartment's main dining hall on Sunday. But after he bought his gun, he took a seat at a hall table with his daughters. Guests remembered him distractedly slamming the door as he came in. He ate nothing, only tasting a pickle. His daughter whispered something into his ear; he smiled at her and then patted down his wild hair with his palms. He abruptly got up and left.[19]

At some time, George penned his own letter, placed it in Mary Cuyler's hands, and told her to deliver it to the local newspaper if she got wind of trouble:

> I learn from undoubted evidence that L.H. Hiscock has forcibly endeavored to dishonor my wife in my own room—obtaining opportunity thus to do through professed friendship to me. He has often since made her the subject of his obscene attacks (in my absence in the army) and by thus implicating her somewhat in his guilt, has ruined her peace and my own. God has been my help and I ask not vengeance, but he shall abase himself to her and to me, and beg his miserable life of me. I hold her not entirely innocent. . . . Mary [Cuyler], I know all the circumstances fully, and it is as I tell you; so do not blame Mrs. Cole unjustly, if you hear anything about it
>   your aff. Cousin, G.W. Cole[20]

Like Mary had done in her confession, George told it as a story of force, of attempted rape at best.

On Tuesday morning, George, his wife, and John Cuyler boarded the train toward Albany, where the convention was opened by Rev. W. B. Sprague, who gave thanks for the recent war, which had been a divine retribution for Americans' "aggravated sins." After asking God to "intensify" the influence of New York on the nation, he prayed for each member to be safeguarded.[21]

At the station, the General noticed an old friend and asked him "if all were well at home," perhaps the only question that mattered to him. The pale veteran then took his seat by his wife. Fellow travelers recalled a veil over her face and the General anxiously tugging at his mustache. They leaned together, periodically sobbing along the journey. He continued to tremble. He once rose to fumble through his pockets for his missing ticket stubs but fell back into his seat after failing to hunt them down.[22]

When the train pulled into Albany, George announced to his two companions that they would all be getting off and that he would only need a few hours to take care of business. George had Cuyler check himself and Mary into the Delavan House hotel, the place of choice for legislators with teetotalling commitments. George did not check himself in at first but sometime after had "Dr. and" added next to "Mrs. George W. Cole" in the hotel register. It seems to have been unclear to him where he would sleep that night.[23]

Some maintained that during that day, Mary relayed a message to Hiscock, who was at the convention, warning him and perhaps planning an escape; the *New York Tribune* reported that the note urged him to meet at the People's Line steamboat landing, but it apparently reached him after the appointed hour.[24]

George had it in his mind to first talk to his wife's stepbrother, Henry Barto Jr., who, as it turns out, was still at the convention.[25] Barto quickly came when called. Something transpired in their meeting that infuriated George. The two had had a falling out since George had accepted his commission in the "Abolitionists' war" under Benjamin Butler. George laid out some plan that required Barto's complicity; he promised he would not take Hiscock's life but only make him beg for it on his knees "like a dog." Barto rejected his rash scheme, telling him, "You will think better of this in the morning," urging him instead to talk over the matter with ex-governor Thomas G. Alvord, a political ally and personal friend of Hiscock's.[26] (It had been Alvord, along with Hiscock, who had engineered George's promotion to brevet major general.)

After his meeting with Barto had not gone as planned, George asked Cuyler to go and watch over Mary, fearing that "the poor, sinful woman" was going to take her own life. Cuyler went and found her at a table before an open bible, a book she was not known to consult much.[27]

The General went to the hotel's hall and took a seat at a table. He still could not bring himself to eat. Along with other half-spun plans, he had envisioned bringing his two guns to the convention and challenging Hiscock to a duel or giving him ten days to leave the country.[28] Too much time had been frittered away for that to happen. He left the hotel and emerged onto Broadway. He made a two-block beeline for the prominent Stanwix Hotel, where many politicians took rooms and socialized in the lobby.[29]

The sun was sinking. Gaslights were lit along the boulevard stoops. Hiscock stood behind the lobby glass, standing in slippers, talking with his lawyer cronies, his lips moistening an evening cigar as he leaned against a pillar. He had just taken tea and still had his studs in his shirt. George walked along and past the hotel's main entry, rounded the corner, and slyly hooked back into the hotel side door.

Trancelike, the General cut a long arc through the lobby toward his family attorney. From about twelve feet off, he reached into his jacket and raised his arm as he approached. His throat tightened like the skin on a battle drum. One man thought the General was offering him his hand until George took aim. By then George was nearly touching Hiscock when he discharged the Derringer into his face. Hiscock staggered a bit, with hands reaching outward. He gasped and then fell, friends recalled, "like a bullock," with his "life blood oozing out."[30]

George backed off a bit and slid the gun into his pocket. Moments after the shot (which rang out for two blocks), a crowd began jamming itself into the lobby, pressed from behind by watchers in the street. Hiscock's close friend Moses Summers—a lawyer and local newspaperman—grabbed the General and demanded an explanation. In a daze, George told him what Hiscock had done to Mary.

When Summers questioned how the killer could know such a thing, George pointed to the confession in his breast pocket. Summers, who knew the murderer well, told him he would have to be detained. The veteran calmly responded that he was ready to surrender himself and face the consequences, even execution, for his deed.[31]

A physician rushed in to examine the body while politicians and close friends heaved it upstairs on a stretcher to a second-floor bed. Hiscock was long dead and had been nearly so before he hit the floor. After doing what many believed he had come to do, the General waited almost serenely for the police. He had no intention of fleeing the scene, and had bet his life that no jury composed of red-blooded men would convict a soldier for killing a false friend who had trespassed a soldier's marriage bed.

On the short walk to the station house, his emotions got ahold of him. He halted at times and threw his arms into the air; agitated and incoherent, he cried out into the darkness, asking the heavens what would become of his two young daughters.[32] He began a garbled account of how his innocent wife had been ravished while sick. He said that he had done the deed purposely but then said he had only planned to humiliate him. Those plans vanished, he claimed, the moment he laid eyes on Hiscock.[33]

At the station house he wrote a letter addressed to "my darling Mary" and then asked Summers to personally deliver it to her in her hotel room. "Be kind to her," he said. Mary learned her worst fears in the letter—that George's heart was "on fire" and that he had met the person who had "so grossly wronged" her. Now that Hiscock had finally atoned for his evil "as far as he could on earth," he wrote, she needed to go to Brooklyn to live with family.[34]

She rushed off the first call for outside help, a Western Union telegraph to George's brother, Cornelius:

GEN GEORGE W COLE IS IN PRISON & SERIOUS TROUBLE & WANTS YOUR ASSISTANCE COME IMMEDIATELY MRS. MARY B. COLE.[35]

With her marriage, reputation, and hopes dashed, Mary set out to help men manage their crises.

CHAPTER 15

RISING MEN (WHO NEARLY NEEDED GOD)

WITHIN HOURS PRISONER COLE DELIVERED a crafted statement to the reporters and onlookers gathered at his cell. "I had a friend, L.H. Hiscock," he began. "I thought him the best friend in the world. I have a wife and two children; she is as pure as snow, or was before [Hiscock] became acquainted with her in 1864. I was in the army, first as a private, and last as a Major-General."[1] Choking back tears, he went on to say that his close friend had assaulted Mary Cole in what she feared was her deathbed. She had called on Hiscock to help her finalize her will. She lay helpless when the attorney raised her up and forced his mouth on hers. She resisted and later forgave him after he begged her for mercy; but, George continued, Hiscock repeatedly returned on the "guise of business," once locking his arms around her and disrobing her. When the General had recently left town, seeking employment in Washington, DC (when he had an emergency attack of his bowels), Hiscock had tried, and had failed, to have his way with her again.

George had already altered his story. On the way to the jail, he cried that she had been "ravished." Now, he clarified, she had denied Hiscock all that he wanted. She mostly resisted the "destroyer," though his repeated attempts brought her shame and depression.

When the statement came to the killing, he broke down in unremorseful tears. The true victim had been "poor heartbroken" Mary, who, he said, flashed in his mind during the slaying. When he approached Hiscock, with only the intention to shame him, an image of Mary and his disgraced daughters "rose up" in his thoughts. He couldn't speak as he raised his gun. Mary and the girls were all he could see as he stepped toward their destroyer. He couldn't utter a word. "Something was in my throat."[2]

★

HISCOCK'S DEFENDERS IMMEDIATELY RESPONDED to the prisoner's statement. They were guarded in their defense of their friend's supposed sexual misdeeds. They instead focused on George's matter-of-fact summary of his war record: "I was in the army, first as a private, and last as a Major General."

The *New York Times* challenged the prisoner's claim, saying that in fact he had begun as captain and ended as brigadier general. The *New York Tribune*—one of a few papers that initially defended the prisoner—vouched for George's claim. It assured its readers of the soldier's distinguished war record and then embellished the original statement. True, he was "mustered in the service" as a captain, but he first "enlisted" as a private (a distinction offered by the paper with no clear difference). During the prisoner's rise in the ranks, each promotion had come unexpectedly and "entirely" without his solicitation. He had not been desperate for success, argued the *Tribune*. Indeed, he sacrificed his thriving business to save the Union.[3]

The *Syracuse Journal* then took issue with the *Tribune*'s account. It warned readers that the murderer's army record and previous accomplishments should not color how Americans viewed the crime. The murder was a question of law and order,

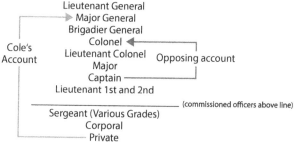

Ranks of the U.S. Army in the Civil War Era

George Cole conveyed his worth as a man by deploying partial truths and exploiting the confusion inherent in the Union army's system of rank and grade. Note that Black soldiers could not rise beyond the line that divided commissioned officers from the rest.

not of the prisoner's military rank. But then—essentially conceding that the original military sketch mattered dearly—over half of the article challenged the "cardinal virtues" of the prisoner's supposed promotions and business success. He had not enlisted as a private, the author wrote, but started as captain of Company H in the Twelfth New York Volunteer Infantry; and he was merely *breveted* a major general just before mustering out of the army. His promotions had not come unexpectedly. The paper threatened that if needed it would provide evidence to prove Mary Cole's "anxious desires and active efforts" in getting her husband promoted.[4]

George's enemies mobilized over these details because they knew what he was up to as he sobbed from his cell. His summary of his promotions, spoken in a uniquely American vernacular, was a powerful code for his character and worth as a human.

According to the code, every leaf, bar, and star on the General's uniform mattered. What mattered most, though, was that he had first worn an undecorated private's jacket. Every rung counted between his current perch and that of his former lowly self. The span of one's ascent said more than one's final altitude.[5]

The following day, after the Constitutional Convention reconvened amid buzzing crowds, Hiscock's cronies spoke the code flawlessly as they eulogized their slain friend. For them, the code was about rising above one's own family. Hiscock's key political ally, Thomas G. Alvord, said that though the corpse would soon be returned to the arms of kin, Hiscock had long outgrown his childhood village. Though born into a "crowded" household in rural Pompey, this son of a farmer and common field laborer soon "emerged" from his humble position "anxious and desirous to permit his intellect to grow and expand." George's victim had "stood outside of the family circle and with his own hands and with the work of his own brain, brought himself to the position which he occupied but yesterday." He was eminently a "self-made man, working out with his own intellect and with his own arm all positions which have been given him."[6]

Days later, prominent attorneys gathered at the Onondaga Supreme Court to pay Hiscock their tributes. They decried a murder that had snuffed out potential greatness; it ripped out the back half of an autobiography, violently interrupting Hiscock's story of overcoming local, small-town restraints of family and farm. He had just begun to shine. After he had briefly practiced law in a village, they said, he had moved to Syracuse, "thus changing a limited sphere for a wider range of usefulness, and one better adapted for the display of his abilities and capacities."

A friend added that just days before, the slain had been engaged in "the great struggle for successful life." Another said that Hiscock was "a *rising* man." Another, that in the legislature "he rose very high." Like every self-made man, he "was not controlled by passion. He was possessed of extraordinary self-control." Such rising therefore made him incapable of the deeds he had been accused of committing. Their message was clear and in lockstep. Hiscock had traded his farming community for the broader possibilities of the city; without aid he had moved beyond his kin. This was proof of his grand soul.[7]

For these men, this was the highest praise one could heap on a dead man.

PRISONER COLE'S FIB ABOUT HIS military career was an exaggeration, but one he rightly believed he could get away with.[8] George might have learned it from General Benjamin Butler who at least once proclaimed to one of his fellow commanders that "the trouble with you West Point officers is that you never were in the militia." He had started from nothing in the militia. "I rose from a private to a major-general," he boasted, "it isn't everybody that knows it, but I did."[9]

George and Butler used the grade of "major general" to accentuate their rise from humble privates. The title implied towering authority. Only Ulysses S. Grant had ascended higher than the grade of major general during the war when Abraham Lincoln appointed him to lieutenant general, a stature that, in America's military history, only George Washington had reached. (Grant sometimes wore a common private's jacket with his lofty insignia stitched to it.) The creation of the volunteer army, though, had introduced some confusion for military titles. After Lincoln's repeated calls for volunteers, throngs of professional officers took leave of America's small standing army—the Regular Army—for commands in a volunteer army in need of trained commanders. Lower-level regular officers, such as sergeants or captains, could hope to become volunteer majors or colonels. Majors might become generals. Prestigious officer titles once out of reach for all but a select few suddenly could be had.[10]

Prisoner Cole understandably did not emphasize that his meteoric rise to major general had happened in the volunteer army. (His critics made sure to fill in the blanks.) His silence was more misleading, though, when he failed to add that he had been a major general "by brevet." Though both volunteers, George and Butler had not been the same kind of major general. A brevet was akin to an honorary title, though also a permanent appointment, that did not change one's actual grade or pay. It was by nature confusing, and only grew more so in the closing months of the war with the avalanche of brevet requests and paperwork that overwhelmed the Adjutant General's Office and Military Affairs Committee. George's critics in the *Syracuse Journal* rightly revealed what many did not understand about the politics of promotion in Lincoln's army. They "pricked some of the bubbles blown." There was a yawning gulf between an actual general and a breveted one.[11]

The game of utterances—of key silences and qualifiers—was serious business for men trying to establish how they measured up with others. George's claim to be a major general was an audacious brag; but similar claims had become commonplace after the war. Hundreds of other men had come home imprecisely referring to themselves as "generals"—and many thousands more misleadingly called themselves "colonels," "majors," and "captains."

So many breveted veterans casually referred to themselves as simply "general," or "colonel," that Americans (and subsequent military historians) used new prefixes to help distinguish genuine officers from the rest. Since the emergence of the earliest practice of breveting in the American military, nonbreveted officers had begun creating and using prefixes like "actual," "effective," "permanent," "ordinary," "full," and "real." One journalist correctly stated that the prisoner was a breveted major general but then wrongly corrected himself, saying that George had been "promoted to a *full* brigadier general—instead of brevet" as had been stated in his previous dispatch.[12]

George obtained his brevets in his final days of service.[13] Eleventh-hour brevets were legion. Summing up how the brevet had been cheapened by the end-of-war profusion, one veteran wrote that the government "appeared not to know where to stop in the bestowal of these military honors. . . . Brevet shoulder straps were showered down 'as thick as leaves in Vallombrosa.'"[14] (Actually, and telling of the confusion, brevets were not supposed to come with new shoulder straps or any official change to an officer's uniform.) By the war's end, largely due to breveting, the army had given over three times more brigadier generalships than common sense warranted.[15]

Just months after George's statement from jail, the US congressional House Military Committee began debating, as it had in the past, what to do about the war's excessive breveting. The committee prepared a bill that would abolish brevet promotions except for soldiers who had acted heroically on the battlefield. It also sought to stop the growing problem at parades where brevet officers wore uniforms that made it appear as if they had been awarded the actual grade.[16]

When, from behind iron bars, "the General" stretched his military promotions to their credible limits, he was merely pushing his fellow Yankees into the hall of mirrors created by the war and its seductive promise to make men makers of themselves.[17]

★

THE DAY AFTER THE KILLING, delegates at the reconvened Constitutional Convention agreed to adjourn until the following Tuesday, lower the flag to half-mast, wear tokens of mourning for thirty days, and form a committee of eight to accompany the body back to Syracuse. One friend of Hiscock pushed for an amendment. He urged that they write that Hiscock had been "stricken down by the hands of an assassin." When a few questioned such prejudicial language, Hiscock's defender backed down but warned that spineless resolutions could someday lead "philosophers and philanthropists of the world" to paint George Cole as a hero.[18]

The painting had already begun—not by philosophers but by ordinary men and women who viewed George as something like a knight beating back the spread of modern infidelities.

Earlier that morning, Luther Hiscock's brother, Frank, had taken a train from Syracuse to Albany to retrieve the body. Along with the corpse, the coroner handed over bank notes (one reported to be $1,000), silver shirt studs, various papers, letters, a silver lighter, and photographs pulled from Luther's pockets.[19]

At the preliminary investigation, George's attorney, William Hadley, secured a subpoena for the personal effects.[20] Hadley cross-examined Hiscock's friends about possible "female cards" and other objects in the dead man's pockets. Hadley and a few newspapers would soon depict the missing pocket items as a rake's bundle of lusty letters and erotic photographs. Others, though, insisted that the possessions were nothing but business papers and some sentimental letters and photographs of his daughter and loved ones. One, they claimed, was a likeness of his dead wife, Lucy.[21]

Frank Hiscock refused to cooperate in handing over his older brother's effects. Only he and the coroner, and perhaps the men who were present at his death, knew what was in Luther's pockets. For everybody else, it was not clear whether they were the private effects of a grieving widower or the traces of a serial seducer—or the shuffled papers of a man who was both.[22]

The next day, Frank returned to Syracuse with the corpse in its ice-packed metallic casket. He, a group of friends, and convention delegates arrived at the station to an awaiting crowd that accompanied the remains back to Frank's home.[23]

★

Two days after the murder, Rev. "Dr." Sherman Bond Canfield, who counted Mary and George part of his flock, traveled from Syracuse to tend to their grieving. He was not the hard-nosed pastor he had once been. His Calvinist theology had recently petered out. He had once been a Yale-trained guard dog who stood ground against the spreading doctrine of perfectionism—the belief that humans held salvation in their own, impressively clean hands.

He ceased delivering razor-sharp sermons about the corrupted human heart when, on a recent Sabbath morning, he had stepped to the pulpit as if he were Saint Paul repenting for trying to convert the Athenians with naked reason. He penitently stood before his congregation and promised them just the sweet message of the gospel. "Henceforth," he announced, "I shall try to preach to you Jesus." Like many pastors of his day had done, he embraced the seductive doctrine that men, who from time to time strayed from the course, only needed the abundant love of Jesus.[24]

He tried to bring that love to the jail cell when he succored Mary and George, his wayward lambs. He feared they were headed for more trouble. The papers had already spread details about how, right after the murder, George had tried to conceal a small spring-back knife tucked in his vest. They speculated—as his own family did privately—that he had plans to slit his own throat. Canfield counseled the couple and secured an oath from the prisoner not to magnify the tragedy with more needless blood.[25]

The next day, mourners gathered for the funeral. The ministers in attendance, like the one who visited the Coles, represented a kind of Christianity that emphasized the power of human goodness over evil and the "spirit of the law" over obedience and justice.

The prayer was offered by Rev. Ezekiel Mundy, seen by some as a radical young minister in Syracuse whose sermons one friend described as "a simple philosophy of good living."[26] Pastor S. R. Dimmock and his choir from the Plymouth Congregation Church provided the hymns and sermon. Dimmock's church had borrowed its name and upbeat gospel from the famed Plymouth Church in Brooklyn. The Brooklyn pulpit, made famous by Henry Ward Beecher, the most celebrated pastor of the day, was known for its abolitionism and its increasing preference for the gospel of human goodness over Calvinistic depictions of human depravity. (In the years that soon followed, Beecher would find himself mired in two scandals concerning adultery.)[27]

When Dimmock stepped before the long-faced mourners, the tension would have been palpable. Before devastated loved ones, he had to speak at length about a murdered man who had been accused of desecrating another man's bed—with seduction or perhaps rape. The pastor had been suffering for years from asthma and severe catarrh. Inflamed membranes nearly sealed off his infected nasal cavities. He struggled with depression and languor, and worried about what he referred to as his "repugnance to society"—probably the odor of his breath, which passed over the corrupted discharge in his throat and nose.[28]

On Sundays, though, the weary minister could at least assure himself that his fetid mouth delivered the gospel of human goodness, the fresh air of optimism. His words, he could tell himself, were like honey from the rotting lion's head in the biblical account of Samson. Still, though he was the kind of minister who rejected the religion of damnation and depravity, he unhappily found himself in the middle of a regional tragedy, staring into the abyss of human sin.

And so, with Hiscock's corpse lying nearby in an open casket, Dimmock, more than he was accustomed to doing, addressed the reeking truth about the caverns of the human heart. He did not dwell on adultery and revenge. To the disappointment of some, he did not vilify the killer. Instead, he first traced the tragedy back to places like Shiloh, Gettysburg, and Cold Harbor.

He sniffed his first words into the hushed room. "War is a scourge to any nation, even if the cause be just and the result success." Only the war, he believed, could explain the shocking evil. It somehow lay beneath it all.[29]

Many Americans, he admitted, had expected war to compromise the standards of the lower sorts by sowing seeds of profanity, drunkenness, Sabbath breaking, and sexual permissiveness. In this, he said, "we have not been disappointed." But Hiscock's sudden death had "forcibly reminded" Americans that the war had degraded the better sorts too. The result of the war was to "cheapen human life." And though the General had fought on the right side of the conflict, the war had made life disposable in his mind. "To a soldier, who has been five years in bloody conflict," he continued, "it is a light thing to deprive his fellow of mortal existence. The springs of humanity are dried up, and the susceptibilities blunted, so that, even on the slight provocation, one will assume the prerogative of God alone." War makes soldiers temporary gods and some veterans can't relinquish the power.

The preacher had to watch his words. He couldn't allow his listeners to confuse killing during battle with murder from the hand of a soldier after war. Yes, the government had justly killed through its soldiers. Those same soldiers, however, could not assume power over life even if to vanquish evil in their private battles. "When human life is taken by a magistrate, there is the delegation of divine authority."

He did not see, or would not dare confess, that for men like George Cole and the many who held him as a hero, the line between what he did for America by killing rebels and what he did for humanity by killing Hiscock was razor thin. For the many who supported the prisoner, imperiled unions of whatever kind justified force and gunpowder.

After saying what was often feared about the war but rarely confessed publicly—especially by well-heeled Republicans like those in attendance who viewed Union victory as the triumph of good over evil—Dimmock then preached what would become a standard denunciation of the murder. He said that regardless of Hiscock's purported behaviors, the General's act of revenge could not be approved by law-loving people.

The preacher exhorted the "great concourse" in the house, but really the masses that he knew would read his sermon, to postpone judgment and keep in mind that Hiscock had been robbed of his right to tell his side of the story. The prisoner's evil act punished innocent children from both households and forever tarnished Mary Cole's reputation. It erased the veteran's own military achievements. "He has earned laurels by five year's patriotic service" but with one act of cowardice "has torn them from his own brow." George Cole, he said, represented "the suicide of honor."

Dimmock had softened his theology but was not what conservatives called a "loose" minister. The Democratic *Albany Argus* argued right after the murder that part of the crime could be traced to "the doctrines of Free-Love" promoted by "the yellow-covered literature of the day" to which "loose" ministers contributed. Prisoner Cole referred to them as "weak-kneed clergy"—sentimental pastors who could not understand how violence and discipline from time to time were needed to purify a sinful world. These descriptions did not fit Dimmock;

but his ministry reflected nineteenth-century Christians' increasingly tolerant stance toward sin, a stance that emphasized the core goodness of human feelings.[30]

Feelings stood at the center of the Stanwix tragedy. The whole ordeal could be boiled down to humans following the deepest impulses of their bosom. Some said that Mary Cole and Hiscock had followed their hearts outside the legal confines of marriage; others said that feelings from domestic love drove George to murder.[31]

Feelings, Dimmock told the mourners, needed to be restrained by law. The murder of Hiscock was the result of lenient laws. He urged the New York State Assembly to make adultery a crime. He marveled about how property and reputations were protected by law but marriage, the most sacred bond of humanity, was not. And—just as George's attorneys would argue later—the fact that there were no adultery laws in New York made murderous revenge a logical step for jealous husbands who had no legal recourse for what other men might do to their marriages.

After he teetered on blaming legislators for George's deeds, Dimmock turned to the soul of the deceased. He strained to shower him with faint praise. The slain had been a "judiciously indulgent" father. Once when Hiscock's daughter was dangerously ill, his manly heart quaked while his "tears flowed freely as a woman's." Though Hiscock had made no profession of faith, he did have a kind of "intellectual faith." He exhibited no skepticism. No scoffing of religion had ever fallen from his lips. He had always admired the pure faith of his deceased wife, Dimmock added. Hiscock had wanted his children to be in good graces with Jesus.

But—as all of the reverend's words suggested—Hiscock had never submitted to God. The pastor spoke as if he had first applied the obligatory ointment for a wound, only to wipe it clean for necessary airing. Hiscock had never experienced conversion; he instead had a secondhand relationship with Jesus through his wife and children. The preacher made sure everybody in the room knew that Hiscock was no regenerated Christian.

Dimmock closed his sermon by using Hiscock as an example of the kind of detached Christianity of men who too often relied on the piety of mothers and wives. The preacher criticized something that he and many fellow ministers had witnessed from the pulpit. His brand of Christianity, after all, was one in which ministers and women emphasized the feminine attributes of the gospel, enabling many men (like George and Hiscock) to lean back from matters of religion.[32]

The reverend had spoken directly, perhaps too baldly for loved ones. The murder was the bitter fruit of war, of weak laws, and of decent men who refused to submit to Christ. Hiscock was a loving man, but a lukewarm Christian. The sermon had partly, briefly drawn back the silken veil of liberal Christianity that masked human ugliness. But the preacher had also painted a sentimental portrait of Hiscock as a weeping father who found Christ vicariously through his children. Some—including the preacher himself—might have wondered if Dimmock had come to comfort mourners or call mankind to repentance.

When the reverend finished speaking, mourners stepped toward the casket to view the mortician's art—an art much advanced by the recent need to make the war's cadavers appear to have parted the world in peace. A correspondent noted that despite the "certain work of the assassin," Hiscock's embalmed and touched-up features looked calm and natural. He looked like a "noble-faced man in quiet, peaceful slumber."[33]

After the casket was closed on the "slumbering" body, a wreath and cross were laid on the lid. As a friend put it, Hiscock's "manly form" was then "placed beneath the sod forever."[34]

Somewhere a stoneworker had been commissioned to chisel an epitaph into the base of Hiscock's tombstone. The words were taken from the poem "Immortality," by the contemporary English poet Matthew Arnold:

> He who flagged not in the earthly strife
> from strength to strength advancing.

For those who cherished Arnold's poetry, the meaning was clear. Hiscock had not flagged or lost vigor in his worldly labors. He had advanced with force.

Arnold's poems and writings were steeped with a sense of traditional Christianity in decay. In this poem—beloved either by Hiscock or by his closest friends—man need not wait on death and heaven to make himself right; man did not lack God to raise him up or free him from life's miseries. Arnold taught through this poem that man gains his own permission to continue his upward trajectory into heaven by first advancing himself on earth. A "well-knit" soul was the possession of men who win life's battles. That kind of man advances himself, the poem goes on to declare, and then "mounts" to eternal life, "and that hardly." Driven men of the world, in other words, would escort themselves into the kingdom of God. Hiscock's detached faith didn't matter. He had made his own salvation.

CHAPTER 16

the DOMESTICATED PRISONER

MARY COLE WAS DETERMINED to nurse her husband through calamity. She pleaded with the jailer to allow her to board in the jail instead of the nearby hotel, as if she could or should share the punishment for her husband's deed. Until Cornelius Cole arrived nearly a week after the murder, she dutifully waited on the prisoner.[1]

As George pondered the fate of his children and confronted the sharp denunciations in the papers, he sank further into the hole of depression. Suicidal urges badgered him.

FOR HELP HE TURNED to his most trusted confidant, his sister-in-law Olive, wife of Cornelius. Olive came from the same world as the Coles. She was the daughter of aspiring Lake Country farmers. She graduated from a local academy and continued on to a female college. She caught the eye of young and ambitious Cornelius when she was singing a Methodist hymn in her family church pew, standing in her dark-blue velvet dress and undersleeves of white silk muslin. She later described herself as having a "Puritan soul," but her religious sensibilities, like those of so many around her, were hardly so. She was a Methodist girl with ambitions in the world.[2]

Prisoner Cole wrote her that he had held himself together as well as any man could in such a catastrophe. Still, "I am awfully lonesome and cast down and hopeless," he said. "But don't fear my manhood, I shall acquit myself as a man." He clung to the belief that Mary had been raped and that she was not Luther Harris Hiscock's only victim. "His friends are moving earth for my blood," he wrote, but Hiscock's acts were "coming out daily in <u>awful blackness and fullness</u>." He had ruined other families, even young girls. "He used force," George wrote, "only a few months ago on a young girl 14 years old in St. Charles Hotel, Syracuse." George wanted to believe this, though he knew that there were other tales circulating about Mary's guilt.[3]

Shaken by George's letters, Olive told her husband that she needed to see her brother-in-law before it was too late. She didn't think George was strong enough to resist killing himself. "His sole thought is for his children," she wrote, before adding her frustration. "A pity he did not think of [his daughters] before" acting on his rage.[4]

Two weeks later, George began a dire letter to Olive. "Dear Sister, I am failing & shall soon sink under my agony (my children's disgrace). I try hard to keep up but I cannot. I have not heard from Mary or the children since a week tomorrow and I think she too has deserted me in my imprisonment." Mary had dependably called on George each day from nine o'clock in the morning until just before noon and frequently returned in the evenings. She brought him books and papers. At first their visits were monitored by the jailer, but their regularity convinced the jailer that he could lock them together in the cell. He never saw Mary sit on or lie in George's bed; he said that the prisoner always kept his robe on and that Mary had only removed her shawl and bonnet.[5]

Now that Mary had abruptly stopped coming, George pleaded with Olive to go to Trumansburg, where Mary had recently begun staying at her stepbrother's home, and to bring her back to Albany, where she and Olive might stay at a "nice boarding house" near the jail.[6]

He had recently turned to scouring old letters from Mary, using hindsight to pry loose clues about what he was just coming to see as her shameful connection with Hiscock. As if drawing from a well-known reading, George wrote a curious passage in quotation marks:

> "I am compassed about by enemies & bitter water overwhelms my soul."

The quote, which seems to have had no exact literary origin, reads like a biblical hodgepodge taken from various suffering souls in ancient Hebrew texts. It sounds like wayward David crying to his God about his fall; Job stunned by his abandonment; and the wandering children of Israel complaining about the bitter waters of Marah.[7]

The words apparently sprang from the prisoner's intense, if passing, relationship with the scriptures in his cell. Unrestrained by rigorous scriptural precision, and writing like a lamenting prophet himself, he mapped the cries of David onto his own life. Four days later he wrote Olive that he hoped to "relieve" her anxiety about his condition. Despite the depression, which he blamed on his wounds and monotonous confinement, he had turned a corner. "I have a new lease of life," he assured her. He felt relieved that Mary planned on returning any day. He seems to have taken renewed pity on her. Still, he yearned to see Olive in person. He had something urgent to share with her.[8]

He had just experienced something that he seems to have needed her—or perhaps any pious Christian—to help him interpret. "I want your advice on a <u>delicate matter</u>," wrote George, referring cryptically to something that had happened in his cell. George had apparently tried to kill himself or, because of his wounds, had felt one foot slip into the grave. "I was <u>mighty</u>

near escaping a trial a few days since & to be tried before a bar more high & more merciful than the earthly tribunal," he wrote. He had dodged death.

George did not often talk like this. He did not strike the slightest evangelical tone in any of his surviving letters from the war, or after his trial. Like Hiscock, he had loved women who loved Jesus, but he could never quite speak or believe like them. But after the "delicate matter" in his cell, he used phrases like "for my advocate will be Christ." An advocate and friend, this Jesus was the kind of personal companion that had become so familiar to Victorian Christians, the kind that so many ministers who played background roles in George's drama had embraced. "I am employing him often daily," he continued, "& he is very encouraging to me." For at least a few days, God had chased from George's cell those dark spirits that bedeviled Job and David.

Having come close to meeting his maker, the prisoner was left with a serene perspective on the entire drama. His brush with death and his spiritual epiphany left him to drift off into reveries. After addressing the "delicate" experience, and before uncharacteristically closing with God's blessing on Olive, he added, "I am alone nearly all the time with my thoughts and memories & grow nearly distracted at times."

During a short respite provided by Jesus, he didn't need other men. He did not need vindication from the State of New York, his army commanders, popular opinion in the press, or a jury of peers. He had discovered a merciful God and relished his life memories. He only lacked a pious woman to help him make sense of it all.

Knocked-to-the-ground evangelical conversions in the nineteenth century often did not last. Even so, George's spiritual flame, and the peace it brought him, was unusually fleeting. With every day it became clearer that God would not free him from the tedium of his imprisonment, the maze of courtroom procedures, or the venom of public scrutiny. It dawned on George—perhaps with the help of his proud attorneys—that he didn't need the merciful intervention of Christ so much as a well-honed legal defense. If he and his lawyers told his story just right, he might convince his peers that he needed no forgiveness at all.

★

AFTER GEORGE'S INDICTMENT, his attorney had argued that if the prisoner was not moved from his original cell, he would die from his war wounds. The judge agreed and George was transferred to an upstairs cell set apart from the cramped inmates, some of whom were chained together in gangs. Cornelius Cole recalled, after he first arrived to find Mary and George weeping together, that Mary took "some pleasure in keeping every thing exceedingly neat about the apartment"—as if tidying her husband's quarters could somehow bring order to their crumbling lives.[9]

His new cell had once been occupied by Mary Hartung, who was of enormous local fame for having poisoned her husband before the war. George's attorney, William Hadley, had defended Hartung and ultimately got her released despite a conviction in court. Hadley may have used his familiarity with the jail to secure the General a cell once designated for female inmates and debtors. It was not unusual for jailers, pressed for space, to house male and female inmates in ways that violated codes of Victorian decency—with only a metal floor grate or door separating them. Whatever the case, his quarters, though still described as "small and destitute," must have seemed like a refuge from the revolting scenes that others reported throughout the jail.[10]

For years, reformers had called for the Albany jail to be razed because of its wretched conditions. It lacked proper ventilation, had no library, offered no way to wash one's entire body, and provided no means of exercise for the inmates. Many of its prisoners, a good number of them ex-soldiers, spent their days gambling with cards. Sometimes three or four prisoners were jammed into a cell less than five feet wide and seven feet deep. The smell of manure from the adjacent stable wafted through the grated windows. For some reason (perhaps to prevent communication between cells) the ventilation ducts had been stopped up. At night inmates relieved themselves into containers on the floor. Though the floors were regularly cleaned, the air could be repulsive.[11]

Like the majority of New York's jails, and despite laws requiring such, Albany did not provide a copy of the Bible in its cells. During a period in 1863, at least, a chaplain offered sermons on Sundays. But even when services were held in front of the motley inmates, jeering often drowned out the hoped-for quiet whispers to the sinner's heart. Some years before, many of the Albany inmates began sleeping on straw mattresses laid out on the floor. They once had iron bedsteads until some prisoners began breaking them into weapons, using the bars and rods to attack the jailer.[12]

Henry Smith, the district attorney leading the prosecution, had once written a report about the jail's "appalling horrors." He had witnessed some sixty men and boys huddled in a room where first-time offenders, and the wrongly accused, spent long days in close company with "the most depraved." A third as many women were crammed into a smaller room where inmates, who varied from "reasonably tidy" to "repulsively filthy," shared intimate space. Reformers worried that such conditions helped criminality spread like lice as novice wrongdoers were "initiated into all the arts and mysteries of crime." Because he could, George moved to a new cell that distanced him from the horrors.[13]

★

GEORGE FORBADE his two young daughters from visiting him. He worried how images of a confined father would assault their feelings. "Their young minds," he said to a visitor, "would always be impressed with these cheerless surroundings of my being in prison; and I will bear the agony of their absence rather than this." He "only wished" he could lay eyes on them. He hoped he could shelter them, not only from the scenes of his imprisonment but also from the rumors outside the jail. He trusted only Olive to explain to them why their father was in the newspapers. She assured George that nobody had "prejudiced" them about the tragedy.[14]

He knew as well as anyone that his degradation was on display at every newsstand and in every hotel reading room. With the daylight that shone through his barred windows, he perused the scathing reports that filled the papers. As Cornelius put it, "the hounds" were still after him, and "of course [the General] feels it."[15] The best he could do was shape public opinion and perhaps in that way salvage himself before his fellow citizens and in the eyes of his girls.

And so, with the eyes of countless upstate New Yorkers and other Americans upon him, prisoner Cole, at first with the help of Mary and friends, transformed his cell into a museum of his embattled life. Over the next months, he became a curator of his public image—a domesticated father, and some relic of endangered manliness. He welcomed and entertained many visitors—how many is not clear, but so many that he took their frequent visits for granted. Cornelius noted in one letter that though women had traveled all the way from Syracuse to call on the prisoner earlier that day, during Cornelius's two-hour visit with his brother, George "said nothing or next to nothing about" his previous female admirers.[16]

As a former book merchant and owner of a photography gallery, he understood how men and women were sized up according to their appearance and belongings. Avid readers everywhere in the region and beyond witnessed his closely managed quarters through the public gaze of newspaper accounts. Like any good Victorian who filled his or her parlor with sentimental knickknacks and possessions of refinement, George decorated his cell with proof of his affection for family and with books and artwork that conveyed his good tastes.

He welcomed his visitors and reporters as if he were a father in his private study. In entertaining one journalist, he dressed in a robe with his feet clad in a pair of "very handsomely embroidered slippers" that matched his suspenders. He could not control how visitors saw him, though. The same reporter who noted that his eyes "glistened with tears" when he spoke about his children also wrote that his mustache had grown scraggy and his complexion oily. His "saddened" eyes had less to do with his love for family, the journalist wrote, but instead suggested he was a "man of impulses, rather than will and character." (If so, George had failed to become the kind of self-directed man into which Wesleyan University had tried to mold him.)[17]

It was George's intent to tightly control his image, perhaps, that explains why some of his soldiers were not allowed to visit him in his cell. Several of his former soldiers reportedly showed up to the jail to visit their "Old Commander." When the jailer informed them that they did not have permission, or the proper permit, the group protested in vain until one of the soldiers "burst into tears," exclaiming, "Why in Hell didn't the General call upon us if he wanted to get rid of the enemy[?] We would have performed the work." The report did not say if these were officers or enlisted men, Black or White, or if they were in George's regiment of "bully- boy" raiders, or from his

Black cavalry. They were painted as rougher sorts who left after much pleading, muttering to themselves.[18]

George knew how fascinated the public was with his ordeal. Daily newspapers hung along a clothesline strung across his cell. The newspapers detailed his small living space—a space that was described as strewn with the same newspapers. His life had become the focus of the public gaze, a series of reflections of reflections between opposing mirrors. Through reports, people watched George as he read about how people were watching him. "Oh, wad some power the giftie gie us. . . ."[19]

Readers wanted to know what he read. George had packages of books and papers conveyed from his extensive library back in Syracuse, some of which had likely been left over from his busted book and lumber business. Below his small windowpanes, books of all kinds covered benches and a writing table. George would have been pleased that the reporter noted that on his table lay an open bible and Shakespeare's *Julius Caesar*. The Shakespearean tragedy, about how ambitious patriotism destroyed friendship, was opened to the third act where Marc Anthony proclaims,

> The evil that men do lives after them;
> the good is oft interred with their bones.

Lying nearby was William Jay's *Prayers for the Use of Families*, a book written by an English minister who wanted to stop the feminization of Christianity. In the preface, Jay tells fathers that they had been "placed at the head of families" and called to "rule well" their households of wives, children, and servants. "Behold a church in thy house," Jay wrote, reminding fathers that they had been called to be domestic ministers. Somewhere on the table was a copy of the most influential religious literary work penned in the English language: John Bunyan's *Pilgrim's*

Progress, an allegorical journey of redemption by a lost man named Christian.[20]

After Mary relocated to the home of her stepbrother, Henry Barto Jr., George became the primary curator of the museum that was his cell. One visitor recalled how, upon their entering, the prisoner—with "the grace of a gentleman of culture"—apologized for the "simply furnished" space. Beside the bed in the corner was a crude wooden bench with his "toilet articles." There was a rocking chair and two other seats for visitors. Admiring ladies had sent him letters and bouquets of flowers. At some point, he had a sofa brought in. A flute had been laid out on display as well.[21]

And, of course, he displayed pieces of the war that he still had with him. He kept Mary's war letters. One editor from Troy noted an "iron army camp pot" in the cell that sat at the side of his card table. When two visitors asked him about the war, his face brightened. He related one incident after another, finally ending with a mournful look on his face. "Yes," he said, "I wish I had left my bones on some of the battle-fields."[22]

In late fall 1867, cell visitors reported that he had in his possession a "beautiful finger ring." It had been worn by a soldier named Griffin who had been killed during the siege of Petersburg. Griffin fought for the New York Eighty-Ninth, a White regiment. George showed the relic to his visitors and said he was anxious to restore it to Griffin's family.[23]

(Witnesses gave no explanation why he had the ring three years after Griffin's death. Maybe the prisoner or one of his Black soldiers had found it after the battle at New Market Heights, near Petersburg. George and some of his Black soldiers had returned there near the end of the war to remember where some of the men had been killed—and where Robert Dollard had suffered a gaping head wound. Perhaps a farmer in Virginia found the ring while plowing his field and sent it to the now-famous veteran. Perhaps someone bought the ring on the death-relic market—where ordinary Americans purchased buttons, bullets, and things taken from dead soldiers' pockets—and gave it to George as a gift. All that was clear was that he wanted to bring comfort to the soldier's family.)[24]

★

HIS CELL was an exhibit of the ardent love of family. Tacked to the wall, across from the table, hung two photographs of his daughters "in sight of him all day long." On the wall next to his bed, an "anchor of hope" made from moss and white rosebuds hung from a blue chord above his pillow. Alice, his ten-year-old girl, made it and had it put in an oval frame made of black walnut. In antebellum ladies' guidebooks about flowers, the dried white rose symbolized that, for a "true woman," death was preferable to losing sexual purity. What this implied about Mary, reporters did not say. Attached to the anchor was Alice's "pathetic note" expressing her love for her absent father. She wrote that she wanted to make her father an emblem of hope. She made it with her own hands but worried that the frame she bought in the little town of Trumansburg was not high in quality. "We are well. From your loving Alice."[25]

George allowed at least one visitor to read his response to Alice, a poem he wrote not long after he had a spiritual crisis in his cell. Two verses from it read,

> My Darling, your present came safely to-day,
> Made by your industry and art;
> As, in coming, it was not delayed by the way,
> It delayed not in reaching my heart
>
> ...
>
> How it makes my hand tremble; God bless you, my child

Prisoner Cole curated his jail cell in ways that reminded the public of his refinement, love for family, and sacrifice in war. His daughter's handmade anchor of hope hangs on the wall above his head. On the floor and at the far wall, we see cages he made for his mice and birds, tables with books, and an army chest. This depiction makes his cell look much larger than it was reported to be in other publications (measuring a mere six feet by four). The artist omitted the clotheslines strewn about the cell on which George hung his newspapers. Compared with reports from other newspapers, the prisoner appears dressed in unusually refined attire, befitting a genteel man luxuriating on a sofa. Frank Leslie's Illustrated Newspaper, *May 23, 1868, 149.* Image from Internet Archive

> And watch well your innocent rest
> When I think of my children my heart is 'most wild
> To press them again to my breast

The poem went on to place Alice's safety in God's hands and promised her that her father would look fondly upon the gift daily.[26]

The odors, sounds, and images of vice and dissolution throughout the jail provided a foil for the domestic tranquility in the prisoner's temporary home. His cell would become one of the most permanent dwellings he had known since the day he left his parents' farm for boarding school. In search of something—better soil, a boom town on a promising canal, social life, glory in war—George had moved from one place to the next. He had finally become a settled presence in his girls' lives. He just couldn't stand for them to witness how this came to be.

CHAPTER 17

CONFESSIONS

ONCE THE LIGHT of merciful Jesus faded from his cell, George began to think that Mary Cole's sins were crimson stains that could not be washed away. He had a growing suspicion that Mary had gotten caught up in Luther Harris Hiscock's attentions, and that she was equally at fault.

HE SENSED, as others did, that the carnal misdeeds of Hiscock traced to Mary's money. Before the body of Hiscock had been buried, doubt had been cast on the true motives behind the tragedy. It was "quite possible, if not probable," one letter to a newspaper claimed, that neither adultery nor rape had been the true root of the General's rage. Instead, the anonymous author wrote, it had to do with the making of Mary's will and the money she had inherited from her father—money that was legally hers alone. "Mrs C possesses a considerable estate in her own right—$20,000 is the lowest amount we have heard named."[1]

The letter claimed that because of George's business failures, he had pressured Mary for the "use and control" of her estate. Hiscock stood between him and his wife's money. "Mrs. C," the writer continued, "may have been advised [by Hiscock] to keep it invested where it was safest. She was doubtless anxious to provide for her children." George brooded over these "imaginary wrongs" until fancy took possession of his mind. His fears about losing control of her money, in other words, led to imaginary fears of losing control of her sexuality. The author, who was surely out to repair Hiscock's legacy, went on to say that Mary had amended her own will after spending hours altering it in Hiscock's office. In this new will, she had only bequeathed George the income received through various investments, and only with "certain contingency." George, humiliatingly, had been written into Mary's will like wives had been traditionally written into the wills of husbands.

The letter's author admitted that Hiscock had paid a visit to Mary as she lay sick in her bed. But accusations about Hiscock's unwelcome advances were "incredible" because, the writer reasoned, seven months after the supposed deathbed "ravishing," she visited the attorney's office to have the will amended again. In Hiscock's office, she dictated the terms of the codicil. Hiscock kept the copies. The person who wrote the letter had unusual access to details. It was probably written by one of Hiscock's close colleagues in the law, or perhaps by his brother, Frank (who was a lawyer). The author made a compelling case that money was central to George's grievances but was less convincing about the nature of Hiscock and Mary's sexual encounters. "Was this the conduct of a woman," the writer asked, who had truly been raped?

It likely was.

★

HISCOCK HAD POWERS that Mary needed. As much as any man in Syracuse, he knew how to help a wife keep her money from her husband. George had confided to his Albany jailer that he initially guessed that Hiscock "had been cheating him in some money matters conducted with his wife's estate." The jailer also heard George say that he assumed that Mary's "coolness" to him—no doubt a euphemism for sparsity of sex—"had its origin in the question of property."[2]

A wife's body, like her money, was never securely or entirely her own. Mary may have wondered whether she could permanently say no to a man who was determined to have what he wanted. In the eyes of the law—through the legal fiction of coverture—a married woman did not possess the power to consent to, or resist, the sexual advances of her husband. A wife relied on her husband's kindness, his common sense and moral grounding, to respect her wishes. But in the eyes of the law, her body was his, waiting in some permanent state of consent. Theoretically, there could be no rape within marriage.[3]

Rape was something that happened outside marriage and was seen as the result of men losing control of their passions. It was the most passionate act on a spectrum of sexual desire, a few dreadful steps beyond the sins of fornication and adultery. It was universally condemned at the pulpit and by moralists, though seen as springing from natural desire. The sinful deed was not spawned by a depraved heart, hunger for violent power, or sinister motives. It was the horrifying result of a man's ungoverned sexual longing.

For more than a century, legal arguments and literature had depicted sex as something that might require some physical force. In the minds of many, consent and force were not mutually exclusive. Force and violence were *not* the determining factors for what constituted rape; postrevolutionary almanacs, poems, and jokebooks told stories of women who wanted sex, pretended to resist, but coyly meant yes. Amorous husbands just needed to press on with patience and persevere through the ritual of initial refusals.

Further blurring the lines between consent and coercion, newspapers and literature used the word "ravish" as a synonym for rape. Yet to be "ravished" in a more general sense meant to be overcome with rapturous joy, often by some irresistible and awesome power like God's love. The word "ravish" itself lent a perverse meaning to rape as some exquisite power and pleasure that, like divine grace, a woman could not refuse for long.

In previous centuries, women had been widely seen and depicted as volatile, sexually dangerous creatures. They were Eve's daughters, destined to fool by flattery and lure man into the fall. But after the American Revolution, and especially with the rise of commercial towns and cities, women were often exalted as moral creatures, more sensitive than men to God's call and less driven by the lusts and ambitions of the world.

The age-old caricatures of women as Jezebels and temptresses endured, of course. The images of the hussy and virtuous mother existed side by side and could be selectively evoked to defend sexual aggression. A determined man could tell himself that because pure women were always dutifully resisting, men had to take the initiative. And because a woman was half angel, a man only needed to take her protests half seriously. When she gave in, or seemed to relent, it served as proof that she had never been entirely pure.

If Hiscock did rape Mary—meaning that he used force or coercion to penetrate her or to realize some sexual desire for which she had not wished—her futile protests would have only proved to him that she was partly angelic and needed a man to take charge.

If she had been raped, Mary had reasons to keep silent after the initial encounter; reporting rape, a serious accusation of crime, meant revealing traumatic details to various male authorities—to the sheriff, the judge, the jurymen, and, for Mary, her war-shattered husband. In the nineteenth century, White women who accused White men of rape had to prove penetration and undergo scrutiny of their past record of virtue. A woman who had a history of unseemly sexual relations, of flirting, or who belonged to a family of low reputation would likely be deemed incapable of saying no. Fallen women could never truly reject a man's advances. Only a woman proven to be pure could be raped.

Given the powerful, and unreachable, ideal of pure womanhood, Mary possibly wondered to herself whether she was worthy enough to accuse such a well-regarded attorney of rape or whether, instead, she had somehow brought the ordeal upon herself.[4]

★

MARY'S FIRST CONFESSION NOTE WAS A PROBLEM. It depicted scenes of "partly" accomplished rape. The timing is hazy, but likely on the morning the couple boarded the train to Albany, George had urged Mary to amend her confession. Along the top, in pencil, she added, "But upon my soul [Hiscock] never had an entire connection with me, nor did he ever enter me entirely." The penciled words had to have been written in a moment of haste, away from home, when a new confession could not be properly written. The details only added to the confusion. For her husband's sake (and for the millions of people who would soon know), she said that Hiscock had never "entirely" entered her. She had been raped, it still seemed to say, but inches from becoming his total possession.[5]

This amended confession seemed to prove—if only in the prisoner's mind—that Hiscock had never captured Mary's soul through sexual unity. The two never shared the kind of spiritual and emotional bonding through bodily pleasure that many Victorians held as proof of authentic love. It had been a half-accomplished rape with no enduring spiritual connection. The confession seemed to leave space for him to forgive Mary, and someday reunite with her.[6]

Evidently, once the General came to his senses after he was jailed, he realized—probably with the help of legal counsel—that Mary's first confession, even with the amendment, put him in a legal bind. Hiscock could have been arrested and sentenced harshly for rape. If it had been rape, as the original confession implied, George would have had a clear path for seeking justice through the law. Adultery, however, was not a crime, and it left a cuckolded husband no way to seek justice through the courts. Any suggestion that Mary had been raped would rob the killing of its justification. It had to be made clear that Hiscock *had* fully connected with Mary. And that it was not "by force" altogether but through some combination of seduction and consensual adultery.

George's defense needed to mop up the strategic mess of the first confession. They needed evidence of Mary's complicity and believed understandably that they could find it. There were, after all, reasons why Mary and Hiscock would have sought emotional refuge in each other. She had been overwhelmed by darkness, coping with a maimed husband who seemed to be heading for a grisly fate at the hands of rebels. If George survived the war, she would soon share her bed with a mentally dashed husband who had begun to repel old friends with his changed demeanor. He had been gone a long time, one-third of their fifteen-year marriage. Unlike George, Hiscock was there, and he was an able-bodied man. His groin had not been disfigured in war. Since losing his wife, he—like Mary—had been mired in loneliness. They were both raising young children alone amid the anxiety of war.

There were worldly reasons that attracted Mary to Hiscock—a man who wielded power as an attorney and had a shot at becoming a leading statesman in central New York. In the last winter of the war, the Third District of Onondaga County elected him to the state assembly. In 1866, at roughly the same time that George returned home, some New York papers mentioned Hiscock's name in discussions of the speakership.[7]

George's younger cousin, Mary Cuyler, knew as much as anybody about the matter. She had lived with the Coles for nearly a decade, helping Mary with the children since she was twelve years old. Her testimony, more than anything, made the killing appear to be about adultery more than rape.

She said that once, during the war, she saw Hiscock enter the Coles' bedroom with the blinds drawn and Mary waiting inside. She claimed that Hiscock entered the Cole home "pretty often."[8] She once noticed that Mary wore a new gold ring next to her wedding band. When Mary left her rings lying on a table, Cuyler furtively examined the new one, discovering the initials "W. & H." engraved on the inner band. It was the mark for Willard & Hawley, a prestigious Syracuse jeweler. (Hawley often went by the titles of "Colonel" and "General" from his time in the local militia.) Something was askew. It was not, as she might have first imagined, an intimate trophy from the war, sent to Mary after one of George's raids in North Carolina. Instead, it had been purchased locally but not from Mary's preferred jeweler. Cuyler confronted her about it, and Mary answered that she had bought it herself. When Cuyler responded, "I did not know you traded with Willard & Hawley," Mary blushed and looked away.[9]

Mary Cole must have convinced herself for a time that she could keep the two troubled relationships as separate as the fingers on her hand. She reportedly had tried for a time to cut off all relations with Hiscock, only to later meet secretly outside the Cole home. It was said that she met Hiscock at her sister-in-law's house and at Hiscock's law office. One man said that he had been paid by Hiscock to take him and Mary up and down Syracuse streets in a covered buggy.[10]

Late in the war, Cuyler discovered a large diagram of the assembly chamber in Mary's desk drawer, a token of Hiscock's prominence. The diagram was an annually printed schematic of the arrangement of desks and seating assignments for New York's senators and assemblymen. It showed where Hiscock sat and politicked with other men of mark. While sneaking a look at the diagram, Cuyler noticed Hiscock's signature in the corner.[11]

The various items discovered by Cuyler—the map of Hiscock's political power and the ring from an esteemed jeweler—seemed to reveal what George lacked as a husband. Some claimed that Mary had gifted elegant shirt studs (that may have once been George's) to Hiscock on Valentine's Day. Along with a silver matchbox, the studs were part of what the prisoner's lawyers called "love tokens"—too refined, perhaps, for her war-calloused husband. Some of the evidence suggested Mary had fallen for Hiscock, or that she had traded her body for legitimate control over her estate, or the sweet taste of success and power.

Even if these accounts were true—and some of them seem to have been—they were suspiciously convenient. Most convenient of all was a second confession note, written in Mary Cole's hand, which was placed in a sealed envelope to be opened in court. The public could not be sure when she had written it. George and his lawyers claimed that she composed it before the murder and had placed it in the care of John Cuyler, who then stored it in a safe. More likely, she wrote it under the guidance of her jailed husband and his counsel.[12]

George's fate depended on the new details:

> I acknowledge of my own free will I have had criminal intercourse, at Syracuse, with Mr. L. H. Hiscock, at various times—first about the fall of 1864, and last about the Fall of 1865.

"Criminal intercourse" meant adultery (though not criminal in New York). Mary was now an adulterer.

> I make this acknowledgment of guilt to my husband
> hoping by truth and frankness to obtain forgiveness.

Then Mary wrote what George must have desperately needed her to say:

> I acknowledge that since that time, I have, when my husband was at home, seldom permitted him those favors due in married life, more than once a month, though he has never refused my slightest solicitations to such favors. I acknowledge he has often asked the cause of such coldness and complained of its injustice
> Mary B. Cole

To this second confession she added another amendment to salvage the first. It helped reconcile this new story with the original. She wrote at the bottom,

> My criminal connections with Mr. Hiscock were at my own house, and only took place after repeated calls, and at first against my remonstrance.
> Mary B. Cole[13]

The second confession was designed, it seems, to save George the prisoner from execution and George the man from emasculation. He had killed a man not for raping his wife but for sexually enticing her away from her virile husband, who—it was made clear—always stood ready to partake in her meager carnal offerings. No more could others casually speculate about how the war had disfigured him and ended his manly desires. Mary, the confession made clear, had not turned to Hiscock because her husband could not satisfy her sexual appetite.

Even with the evidence that Mary at times welcomed Hiscock's advances, force and violence cannot be ruled out. Shame, secrecy, and the truth-shifting tactics of courtroom lawyers obscured the true nature of the sexual encounters. The only thing that seems clear is that what happened between Mary and Hiscock was warped from the beginning by the forces of coercion, ambition, depression, loneliness, and, most of all, coverture.

Private letters between the prisoner and his family show that they increasingly placed blame on Mary too. Perhaps George was finally getting to the truth of his wife's betrayal. But perhaps he believed in her guilt because, if he hoped to escape the noose, he needed it to be true.

As for what Mary needed, that was a question few dared to ask.

CHAPTER 18

MARY. WIFE. SELF.

For years, Mary Cole's sexual desire for George had been on the wane. In their early marriage, she had justified her dampened passions with her fear of pregnancy. After she almost died following the birth of their first child, George had—in his own words—tried "kind remonstrances" to no avail. His kind complaints only led to fewer privileges. After years of grousing, he came to believe she was "naturally very little given to the pleasures of married life." He insisted that even with his frustrations, he had always been tender with her and had governed himself, thinking she was "less robust and healthy."[1]

George confided to Olive that in the final year of the war, Mary had been "very loth to grant" his desires. And, as he was coming to believe, she had half willingly granted her body to Luther Harris Hiscock. By the time he returned from the war for good, she had almost denied him entirely what he called his "marital rights."

From his lonely cell he wrote that he had always been tender when he could have demanded sex as some husbands did. He eventually came to terms with the infrequent sex. But when he began to believe that she had partly offered herself to Hiscock, her sexuality was at once a searing contradiction. Either

Mary had given to Hiscock what she chose not to give to her own husband, or Hiscock had used the force that George had the "right" to use but had chosen not to. Months of stewing over it brought him to conclude that her coldness had been caused by a "sense of guilt and grief."

His sexual frustrations, and the tensions in the Coles' marriage, were theirs alone—private matters only known to him and Mary, perhaps to a few intimate friends, and maybe to Hiscock. But from a wider perspective, their intimate negotiations were something shared by many of their American peers. Women from Mary's privileged circumstance were having fewer babies; they were congregants in what Elizabeth Cady Stanton called the "gospel of fewer children."[2]

For over fifteen years Mary had checked George's sexual appetite by vocalizing her fear of childbirth. She bore two children, few for her day. Death was a mocking absurdity for middle-class Christians in the nineteenth century who had grown optimistic about humans' capacity to master nature, as they had done with the electrical telegraph and the steam engine. Death, though, kept rapping its gray knuckles on the bedroom doors of young mothers and children. George pined for more sex but sympathized with her fears. (He had, after all, once warned parents, in his advertisement for his daguerrean studio, to photograph their family members before the grave snatched them away. Mary's deadly pregnancy had weighed on him.)

For potential mothers, sex and suffering were two sides of a coin. After coitus, the specters of pain and death waited in the wings. Women who did survive pregnancy often faced a long road to recovery from birth-related complications such as vesicovaginal and rectovaginal fistulas (holes between the vagina and bladder or rectum from intensely pushing the infant through the birthing canal), perineal tears, infections, incontinence, and lacerations and tears in the vaginal wall or cervix, which often led to a prolapsed uterus, painful sexual intercourse, and increased difficulty in subsequent deliveries.[3]

And then there was the mental pain of raising a child. The bodily pangs of childbirth promised to bring a mother like Mary unspeakable joy—tinged with mental burdens. American mothers increasingly felt pressures that their mothers or grandmothers had not. Enlightenment philosophies and especially liberal evangelical Christianity had rejected predestination and original sin (the belief that depraved children were marked for damnation were it not for the miracle of unearned grace). It was widely accepted, instead, that the destiny of the self was molded by early education, especially by the mother. Child-rearing manuals, sermons, and popular stories echoed the belief that children were not sinful creatures that needed their will broken by discipline but instead unformed clay waiting for mothers to center them on the potter's wheel.[4]

Just as George had learned it was up to him, as a man, to make himself, girls learned that as mothers they could make good children. Public lectures and literature preached strategic mothering. Henry Clarke Wright, a contemporary women's rights advocate and champion of sexual reforms, taught that if Americans wanted to create happy, intelligent, successful children, couples had to avoid the "crime of undesigned maternity." A boy's life was imbued with promise through planned maternity.[5]

Mothers like Mary who feared death, or who worried that they could not pour enough love and learning into their children, had fewer babies. The staggering decline in fertility over the nineteenth century can only partly be explained by new contraceptive methods. Like Mary, many—how many will remain unclear—relied on bridling the sexual desires of their husbands. Some relied on more desperate measures.[6]

★

GEORGE LEARNED from the newspapers in his cell what his family had tried to keep from him. It was all but certain that Mary had an abortion. A California paper revealed that some months after Hiscock had visited Mary in her sickbed, sister-in-law Olive "observed circumstances" that led her to strongly suspect that an abortion had recently been "produced" for Mary. The paper maintained that Olive's knowledge would be used in the coming trial and that George's lawyers wanted her to testify that Mary exhibited evidence of having had "the operation." The author, clearly a friend or reporter sympathetic to the prisoner, intimated Hiscock had been the father and that he had helped Mary end the pregnancy.[7]

The leaked secrets reflected what George's side of the family had been writing in their personal letters. In a private missive to her husband, Olive warned Cornelius Cole not to reveal to George that she knew "the true cause" of Mary's nagging illness. Mary had been covering the effects of a recent abortion, passing it off as some female complaint. Olive didn't want Mary to be picked over by newspaper vultures. "I am bound to know no more than any one else of the matter," she warned. She said she would not allow George's lawyers to call her onto the stand and hoped she could keep the secret from George. Revealing the truth to him would only make Mary seem more evil than the world had already painted her.[8]

These accusations and cryptic discussions about Mary's abortion happened at the beginning of a legal shift in the United States. In 1867, the same year that reports of Mary's abortion first appeared in a newspaper, Illinois banned abortion except to protect a mother's life. Within a little more than a decade, the rest of the states followed suit. For centuries in the Christian tradition, abortion—the conscious act of ending the life of an unborn baby—had been forbidden. But until the mid-nineteenth century, both Protestants and Catholics had not considered pregnancy to have begun until the "quickening," the moment when the mother first feels her baby move, usually in the fourth or fifth month. For generations, women in America and Europe believed that with the quickening, the baby's soul entered the womb. Only the mother knew when life had begun.[9]

Before the quickening, pregnancy could be a time of anxious uncertainty. Midcentury physicians urged women to pay close attention to their menstruations, for in them lay the first signs of deadly reproductive disorders. A stoppage of the menses (amenorrhea) was deemed dangerous, yet it was difficult to distinguish that from the early signs of pregnancy. Women used various methods for "bringing on the menses," but such methods had the capacity to end a possible pregnancy. Popular northern health reforms like "water cures" and widely prescribed vaginal douches also served the purpose of inducing miscarriage, even as they promised health.[10]

For women who suspected they were pregnant and who did not want the child, this confusion brought options. If they hadn't successfully used cow-gut condoms, aloes, vinegar or brandy douches, sponges, pessaries, and other devices to prevent pregnancy during or just after coitus, they could still terminate it over the coming weeks and months—though with increasing difficulty. Countless pregnant women, with varying degrees of doubt (or certainty) about their suspended menses, sought out abortifacients from midwives and "Indian doctors," who administered concoctions made from things like pennyroyal, snakeroot, tansy tea, black hellebore, calomel, iron dust, and savin from the juniper bush.[11]

By the 1850s, "respectable" newspapers from across America routinely ran ads for pills or remedies that vaguely promised to fix a woman's "female complaints." George had stocked such remedies on the shelves of his Havana store. Many advertisers and merchants coyly warned (and thus promised) that taking their product for stopped menses during the first months of pregnancy would lead to miscarriage. The uncertainty surrounding the meaning of a missed menstruation, and the new, aggressive marketing that exploited this confusion, made it possible for more women to end their quickened, or unquickened, pregnancies.

Reports in the press, and revelations in private letters, suggest that Mary knew she was pregnant and sought out some method to end it. The abortion left her gravely ill. Desperate women resorted to drastic measures and often suffered for it. A desperate woman who missed her period and who perhaps felt the quickening might ram a table's corner into her pelvis, pound her own gut, strain herself under heavy weights, induce violent vomiting, have her foot cut for bloodletting, her thighs subjected to a light surge of electricity, or a tooth pulled. A woman who had means, like Mary—often with the help of a growing number of abortionists (especially in America's rising towns and cities)—could have her amniotic sac punctured or her cervix irritated into dilation.[12]

In step with the increasing freedoms in cities, many Americans deemed abortion a necessary evil when sought by unmarried couples or by girls who had fallen into trouble. Such conditional acceptance, though, came under serious scrutiny in the middle of the nineteenth century when it became clear that many White Protestant middle-class mothers like Mary—not young women in dire need—were resorting to abortion to stave off large families or even to cover extramarital affairs. Moralists began painting images of shrinking populations of White Protestants being overtaken by rapidly reproducing Irish Catholic and Black families. Married women of means were denounced for shirking their natural duties as mothers and nurturers. Amid this national alarm, rumors spread about the dangers of Mary's freedom.[13]

★

DURING THE WAR, Mary had moved her family into the Jervis House, a four-story dwelling in the heart of Syracuse.[14] It brought them into sparkling society, just blocks from the Erie Canal, across the street from a park framed by boulevards and avenues lined with shops.

Originally built as an art school for women, the Jervis House was what contemporaries called a "family hotel" or an "apartment hotel." Faced with cutthroat competition, hotelkeepers found that selling yearlong occupancies at reduced rates kept hotels solvent in lean times. By midcentury, many middle-class families, often at the instigation of wives, began residing in hotels or hotel-like apartments.[15]

As the Coles did at the Jervis House, many Americans took dinner in a grand hall, ate food prepared by wage employees, dirtied linens that were cleaned and then pressed in hidden-away laundry facilities, and slept in rooms cleaned by strangers. In such homes, a mother—who customarily worked as her husband's unpaid domestic laborer—could transfer her duties to an army of wage workers who did "women's work" within the hidden bowels of the hotel. Middle-class mothers achieved a kind of equality in the home through inequality in apartment hotels.[16]

Family hotels blurred the line between home and the outside world.[17] In the Jervis House, Mary and George lived in a hive of social and business connections. Families ate alongside more than a hundred neighbors and found entertainment in the main lobby and in the small park just outside its doors—music recitals, balls, and tableaux vivants in which carefully posed residents re-created scenes from literature such as the death of little Eva in *Uncle Tom's Cabin*. There was a saloon in the cellar.[18]

Aspiring women like Mary could find refined society in reading rooms, recital rooms, and lobbies of the family hotel. The renowned A. M. Cobleigh held a dancing school in one of the upper chambers of the Jervis House where women danced to his violin and learned "the refinements" of proper behavior. To be in his club, it was said, was "to be in society." In another part of the hotel, women suffering from tics or nervous disorders could obtain electropathy where an experienced "Lady operator" would be in attendance. The Jervis House was also home to a director of the Female Department of the Syracuse Institute, which offered lessons in French, Spanish, and Italian. The director accepted applications at the hotel desk.[19]

What the Coles lost in income, Mary gained in access to goods and services, and in freedom from having to seek out, store, and prepare food. The family hotel spared her the burden of supervising, hiring, and firing domestic servants. The Coles' daughters took rooms upstairs from their parents' place in a separate apartment, where their aunt Mary Cuyler slept and helped raise them. The Coles had a piano, a clear mark of refinement and taste; yet, if the Jervis House was like most family hotels, they had no washbasin or kitchen.[20]

For these reasons, hotel apartments fomented controversy. Critics had insisted that such living would lead to excessive freedoms and moral drift. It endangered the family, they said, by distorting the roles of men and women. Middle-class women led artificial domestic lives in hotel spaces, separated from the domestic work that supposedly flowed from their maternal love. Worse, it was feared that bachelors in the hotel would put off marriage so long as they could get their shirts and sheets cleaned by hotel staff. And these bachelors would exploit the open atmosphere to make adulteresses out of the wives of other men. Common tables and shared hallways, critics warned, turned apartment hotels into dens of flirtation and worse.

Some warned that motherhood itself—the sheet anchor for a republic tossed to and fro by ambition and vice—was imperiled by the family hotel. In his investigative tour of boarding houses in pre–Civil War New York, Thomas Gunn dedicated a chapter to an unnamed opulent family hotel on Broadway. The establishment was filled with wives and "egoistic old bachelors" who showed an "indifference to the pleasures and sanctity of home."[21] In March 1864, about the time Hiscock made his first advances on Mary, the New York Times published an article about the need for more single homes, not hotels, in New York. The city needed private homes and "families with the grace" to occupy them. "There can be nothing worse for women than an idle life in a hotel," it warned. Children and mothers would be denigrated by the "folly, frivolity, and vulgarity of the promiscuous crowd that throng them."[22]

This wood engraving from Gunn's exposé of housing in New York City warns how bored wives, freed from their domestic calling, would mingle and flirt with other men who breezed in and out of the family hotel. "Stroll into the drawing-room on an evening, you will see they know how to amuse themselves. If Mrs. A is coquetting with B, who can blame her? She is young, and pretty, and rather neglected by A [her husband]. . . . And if C (who is a married man, and ought to know better) is talking eloquently to Miss D on some subject which brings the blood to her cheeks (rendering her rouge unnecessary for the moment)—people must be sociable when they meet in the same saloon, evening after evening." Notice the placement of the ladies' fans. Both women are holding them in such a position that they remind readers of the sexual intentions of the men at their side. *Image and quotation from Thomas Butler Gunn,* The Physiology of New York Boarding-Houses *(New York: Mason Brothers, 1857), 169–70*

★

THE DETAILS OF MARY'S LIFE made many men and women uneasy. It challenged the ideal of middle-class womanhood, an ideal in which a mother buried her sense of self in family and Christ. Mary's life was a warning that the worldly ambitions that had goaded men like George and his friends into business ventures, across frontiers, and even into war had begun to spread into the hearts of American wives. Such women did not properly support the self-making illusions of husbands. To many Americans, Mary was a warning about what expanding freedoms, and even female aspiration, might do to the family—and especially to men smitten with worldly visions.

George's sister, Mary Stewart, who grew physically sick from worry over her imprisoned brother, struggled to contain her contempt for Mary Cole. "Poor blind woman," she wrote, "will she ever get self out of eye?" Mary Cole's demise, and her blindness from *self in the eye*, was a warning to peers that growing prosperity, and ideals like the pursuit of happiness, lacked moral mechanisms at their core to govern excesses of the self. The thorny problem of "what" would keep ambitions from undermining the common good had been partly resolved by assigned roles of "who" would keep selfism at bay. Selfhood—and its connection to freedom, ambition, and the pursuit of happiness—was that dangerous fruit that only men-on-the-make were supposed to taste. Mary was a warning that such an agreement could never hold.[23]

CHAPTER 19

LIFE IMITATES ART

GEORGE COLE'S TRIAL was delayed for months because Mary Cuyler, the cousin who was a key witness to the love tokens, had a serious illness related to her first pregnancy. The delay gave the prisoner and his counsel more time to craft the story they wanted to tell.[1]

ABOUT FIVE MONTHS AFTER THE KILLING, the prisoner believed he had found a way to tell his story. It leapt out at him from the pages of *Amelia*, an eighteenth-century novel about marriage in London. The similarities were uncanny. Over a century old when George got his hands on it, *Amelia* was Henry Fielding's last and least celebrated novel. Eclipsed by the author's earlier comedies, *Joseph Andrews* and *Tom Jones*, *Amelia* was widely panned in its day and largely forgotten soon after. Fielding's other narratives, especially *Tom Jones*, had a picaresque quality. Roguish young men stumbled their way through debauchery and sexual pitfalls only to be rescued by marriage to pure-hearted women.[2]

In *Amelia*, marriage is not the happy solution to man's fallen nature but more proof of how far he had fallen. Though it had been a literary failure, the novel must have seemed like a gift from God to the prisoner. In its pages, he discovered a bizarrely close reflection of his life. The book begins with the arrest and imprisonment of a luckless soldier, Captain William Booth, who has a strained marriage. In a jail filled with the dregs of London society, he recounts his troubled past to the reader; he had bad luck with money, a frustrated military career, and war injuries. He also has a pure-hearted wife, Amelia Harris, who attracted the attention of sexual schemers while Booth was at war. Like George, Booth had two young children. And when Booth was wounded in battle, Amelia—like Mary—came to the war's front and nursed her husband. Like Mary, Amelia inherited a large sum of money.[3]

It was a story that George believed he could use to better tell his own. George took an elongated pad of lined paper and wrote three cramped pages, weaving together, with various alterations and omissions, passages taken directly from the novel. Fielding's words spoke to his struggle. He wanted those words spoken in his approaching trial.[4]

There was one problem, however. The fictional Amelia resists the sexual traps of her seducers. George focused almost entirely on one part of the novel, on a letter within the story written by a pastor to Colonel James, the man who tried to seduce Amelia. In it, the pastor argued—as would George's lawyers during the upcoming trial—that even if the Bible had not forbidden adultery, the law of nature made its evils plain to all men's hearts. Nature was so certain in its condemnation that even non-Christian societies punished it with "the most exemplary pains and penalties." Adultery, the pastor wrote, was "robbing" a husband of his property.

In the novel, the person reading the letter interjects sarcastically, "Mind that, ladies, you are all the property of your husbands." George edited that part out, knowing full well that his lawyers couldn't talk this way in a New York court of his day. Otherwise, he copied the fictional letter nearly word for word. He copied the part where it says that if seducers were allowed to poison that fountain from which a husband "has a right" to the sweetest pleasure of life, married men would become "lost to all industry, and grow careless, of all their worldly affairs." The jury, he thought, would get the point. The wife's domestic balm—her sex—somehow gave men the strength to strive.

Without a wife's sexual fidelity, George's copied notes continued, husbands become "bad citizens, bad relations, bad friends, and bad men." Wayward wives lead to hatred and revenge, and "murder and suicide often close the dreadful scene."[5]

Revenge. Madness. Murder. It spoke prophetically to the prisoner's experience.

What, asked George (copying the words of the pastor), was so irresistible about a sexual delight certain to inflict misery on one man and death on the seducer? Some of the fictional letter didn't suit George's needs. He kept a part about adultery as a foolish "pleasure of a moment" but discarded the more permanent-sounding phrase "the possession of a woman." (Mary's confessions made clear that she had never been fully possessed.) In one part, he kept the word "friend" to describe his relationship to Luther Harris Hiscock. In another, he cut it out.[6]

These editorial decisions revealed a mind, half a year after the killing, not quite settled on how to explain what happened between Hiscock and Mary, and to what degree Hiscock had really been a friend. When the fictional letter begins praising the unbudging fidelity of Amelia, George could not use any of it in his proposed defense. Amelia had withstood the designs of men. Mary had not. In the story, the pastor claims that in pursuing Amelia, the evil Colonel would face "the difficulty, I may say, the impossibility of the success" in seducing her. George knew that Hiscock had obtained some portion of "success."

George skipped past the strongest praise for Amelia: "You are attacking a fortress on a rock," the letter from the book warned. Amelia had a chastity "so strongly defended," by a good mind and "the strongest principles of religion and virtue." Mary had not been a fortress on a rock. Her "principles of religion and virtue" had failed her. Over the months since the murder, George had come to fear that she had willingly lowered the fortress bridge.

The pastor's final words about Amelia would have been painful for George to read. He left them out of his defense. Though only words from an imaginary letter, about an imaginary Amelia, it cast blame on George as a husband. The pastor said that even if Amelia *had* been less pure, her husband's "firm and constant affection" would be enough to ensure Amelia's fidelity. The love from a husband, in other words, would rescue a straying wife from her self-destruction. Fiction gave the prisoner a powerful way to tell his story; it also cut him to his heart.

★

WHENEVER CORNELIUS COLE could, he left political affairs and family in Washington, DC, and hurried to Albany, where he spent long days interviewing potential witnesses and consoling the prisoner. He talked with his brother late into the evening, sitting nearby as George lay on the couch stripped to his underclothes.[7]

On one visit George told Cornelius about *Amelia*. The bookish prisoner must have told his brother about the eerily familiar plot. "Gen'l is reading Fealding's 'Amelia,'" Cornelius wrote Olive. Though he misspelled Fielding's name, he assured her that it was "a fine story."[8] The General must have told the story well, because Cornelius urged Olive to "get [*Amelia*] when you are through the present work in your hands."[9] It was the kind of book a man of worldly ambition would be anxious for his wife to read.

Olive didn't need to read "Fealding" to understand the prisoner's troubles. She used another tale to make sense of the family crisis. To help her say what she couldn't or wouldn't say directly, she clipped a story from a California newspaper and sent it with a letter to Cornelius.[10] The short story, "Husbands at Home," gave Olive a way to broach the topic of Mary's unmet sexual appetite. Before others did, Olive came to doubt the original confession, which limited Mary's guilt. "I think your brother has been unnaturally noble in his conduct towards Mary," she wrote. "Almost any other man in the world would have believed her guilty of unlimited crime, but he confines his estimate of guilt to her own confession."[11] In other words, George pitifully clung to the belief that Mary had mostly been an innocent victim.

The newspaper story was written by "Mrs. Patty Spangle" for the sake of young wives. In the account, when Patty originally met Mr. Spangle he was attractive, from good stock, with unimpeachable habits and character. She could not resist him. He made regular visits and wrote her daily love letters. He courted her madly until she gave her hand in marriage. Their honeymoon was "short and delicious." But soon came the "realities of life" when a young bride steps from "a garden of Summer flowers into the region of perpetual Winter." The storyteller warned that if a young wife does not employ her "good sense and philosophy," she will regard herself deceived "for the balance of her life."

After the honeymoon period, Mr. Spangle began directing his energies into making his mark in business. He "took a tilt at the world, determined to wrest from it not only a competence, but a fortune." He thought doing so would secure Mrs. Spangle's happiness. But the world crushed him instead. During bouts of failure, he often unloaded his worries and trials on her. And during his feckless hunt for success, he gave her less and less physical affection.

To Olive's eye, it seemed to describe George's marriage. It also articulated what Olive wished to say about Mary's sexuality. Mrs. Spangle, the tale continued, longed for her husband to grab her hand as he had done during their courtship when there was much "romance and adulation." Mr. Spangle assured her that he loved her and wondered why, with so many assurances, she could doubt that love. For Mrs. Spangle, a wife of twelve years who treasured their "delicious" honeymoon, words no longer sufficed. As she put it, she "also knew" that there was "plenty of flour and bacon in the pantry." But such knowledge "did not satisfy [her] hunger." Knowing through words was not knowing it through tasting, smelling, consuming. She craved sexual and romantic tenderness from her husband.

There was more. Mr. Spangle adored his children but did not wake to calm the babies through the night. He depended on her to gather his boots, lay out his clean shirts, remove his cuff buttons, and provide him, "like any other child," with a proper washing and grooming. He had a lack of empathy for the pains of others yet, when suffering, groaned as if he were dying. In those moments, he could barely "suffer [her] to leave him for a moment."

Olive might have been mapping the story onto George's depleted health, his war wounds, and the veteran's rough demeanor. She was, no doubt, mapping the story onto Mary's sexual needs. Somewhat cryptically, she wrote, "If you can understand what was lacking in 'Spangle' to render Mrs. [Spangle] contented," she wrote, "you will know" what may have rendered Mary "dissatisfied."

The story only used the word "satisfy" when Mrs. Spangle complained of her husband's lack of physical interest in her, of his not touching her in gentle and amorous ways as he did in their dizzying courtship. He continued to declare his love for her while struggling to make his mark in society. But like bacon and flour in the pantry, they did not "satisfy" her. Not until they delighted her palate and satisfied her gut could they appease her cravings.

"It is hard," wrote Olive, for George to think of Mary differently from how he has always been accustomed to—that is, as a "pure faithful wife." She continued, "He cannot appreciate a certain kind of female character. Only 'men of the world' can." Had George better understood Mary, "he could have more fully gratified her natural desires." Olive asserted that Mary had erotic needs that George could not fathom. (Olive did not broach the possibility that George's war injuries had left him incapable of satisfying Mary's hunger.) He had come to see Mary as a woman who was not drawn to sexual pleasure. Emboldened by the clipping's directness, Olive offered the boldest of explana-

After much searching, I have been unable to locate a picture of Mary Cole, but we know a great deal about her personal life thanks to the letters of Olive Cole, George's sister-in-law, pictured here (*center*). It was Olive who spoke frankly about Mary's sexual needs, the stupidity of the murder, and the wrongheaded arguments made by George's attorneys. *UCLA Library Special Collections*

tions: the General, a man who spent half a decade among the roughs of the army—an army beset with prostitution, male banter, and venereal disease—was not "worldly" enough to understand and provide for Mary's physical desires.

Hiscock's friends had questioned the purity of Mary too. But their intention was to clear the name of their friend, not understand her. Only Olive dared to suggest that the supposed purity of Mary—a purity that would have given her more power to control sexuality and pregnancy within her marriage—did not reflect her true desires. Mary was not a simple Jezebel or a serpent (as she was painted by some) but a woman with natural cravings that did not jibe with the sexually passive role attributed to Victorian wives and mothers. She was no Amelia. In Olive's telling of it, Mary had not failed in her divine calling as a pure woman. Rather, the cult of purity had failed to capture Mary's nature, and George had failed to gratify her. He, like so many Mr. Spangles, did not understand his own wife's body and mind.

★

THE STANWIX MURDER POWERFULLY RESONATED like a Brahmsian chord with Americans who were coming to terms with the expanding sexual liberties of urban men and women. Fears ran wild about wives' waywardness and husbands' ebbing power over them. The murder evoked fears of sexual licentiousness, even as it fed the public's curiosity about the secret life of others.

The only surviving visual depiction of the murder teems with erotic imagery. The woodcut image was published in the *National Police Gazette*, a widely read men's weekly that exposed the brothels, crimes, and haunts of the urban underworld while, in truth, providing titillation for its readers. The *Gazette* posed as an aid to law enforcement while providing salacious reading. It straddled the line between exposing and reveling in immorality. By sticking close to courtroom revelations and police blotters, the *Gazette* maintained the thinnest veneer of respectability.[12]

The Stanwix slaying was low-hanging fruit for the *Gazette*. But in depicting the murder, the paper had to render the sexual aspects of it inconspicuous. By the 1850s, this sly lewdness—hiding beneath the cloak of rectitude—could be a matter of survival for the *Gazette* and like publications. Starting in the 1840s, with the astonishing proliferation of prostitution and pornography in New York City, Gotham's police and courts cracked down on abortionists, "fancy" booksellers, and publishers. And they waged a targeted war against the most openly pornographic weeklies, called the "flash papers."[13]

Bawdy publications had to adjust. The image of Hiscock's murder, at first glance, appears to be an attempt at capturing the crime as it happened. In the woodcut depiction, George stands with crazed eyes, smoke wafting from his pistol. The witnesses watch as Hiscock lies on his back, having just received the life-robbing bullet.

Upon closer examination, the image is brimming with vulgar hints of how increasing sexual liberties vexed relationships between men. Parallel lines run along the General's pelvic area, forming an erect penis and a scrotum. (One faint line gives it the appearance of a pistol and handle.) The killing, as depicted by the woodcut artist, reduces Hiscock to a violated woman. Silenced, he is on his back, left with the consequences of George's exploding gun. His hat lies with its opening orifice facing the viewer. The toes of his dainty feet seem to point upward, not quite touching the ground. The shadows on the crotch of Hiscock's business trousers evoke a woman's labia with an escutcheon of pubic hair.[14]

Each of the living men stands with one stiff arm elevated to a different angle, the three arms forming a triangle with the

The only surviving depiction of the murder, an erotically charged woodcut with inset. National Police Gazette, *August 17, 1867*

apex turned downward. If this was intended to mean anything, the shape probably referenced the love triangle that produced the tragedy. Or maybe it was an allusion to the widely known fraternal triangle—now turned upside down by betrayal—that was featured in the bonding rituals of Masons and other nineteenth-century fraternities. The Sons of Temperance, an organization of household fame, used as its emblem a triangle whose three sides together proclaimed, "love, purity, fidelity."

In a period when reformers were beginning to make war on pornographic literature, the engraver could make a case that these graphic allusions were nothing more than crude pleats and shadows. A reader who was unschooled in the erotic wiles of New York flash papers would have seen nothing beyond the slaying. For those who had eyes to see, the image was a half-serious warning of what awaited a man who beguiled another's wife. It revealed how urban life threatened the very men who were making false fraternal oaths.

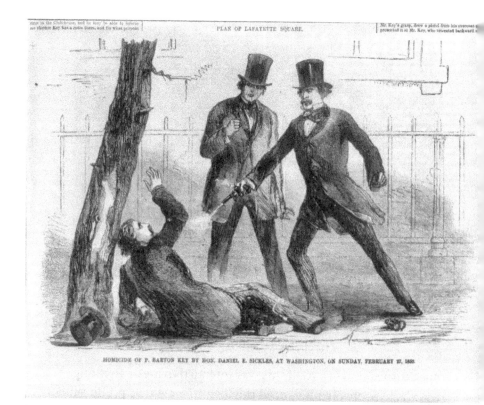

A woodcut depiction of the murder committed by Sickles with its own sexually charged message that violence against seducers rescues the manhood of other men. National Police Gazette, *March 12, 1859, 169*

The man standing at Hiscock's ballerina-like feet appears to have a semierect penis along with the murderer. This was likely no coincidence. When the *Gazette* depicted the 1859 murder of Philip Barton Key by Daniel Sickles—who, like George, had killed a man in the open for sleeping with his wife—the *Gazette* artist placed Sickles's exploding gun directly over the clothed groin of another man watching the murder. Such violent deeds rescued other husbands' virility. George's act saved married men. It preserved their threatened sexual powers.

As George's attorneys were prepared to bet, there was a shared sense—as seen in the erotic, deniable message of the woodcut—that the Stanwix murder had protected ordinary men from the new dangers of urban life.

Olive's clear-eyed view of things, that the story had to do with a woman's unmet natural desires, had little place in a courtroom controlled by men.[15] To win in court, George needed lawyers who stoked fears about modern manhood. He needed spellbinders to stand before a jury of male peers and convince them that what George did to Hiscock was a precious gift for mankind, especially husbands struggling to keep their families intact while chasing success in America's cities.

CHAPTER 20

SOME MAGNETIC POWER

MARY WAS EAGER TO PAY George's lawyers with her own money. Olive warned against it. If he used any of Mary's "oro" and was acquitted, he would be obligated to live with her again, an unacceptable option if he and his lawyers painted Mary as a fallen woman. Olive wrote as if George were a kept man, with a wife who held the purse strings and gave him a certain allowance. If he wanted any of the money that Mary "had in keeping for him," Olive advised, he had better be businesslike and take "only the balance due him allowing a liberal margin for 'extras.'"[1]

RIGHT AFTER THE MURDER, Olive urged the men to pursue Benjamin Butler for the defense counsel. One newspaper painted the possible retaining of Butler as a cynical scheme to make the trial more about the prisoner's war record than about the murder itself.[2] Maybe out of desperation, George initially agreed to pursue his commander. "I much desire Butler, for he knew me and could speak well," he wrote to Olive.[3]

Prisoner Cole's lawyers wisely feared that some of the members of the jury would be repulsed by Butler. Hiring him, they worried, would harm their case by stirring up hatred from "copperheads"—those Democrats who had denounced the war and emancipation of enslaved Americans. Butler would trigger bitter feelings about military corruption and, most of all, about a war that was initially waged to defend the Union but turned into a fight for abolition.[4]

Olive sent a request to Butler anyway. She began her letter by saying that she was only writing because her husband had advised her to solicit Butler's services. (In other words, she was not a woman meddling in men's affairs.) She confessed at the end of the five-page letter, "My first thought was of you when looking for sources of relief." She knew that George's case—with its obvious premeditation—was going to require oratorical genius. She reasoned that "nothing must be left undone to save him" from the probable execution that awaited him.[5]

Butler responded warmly that his respect for George and their "relations in the Army" induced him to offer any assistance that lay in his power. At the very least, he owed it to a fellow soldier. He offered to meet with Olive and consult over what would be "best for General Cole's interest."[6]

There is no record of such a meeting. There probably was none.

Butler was in high demand, after all. Olive's request was one drop in a flood of sycophantic and admiring letters. In the brief period in which Olive wrote him, he was inundated with letters from ex-soldiers and friends requesting legal advice, government positions, and help in raising funds. One man pleaded for him to use his influence to secure a pension for an invalid soldier. Many asked him to bless them with his oratorical skills at upcoming events. Some asked for help in their business ventures. Most praised him. Because he had recently delivered a "tribute in honor of negro valour," a Black woman wrote to tell him that "coloured people of this district appreciate your friendship." Inspired by Butler's stirring accounts of his Black troops, she wrote a poem about the "charge of the black brigade" and sent it to him.[7]

Perhaps Butler didn't have the hours in a day to take on George's case. Perhaps George's headstrong attorneys ruled it out. Maybe George spoke more openly about his contempt for the man. More likely, Butler had bigger ambitions.

★

CORNELIUS FOUND ANOTHER mesmerizing attorney by trading political favors with railroad magnates from California. He had cultivated friendships with the railroad moguls and served as a mostly loyal ally to them in Washington, DC, first as a congressman during the war and then as a senator starting in 1867. He went to the railroad's vice president, Collis P. Huntington, and secured a pledge of $5,000 to help with George's legal fees. In return, Cornelius agreed that he would do everything in his senatorial power to help Huntington secure the rights to San Francisco's Goat Island, coveted for its potential as the railroad's West Coast terminus.[8]

Huntington helped Cornelius enlist the services of James Topham Brady, son of Irish immigrants, who had a legendary gift for hypnotizing jurymen. In Brady's storied career, he had defended fifty clients who had their lives on the line. He rescued each of them from the gallows, leaving the jury spellbound when it mattered most. He had also successfully defended Daniel Sickles, the famous major general who, before the war, had shot his wife's lover in broad daylight. Brady had helped pioneer the defense of "temporary insanity" to get Sickles off.[9]

George's side could count on most of the jurymen revering his five years in uniform. But some would find his service with Black soldiers repugnant. Here, Brady was an asset where Butler would have been disastrous. Unlike Butler, Brady had remained a Democrat throughout the war, though he resolutely supported crushing the rebellion. In fact, he had taken part in the initial defense of rebel president Jefferson Davis and for a time investigated Butler's rumored misdeeds in the war.[10]

The prisoner also retained Amasa J. Parker, an ex-judge and Democrat. A powerful lawyer and politician in his own right, he too was a sop to jurymen who, it was feared, might harbor ill will toward George's time in the United States Colored Cavalry.[11] Altogether, George retained five attorneys.[12]

The prosecution consisted of three well-connected pro-Union men with sympathies for reform and Black freedom.[13] Because George was a veteran, however, they couldn't leverage their credentials as staunch Union men. They had energetically supported the Civil War, but had to erase from the trial as much war talk as they could. Any mention of it would remind the jury that George had risked his life for the country and that Luther Harris Hiscock had not.

SISTER-IN-LAW OLIVE SAW most clearly the contradictions of George's defense. The General's lawyers had plans to play up a testimony that George believed he was being followed by an agent hired by Hiscock. She warned the defense not to let that, or the inheritance money, or business matters cloud what drove the General to his frenzy. "Don't muddle the minds of the jurors by too many causes or 'motives,'" she chided her husband.[14]

Some "touching pictures must be drawn," she wrote. And who could have done it "so well as [General] Butler," she said with regret. "Some magnetic power must be employed to move the sympathies and enlarge and open the hearts of the jurors."

Her advice was ignored. The defense concocted a story of tangled motives. They planned to dredge up the mental illnesses of George's dead mother and his older sister Asenath.

Olive detested the plan. She also warned that she would not take the stand, even if it cost the General's life, to further tarnish Mary's character concerning the abortion. "God knows," she said, that Mary's reputation was "bad enough."[15]

Cornelius sent Olive a private circular, a document that had been mailed to medical experts to obtain their opinion about whether they deemed it possible that the General had lost his mental capacity momentarily at the time of the killing. It was their first stab at crafting a narrative about the General's supposed flash of insanity. Cornelius warned her not to let the circular out of her possession and to "keep it <u>secret</u>. I send it for your own gratification. It is for the <u>proper</u> physicians."[16]

The circular described the night George fell from his horse. It made clear the attorneys' plan to dwell on his grotesque war injuries. It claimed that George partly recovered, thanks to his "strong constitution." But he never got past the swelling, the constipation, the necessity of dilating his bowels into action by mechanically pumping large quantities of water into them, the bloody evacuations, or the protrusions.

Though George had shown signs of extreme nerves after the fall and had a "sensitive temperament," he "proved himself cool, calm and collected, in the midst of danger, on many a hard fought field." In other words, when he was called on to kill or possibly be killed by rebels, he did so calmly.[17]

After shooting his nemesis, the veteran was escorted to the station house and, the circular said, only then did he become "terribly agitated." When one of the escorts suggested he get ahold of his nerves, the General exclaimed, "Oh, my God, my God! I can't be calm. I have braved danger in every shape. While I was fighting the battles of my country, this man, whom I supposed my friend, dishonored me. It was not my intention to kill him. . . . But when I saw him, I thought of my poor, injured wife, and my poor children, I seemed impelled by some power I could not resist."

Olive detected the fatal problem with telling the story this way. The men defending George were too eager to evoke the war at every chance. She warned against weaving together too tightly the slaying of Hiscock and the General's time as an armed soldier for his country. The fatal weakness in their narrative, she warned, was that George had not shown emotion immediately after shooting Hiscock. All agreed that he had pulled out his Derringer in a calm, even sedate manner. As far away as Vermont, the murder had the reputation of being "one of the coolest on record."[18]

More than any other soldierly attribute, Americans admired coolness in battle, men who charged into combat with determined poise. Panic, dread, and bolting all violated the widely held ideal of manly self-control. Self-made men cooly guided themselves through the crises of life while weaker souls were tossed to and fro by emotion. An officer who could walk erectly and calmly through whistling bullets was deemed a master of himself.[19]

George's lawyers couldn't resist telling the jury how composed George had been in battle. But, as Olive keenly saw, by depicting George that way, the attorneys ran the danger of making the war proof of his ability to kill without feeling.

If the lawyers were determined to dwell on his coolness in combat, they must "show the difference" between what provoked George to kill in war and what set him off in the lobby.[20] Olive wrote,

> I fear it will be concluded that if he was "cool" in the one instance [of war, then] he was in the other. . . . Perhaps no allusion had better be made to his "deliberate coolness" under any circumstances.

Stripped of sentimental patriotism, composed killing on the battlefield looked a lot like icy-veined murder. "If I was employed by the other side," she warned, "I would make all the capital I could out of his 'cool manner of using death weapons.'"[21]

★

AS THE TRIAL APPROACHED, regional papers vied for readers by promising the fullest coverage, with details telegraphed up to the hour of going to press.[22] Yet, starting in early March, the nation's attention, and the front pages of periodicals, was dedicated to another trial, the impeachment proceedings of President Andrew Johnson. The newly resurrected Benjamin Butler, recently elected to Congress, led House managers in the prosecution.

George's upstaged trial began in late April 1868. The deputy sheriff, Nicholas Sigsbee, corralled over eighty potential jurors from the Albany region into the courtroom. After only five of them proved to have open minds about the prisoner's guilt, the judge ordered Sigsbee to summon an additional one hundred candidates from town and country for the next day.[23]

The deputy sheriff himself had already fixed his mind. He told others that he wanted to form a jury from his "countrymen" and would hang the prisoner "like a dog." His feelings were uncommon. The vast majority of potential candidates would have been sympathetic to George, like David Freedlander, the liquor dealer from Albany who lied his way onto the jury by claiming he only held a "partial opinion" from reading the papers. In truth, Freedlander admired the prisoner. He wrote Cornelius letters and brought his family to George's cell so his dependents could behold the hero of Stanwix Hall.[24]

During the empanelment, attorneys from both sides fished for clarification regarding what newspapers the candidates read. George's counsel was on the hunt for candidates with conservative political inclinations, especially men who gave off the smallest whiff of frustration with women's expanding freedoms.[25] They sought to remove any husband who had made peace with his waning powers over his wife and her possessions. Thomas Bedell, of the farming town of Coeymans, first appeared to be an ideal juryman when he claimed that he didn't hold an opinion or keep up with the affair. But when Bedell revealed that he only read an "agricultural paper" and that "his wife own[ed] his farm," George's attorneys moved to eliminate him. An unambitious farmer, who reported without a hint of shame in his voice that his wife owned "his" farm, might lead to a hung jury. George needed jurymen whose hearts would take pity on him and his struggles to claim some ownership of Mary's money and body.[26]

★

AT THE TRIAL'S OPENING, the Albany courtroom was jammed to the walls with spectators herniating out the doorways. Scores took the train from distant villages and cities, especially Syracuse, to see the drama in person. So many women were in attendance that the trial would become an infamous example, in the minds of conservatives, of how courtrooms poisoned the minds of good women with prurient details.[27]

The prosecutors did their best to avoid the poison. The district attorney, Henry Smith, opened for the people, knowing he had to immediately build barriers around the slaying itself and not allow the charge of murder to slip into a debate about sexual acts and military glory. He promised to stick to the murder's facts and not refer to the previous careers of the parties. These things "had nothing to do with the case," he repeatedly warned a room stuffed with folks eager to get to the sordid details and the prisoner's war history. As Smith argued it, the case instead was only about the law and whether a man—any man, regardless of his heroic past—could execute a suspected guilty man instead of establishing that guilt in a court of law.[28]

The prisoner represented the slippery slope toward anarchy wherein any man, in a shifting, urbanizing society, might wrongly imagine that he had been wronged or dishonored.

By pledging not to dig up the past, prosecutor Smith drew everyone's attention to the shovels gripped in the hands of George's lawyers; they eagerly awaited their chance to make the trial about sexual betrayal and heroic war stories, not the murder. Immediately after Smith finished examining some of the prosecution's witnesses, the defense cross-examined one of them, asking, "What did Cole say after firing the pistol?"[29]

Lyman Tremain—the fiercest of the prosecutors—sprang up and fought spiritedly to keep such statements from the court record. He insisted that George's words could not be used as evidence of any "supposed invasion of his marital rights" and that they had no bearing on the slaying. The defense retorted that if the words fell from the prisoner's lips, they would only shed light on the supposed crime. Judge Daniel P. Ingraham admitted that he could not keep the seconds before and after the murder from entering the trial; he had to permit the prisoner's words. As George's lawyers knew, the judge could not stop the trial from eventually unfolding into an expanding panorama of minutes, hours, and years of history.[30]

The witness then said that he remembered the General saying, "He has betrayed my wife . . . he violated my wife while I was at the war." The very next witness recalled his words as, "I considered that man one of my best friends, but he raped my wife while I was gone to war." This was no small victory for the prisoner. These words revealed the major coordinates of where his lawyers hoped to take the jury: Hiscock was once a friend. Until he wasn't. Mary was once a pure wife. Until she fell. And George Cole was a wronged soldier who was compelled by duty and love to do what he did. With these three themes, the most powerful of tales would be told.[31]

★

The prisoner's principal attorney, William Hadley, promised to give "a brief history" of the accused. He spoke for three hours. His comments revealed the power that the war held for Americans; they also showed how merciless the defense would be to Mary. He started by asking the jury to restore the poor ex-soldier not to his home, as "he has none," nor to his wife, but to his children. She was "dead to him as though the cold grave enclosed her once loved form." Only from his daughters could he find a small dose of comfort, until a merciful God relieved him from his agony "by calling his crushed and wounded spirit home."[32]

Hadley then spun the obligatory tales of self-made manhood, from George's farm education to his encounter with and marriage to his once-chaste wife, and from his start as a "private soldier" among volunteers for New York to his grand promotions. He warned the jury that the prosecutors would try to "limit the inquiry within the narrowest possible space." Instead, the General's lawyers would "lay before you the saddest picture of crime, of lust, of seduction, of betrayed friendship, of a desecrated home and household ruin, that the eye of man has ever yet rested upon."[33]

He distilled the prisoner's five years in the army into a long list of deeds that proved his gritty determination and sacrifice. The "name of George W. Cole," he proclaimed, would be "bright and unsullied" among those who fought "with the brave Army of the Potomac." (The Army of the James, where George spent most of the war, was not mentioned a single time by George's lawyers.)[34]

Eager listeners learned that, with "his" own money, the prisoner had helped raise a regiment of Black cavalrymen and faced the dangers of leading them into battle instead of cashing in and brokering them to Northern states desperate to meet recruitment quotas. Hadley claimed—in probably a gross exaggeration of some kernel of truth—that the prisoner had passed over an offer by an "Eastern State" of $100,000, an immense fortune.[35]

There was nary a word in the war summary about mutinies, abandoned refugees, or burning citizens' belongings. There was almost no darkness in the war; at least until Hadley gave the public the first description of George's fall from his horse and the "great disarrangement" of the prisoner's "system." He spared few details. The sum of the wounds—the prolapsed anus, the warped ribcage, the lame bladder and colon, the bloody hemorrhaging—stamped the soldier's mind with a certain kind of delusion and pain that followed him home.[36]

Frank Hamilton, one of the defense's key medical experts, had recently visited the prisoner twice to document the wounds. Looking him over like an auctioned horse at a county fair, he measured his depressed breastbone, examined how his belly was asymmetrically swollen, and probed George's "remnant of old piles"—that is, hemorrhoids—finding his anus to be "crammed full" of hardened feces. He observed the prisoner urinating; the dribbling urine from the tip of his penis revealed a bladder still mostly paralyzed. The prisoner shrank in pain when the doctor touched his sternum. Direct touch to his spine brought shudders. During his second visit, Hamilton noticed blood stains on the prisoner's pillow.[37]

The medical examiner added scientific proof to a bevy of testimonies, mostly from comrades, about the nature of the wounds and how they drove the soldier into a morose state. Then, with little regard for consistency in their reasoning, the defense hedged this central argument, saying that even though the prisoner had been driven to insanity, he was somehow also perfectly sensible in his murderous deed. They seemed to be drawing from George's carefully copied notes from *Amelia*. Their client, up to the moment of the murder, and indeed in his moment of frenzy, had acted like any red-blooded man would in similar circumstances. His flash of madness, they argued, was proof of his stable manhood. Natural law, non-Christian civilizations, Hebrew codes, and centuries of verdicts in the English-speaking world all condemned adulterers to violent punishment. Convicting George Cole, they argued, meant rejecting the weight of history and human nature.[38]

Whatever the world's history was, there was indeed an unwritten law in nineteenth-century America that a husband could kill his wife's seducer. Perhaps because American colonies had statutes that made adultery a crime, cases of colonial-era husbands killing seducers are not found in the recorded memory of American law. But as adultery lost its criminality, and was encouraged by the anonymity and vice of cities, husbands turned to personal revenge. Given the logic of coverture, that the husband absorbs the identity of his wife, the shocking discovery of one's wife in bed with another man (called "in flagrante delicto") was understood as an act of sexual assault on the husband himself. The husband who had stumbled upon the act could kill the adulterer and be convicted of nothing more than manslaughter. It was self-defense.[39]

Daniel Sickles's acquittal in 1859 had proved that jurymen would expand the unwritten law to include a husband who witnessed the seducer merely signaling for a tryst. But George's defense had a problem. He had not stabbed Hiscock after finding the two tangled in bed; he had not intercepted a letter of forbidden love or observed a hand gesture inviting Mary for a carnal rendezvous. Instead, after having suspected something was going on, the General returned to Brooklyn on business, wrote inquiring letters, gathered evidence, took interviews, shopped for a gun, coedited a confession note or two, and rode a train to Albany only to first discuss the matter with his brother-in-law. George and his friends feared that he had stretched the unwritten law so far that no jury would acquit him.[40]

The defense, therefore, argued that it was not the mere fact of seeing the guilty pair in "the actual coition" but the burst of passion "created by the knowledge" of the sexual act. This burst "justifies the taking of human life." The mere reminder that such a thing had happened would push a loving husband toward frenzy. The members of the jury were asked to trust their male instincts: "your experience as men; your own innate feelings."[41]

Another snag in the defense was the fact that the state of New York had made seduction a misdeed for which a father or husband could sue in civil court; a judge could award a father for the loss of labor from his pregnant daughter or for the loss of honor to his family.[42]

Hadley's opening defense boldly swept aside the option of suing for seduction. To accept money in exchange for having his wife's "person polluted" would be tantamount to selling Mary into prostitution, hawking her virtue and George's honor for a price. Hadley mocked the seduction suits, saying that for a handsome fee, attorneys in the city would gladly help any such man coin his "tears and groans into dollars and cents."[43]

The General's lawyers claimed that the mere sight of Hiscock momentarily dethroned George's reason. He was insane for a mere moment. To prove this they introduced various theories about insanity that were drawn from the young, confused field of psychiatry and from witnesses' own interpretations of George's state of mind. The courtroom soon played host to an academic debate about categories of insanity. Papers reported a noticeable sag in public enthusiasm. Over Olive Cole's objections, the lawyers brought in local physicians and family who testified to cases of mental illness in George's mother, a grandmother (who one witness said went insane after losing property during a bank failure), an aunt, and two sisters—some of them "growing out of the loss of a child."[44]

These theories about insanity in one way or another were products of Enlightenment claims, mixed with Christianity's cheerier view, that broken humans were the product of a broken environment and education. Madness was not the result of demonic possession or a nettlesome symptom of the fall of Adam but instead could be traced back to something that had gone wrong: physical injury, depraved family life, dangerous stimulus, irritation, extreme disappointment—all of which disordered a mind and its various faculties. George's own attorney James Brady had developed the controversial terms "moral insanity" and "temporary insanity" to explain how damaged or strained parts of the mind of an otherwise decent human could bring someone to perpetrate evil.[45]

Jurymen, lawyers, judges, and some readers may have genuinely wondered about the nature of George Cole's mind and the limits to which a human could be held accountable for the impulses of one's body. (The public was mostly bored by it.)[46] Some detractors, though, cynically questioned how anybody could be held accountable for any crime given the patchwork of new theories used to throw doubt on the General's capacity for wrongdoing. They claimed that what defense attorneys were explaining as moral or temporary insanity looked a lot like the age-old wages of vice or the moral depravity of humans. One paper mocked the debated theories by reporting that a sermon had been given about how Cain was morally insane when he killed Abel.[47]

Americans had come to believe that appalling deeds begged explanation. They needed new reasons because they had mostly discarded traditional Christian understandings of the fallen self, trading them for upbeat depictions of human nature. For this reason, they obsessed over gothic stories and reports of murder, reading them closely for details and clues of an evil deed's origin. Homicidal evil was a mystery that needed solving, as it could not have sprung entirely from within the human heart. Any horrific deed would have to provide its own unique clues to explain itself. Murder, once a sobering reminder of the gnarled human soul, became a crime scene.[48]

The jurymen, in short, were asked to trace the prisoner's lapse of moral reasoning to some freak injury sustained from a fall from his horse, not a soul knotted with pride or wrath. In fact, there was nothing wrong with the soul of the prisoner. It was his *goodness* that brought on the apparent evil. The General had been "overpowered" by his compassion as he imagined the weeping faces of his motherless children. His deep sympathy for his family brought trauma to a "brain surcharged to madness." Some of the most regrettable acts of humanity, in this new reasoning, were the fruits of love.[49]

Brilliantly, and for the prosecution dastardly, the defense made the General's volatile mind central to their case. His stricken mind, at the moment of the murder, provided a way for the defense to instantly transport the jury (through the fluid streams of George's supposed thoughts and memories) into scenes far removed from the murder: the faces of his daughters, the screeching of bullets in battle, his disturbing wounds, and his years of domestic bliss contrasted with flashing thoughts of Hiscock debauching George's wife.

Judge Ingraham insisted that it was not needful to determine what Hiscock had done with Mary; it had no bearing on the question of murder. The General's well-paid lawyers disagreed. What happened to Mary mattered, but it mattered even more what her husband believed had happened. Any deed, real or fancied, that assaulted his troubled mind was relevant.

The prisoner's fitful mind was a godsend. His body was the problem.

CHAPTER 21

HEROIC WOUNDS

IT SEEMED STRAIGHTFORWARD. George Cole's life-altering injury happened in 1862 when he charged rebel pickets at full speed. He tried to jump from his saddle, his attorneys said, but couldn't because of a "previous wound in the thigh." He suffered multiple wounds from the fall. Not long after the horse injury, he took part in the Kinston Raid in North Carolina.[1]

★

IT SOON BECAME CLEAR that the truth was unclear. The defense attorneys couldn't even establish a consistent timeline of when the accident happened. They strained to link George's groin injury to a heroic, or even recognizable, battle. They lumped it together with the "great Kingston raid" that followed it. (Despite claims of its "greatness," court reporters and transcribers misspelled the Kinston Raid—largely unknown outside of the participants and those in the region—as "Kingston.") The best his lawyers could do was wedge the mysterious injury between an earlier wound and a relatively obscure raid.[2]

Friends and comrades muddied the story. One of the first witnesses claimed George was in the hospital "for a long time in the summer of 1862." The prisoner's tragic protégé, Edwin Fox, testified that George had two major injuries while riding on his horse. The first happened at the end of the summer or early fall of 1862. Fox told how he had personally nursed his commander. Then, in "February or March, '63," recalled Fox, his commander suffered a fall from his horse again. When the prosecution interrogated Fox about the two falls, he claimed that the prisoner had been wounded twice, "both by the falling of the same horse and in the same parts."[3]

A friend, Frank Garrett, added to the confusion. He claimed that in August 1862, he first met the prisoner walking with a cane in Syracuse, where George was recruiting soldiers while on sick leave. Garrett joined George's company, understanding that his captain had recently fallen from a horse—which would place the injury earlier in the summer. But in cross-examination, Garrett admitted that the only injury he was certain about was a bullet wound in his captain's leg, which, he claimed to know, was from an accidentally fired gun. W. H. Palmer, a physician in George's regiment, claimed the fall happened in October 1862 (not the summer), that George was in the hospital for only three weeks, and that as far as he knew there was no second fall. Another doctor recalled seeing him "frequently" in the hospital. Others said he treated himself. George's comrades couldn't agree on much at all.[4]

THE PROSECUTION TRIED to capitalize on the confusion and suggested that the gore and suffering had been exaggerated. His wounds to the rectum, they said, were little more than bloody piles commonly suffered by soldiers. Major Rowland Hall, who frequently saw the soldier in camp, told prosecutors that he had never believed that George suffered more than "all of us from our hardships." Doctor Palmer had testified that the Tarboro Raid of 1863 left George hearing voices; but other soldiers, without such injuries, Palmer admitted, saw visions from hunger and deprivation of sleep. "I was afflicted in the same way," he said.[5]

A doctor called on by the defense said that most soldiers had piles and, in some cases, "there may be a protrusion of one or two inches" and bloody discharge. From what he saw in the army, constipation and diarrhea were almost universal. He was right. Bowel and digestive troubles, perhaps only second to respiratory diseases, were the greatest killers of soldiers. Medical records available at the time concurred that acute dysentery sometimes resulted in prolapsed anuses.[6]

The prosecutors called up several witnesses to discredit the pitiable accounts about George's life-altering wounds. A fellow captain in the raids remembered that the soldier did complain of acute stomach pain; but the comrade agreed with one of George's former business partners that the prisoner left and returned from war "sociable and pleasant." Perhaps the most damning testimony came from Brevet Major General Henry A. Barnum, a local Syracuse hero decorated with the Medal of Honor. He had been a fellow officer in George's first regiment. After George transferred into the Army of the James, Captain Barnum continued on to fight in heralded battles from Malvern Hill to Gettysburg to William T. Sherman's March to the Sea.[7]

At Malvern Hill, Barnum had been left for dead on the battlefield and then captured. His family received reports that he had been killed. While he lay recovering in captivity, kin and neighbors mourned his passing at his funeral. He seemingly came back from the grave when he returned to Syracuse. His fame earned him a commission as colonel of a new regiment. The city feted him in a packed Syracuse City Hall, where Jewish women gave him the regimental flag and Thomas Davis—who (with Hiscock) would later push for George's brevet promotion—presented Barnum an elegant sword etched with famous battle scenes in which the miracle soldier had fought.[8]

Like the prisoner, Barnum had suffered wounds to his stomach and torso. But unlike George, he could put them on display, and had, in numerous photographs since the war. At Malvern Hill a musket ball had burrowed through his lower abdomen and shot out his back. After healing, he kept the wound open with oakum rope and ramrods. His steely resolve had delivered him from what he called the "black vulture of war." He was living proof of manly sacrifice and the highest measure of how a soldier could cope with wounds. After the war, he was rewarded handsomely with the position of inspector of state prisons. He then became the editor of an upstate newspaper. The word of Syracuse's favored son carried weight.[9]

It was a blow to George's case, then, when Barnum testified that he had not noticed anything unusual in George's spirits or health. Barnum recalled interacting with George at a midwar reception for the Twelfth New York, when, according to the prisoner's lawyers, George had been convalescing from his wounds. Barnum remembered him participating in the festivities, where, according to one comrade, George offered a toast and gave a short speech. Barnum didn't recall the toast. But he remembered clearly striking up a conversation after the war with a "robust"-looking George on a Syracuse street. They mostly spoke about promotions.[10]

During cross-examination, the defense cast doubt on the motives behind some of the damning testimonies. Several of them had come from the mouths of Luther Harris Hiscock's cronies who were on the board that had fired George from the windmill company. And his comrade, John Moschell, who remembered the prisoner as sociable during the war, held a grudge against the prisoner for having beat him to a promotion. Moschell had run an advertisement in the city's newspaper to dissuade recruits from joining the prisoner's company. And Barnum, though he crossed the prisoner's path many times

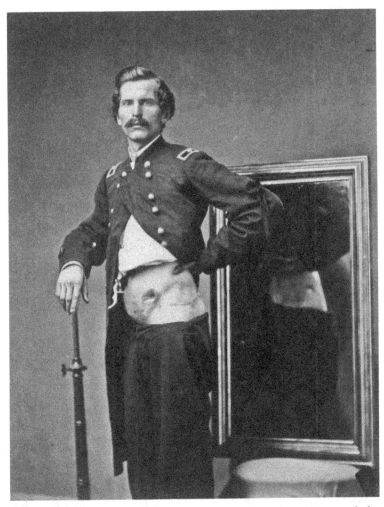

For George Cole, the story of Henry A. Barnum would have been proof of God's arbitrary tender mercies. Their stories were parallel enough to draw attention to how Barnum's good fortune contrasted with George's sorry lot. They both started off as captains in the Twelfth New York Infantry and were breveted to major general. But after George transferred to the cavalry, Barnum went on to suffer various injuries that tied him to epic battles he fought in, mostly with the Army of the Potomac. Some of Barnum's wounds were deadly and strange, like the healed gunshot wound he revealed before a camera here. *Photograph by William Bell, 1865. Smithsonian American Art Museum Collection*

and seemed to be his friend, admitted from the stand that he had been more intimate with Hiscock. He also confessed that his newspaper had published a critical story about the prisoner. He assured the jury that, except for political matters, he had no control over his newspaper's content.[11]

THE PRISONER'S MEDICAL KNOWLEDGE and stubborn pride had something to do with the uncertainty surrounding his body. After he was crushed by his horse, he would not submit himself to the continual care of army surgeons. Just after his fall (whenever it was), the steward in a New Bern hospital fumbled while inserting the catheter into George's penis. He botched the first few attempts before George—delirious from pain and sleep deprivation—snatched the catheter away and worked it into his own urethra.

Witnesses agreed that George had ignored orders for rest. One doctor said that the prisoner had to miss a few expeditions and did not seem physically capable to continue in the saddle. Yet he "generally went on all the raids on horseback" and did so "contrary to my directions." His regimental surgeon recalled that two years after the injury, in the summer of 1864, the soldier was "at his duty at all times, and never in sick bed." Yet, referring to roughly the same time, a tent mate testified that while the soldiers were digging Butler's canal, George "was lying most the time in his tent" when not on duty. In Texas he was often prostrated in a tent with his feet propped up to bring his organs into order.[12]

George had reasons for hiding the full extent of his injuries from certain superiors. He had been hurt at just about the time he stood a chance of getting promoted to major. He never stopped yearning for promotion. His commander, General Godfrey Weitzel, saw him "nearly every day in Virginia." Though their quarters were less than a mile apart while in Virginia and occasionally close in Texas, he didn't recall knowing anything about George's fall from a horse or that he was unusually sick or hurt. Weitzel had noticed Colonel Cole's depressed spirit but thought it was because George had attempted, and failed, a risky move in the field for which Weitzel had promised a promotion if George succeeded. Or, Weitzel figured, it had to do with the fact that for a while in Virginia, the colonel's Black troops had been dismounted and their horses given to another regiment. Weitzel had seen the prisoner lying in his tent a few times with his legs elevated. One time, when Weitzel showed up unannounced at his tent flap, a startled George jumped to his feet "in a peculiar manner" to salute his superior.[13]

Even some of George's siblings were kept in the dark. Almost four months after the fall, his sister Martha wasn't sure what had happened. It wasn't because, George, out of decency, spared his readers gory details. He once wrote about how his regiment chopped a rebel's arm off; and Martha had just read a detailed account of how, during an attack by the enemy, George had watched his bullet pierce a rebel's belly. She believed that George had been in the hospital for "some difficulty in the spine." She had heard from Mary's stepbrother, who had heard it from George's colonel, that George suffered a serious injury to his breast that "was received from a fall from his horse." Otherwise, she wrote, she had "no definite report" as to how his injuries occurred."[14]

The prisoner's groin and chest injuries were not invented by scheming lawyers. There was overwhelming evidence that his body had been wrecked, and with it his mind, and that he carefully guarded his private struggles.[15] For many of George's contemporaries, even in his own circle, his wounds brought doubt and confusion.

★

LUCKILY FOR GEORGE, the outcome of his trial did not depend on proving the exact nature of his injuries or on clearing the haze that surrounded them. His lawyers only needed to reach the hearts of the jurors, and to convince them that the General stood in for all men who felt threatened in their role as protectors of their families.

The larger-than-life Brady summed it up well in his closing remarks when he painted a powerful picture of George, like Christ, ascending the hangman's scaffold and saying to all,

> As I fought to protect my country, so I fought to protect my home. . . . In the blow that I struck and for which I suffer, I strengthened the security of the homes of my fellow citizens as much as I did when I struck against the enemy who would have laid waste our country.

So long as beloved institutions were under threat, a man of duty and love could never rest. "And so," Brady concluded, "if [prisoner Cole] dies, he will die for you, and for all of us." The gallery exploded with applause.[16]

Out of desperation, the prosecution showed its fangs. All the talk about war and military glory threatened to render soldier Cole untouchable. In prosecutor Charles B. Sedgwick's closing argument, he lauded the sacrifice of veterans; it was only honor, he said, that stopped him from asking whether the prisoner had joined the war for patriotism or for ambition and selfishness. Sedgwick was inching onto thin ice. Nobody, he said, wanted to take away a "single laurel from the brow" of a soldier, but promotion was not always a test of merit. "A little influence in Washington," he taunted, "goes much farther than service in the field, or military knowledge, or faithfulness" to duties. The prisoner must have seethed as he sat at his table. "But I have no desire to criticize the military career of the prisoner," the prosecutor said. "The history of General Cole is not a remarkable one," he added, leaving some, if not most, to detect ingratitude or blasphemy in his words.[17]

Then they targeted Mary. Lyman Tremain closed the prosecution by saying he didn't much believe in the myth of women's monopoly on sexual purity. Hiscock had lived a virtuous life. That is, until Mary played the role of Potiphar's wife in the Bible (who, in an attempt to cover her own sins, accused the young Joseph of trying to seduce her). Yet, as if he could not let go of the ideal of female purity, Tremain shored up the myth by arguing that a truly pure woman of Mary's ilk did not need pistols or legislation to keep herself out of the arms of a rake. The fact that Mary was a woman did not make her purer than Hiscock. But still, female purity could have prevented the entire tragedy.

Toward the end of his speech, Tremain began speaking about the war and broke down in tears. Memories of his firstborn son, who was killed in battle, overcame him.[18] When he gained his composure, he then closed by assuring the jury that if they found the prisoner guilty, New York's governor would review the case of the war hero and perhaps spare the veteran from the noose.

George's lawyer Brady shot back that he had never heard of prosecutors urging a guilty verdict while praying for mercy at the same time. He rejected the middle ground; instead, he dared the jurymen to make a choice between the only two options: they must set the hero free or hang him from a rope.[19]

Judge Ingraham, who was agitated by the defense's commandeering of his courtroom, ordered the jury to deliberate. He warned them not to get caught up in the prisoner's history. He pointed out the contradiction in the defense's argument that George was insane and yet had been justified and reasonable in killing a man. "There is no evidence in this case of any adultery—none whatever," he said to folks who had spent nearly two weeks listening to scandalous details of adultery and penetration.[20]

★

WHEN THE JUDGE LATER CALLED on the deadlocked jury, he told them that he welcomed a verdict of manslaughter. The General's attorneys cried foul again. Such middle ground would give jurymen a way to dodge the tough choice of honoring or executing a soldier. Every man needed to decide where he stood, they protested. Unconvinced, the judge dug in his heels and defended the manslaughter option again.

George waited anxiously for the verdict. As his attorneys had argued, he had learned to stare death in the eye and was prepared to "risk it all." He privately feared that his counsel had been too timid.[21]

They had been anything but timid. The defense had dared the jurymen to hang a war hero for defending his honor. It was bad news for the men loitering in Albany's hotel lobbies who had been making bets that the prisoner would hang. Even if the jury chose to send the General to his grave, the defense claimed, the prisoner would serenely submit. Just as Christ had done, George would die for other men, saying, "Not my will but thine be done."

Judge Ingraham's proposed compromise of manslaughter dashed the defense's bold plan. The jurors could not come to an agreement. It was reported that not a single juror wanted George to hang, but at least a few insisted on manslaughter. Many of the jurors came to see the prisoner as some pitiful Christ figure who sacrificed his life for the American family. They were the jurymen who, after the hung-jury decision was read, hurried to the prisoner's table to meet him and his attorneys. They were the men who later visited him in his cell to "shower upon him their sympathy."[22]

CHAPTER 22

RINGS *and* FRIENDS

CORNELIUS COLE WAS CONVINCED that the jury had been bullied by scheming men. He scoured newspapers and recently published investigations, concluding, with only shreds of proof, that Luther Harris Hiscock had played an indispensable role in the New York "Canal Ring." He wrote his old colleague James McClatchy, a newspaper editor in California, to explain the "bloodthirstiness" of the prosecution and the coverage in some of New York's newspapers. He folded some newspaper clippings into an envelope along with the letter. "Now," the letter said, "let me disclose to you the secret spring of this malignity."[1]

In his first draft of the letter, heavily worked over with slashes and alterations, Cornelius revealed the secret: the ring was not made up from one political party, wrote Cornelius, "but from both." As chance would have it, Hiscock had been "one of the most distinguished and certainly the most useful members of this fraternity." The ring needed him "for the consummation of their schemes." Cornelius continued, their raids on the state treasury had to appear legal, and therefore "Hiscock was the man" to arrange the appearances. As a reward, he would share in the "proceeds."[2] In other words, Hiscock had secured favors for the ring while serving on the New York Assembly Judiciary Committee and was expected to deliver handsomely at the Constitutional Convention. His death disturbed the ring's designs. The General had awakened its wrath.

★

THE ACCUSATION WAS PLAUSIBLE. Since its completion in 1825, the state-administered canal had been an artificial river of ambition and corruption. It had encouraged ordinary folks' dreams of prosperity by connecting the crops and goods of farmers and artisans in the interior of America to markets in New York City and the Atlantic world. By the 1840s, though, it was clear that the canal could not keep up with the railroads. Urgent, costly attempts at building lateral canals only postponed the inevitable while inviting mass waste and corruption. Regulations to prevent corruption could not keep pace with the intricate schemes.

In the early Civil War, lawmakers temporarily shut down the shell game by declaring the canal completed. But with the closing of the Mississippi River for much of the war, wartime freight revitalized the canal, renewing the call for expansion and improvements. With the boom of business, legislators in the ring pushed through approvals for improvements called "extraordinary repairs." The wartime prosperity, though, was unsustainable and the hope in the canal's solvency misplaced. Within two years of the war's end, everybody knew the failing ditch was awash with corruption.[3]

There were rumors that some of Hiscock's chums, and his brother Frank, were ring members.[4] Shortly after the killing, many papers had circulated a report (with no accompanying evidence) claiming that Hiscock had been a "prominent" member of the ring.[5] The accusations seemed to be supported in first days of the Constitutional Convention when the "first great debate" addressed the question of whether to continue canal improvements. Hiscock's friends voted in ways that clearly favored canal expansion and opportunities for more graft.[6]

Before convention delegates hotly debated improvements, an independent eight-member joint committee, appointed earlier by the New York State Senate, had begun an investigation that was uncovering "gross" and "monstrous frauds."[7]

When the massive canal report was published, Cornelius devoured the tome and referred others like McClatchy to it. It included more than a thousand pages of testimony from an interminable list of witnesses who often implicated themselves and many others besides. It confirmed Cornelius's contention that the ring operated above party lines, drawing instead from thieves of any stripe. Made up of attorneys, contractors, and politicians, the ring was a conglomeration of self-interests. As the report put it, the canal board had awarded reckless contracts thanks to various schemes crafted by legislators; state agents had used public property for personal purposes; contractors had collected twice for the same job; there were blank vouchers issued, altered contracts, payoffs, and intimidation.

Just months before the lobby floor of the Stanwix Hall Hotel was smeared with Hiscock's blood, "a secret combination and conspiracy" had taken place there. The report found that contractors met there and bid among themselves—that is, they offered payoffs—for the privilege of submitting the "winning" bid. The rest submitted "dummy" bids that would be rejected for informalities. In this ruse, the "winning" contractor originally submits an "unbalanced" bid. He offers to do the major work at fair rates, but at exorbitant rates for subsequent minor repairs. By design, the minor work becomes the primary work. Other contractors won bids to maintain sections of the canal and, after dispersing kickbacks—called "the soap"—to the right officials, neglected repairs entirely. Ring members divvied up the winnings.[8]

The report made clear that it had only uncovered a fraction of the corruption. Cornelius declared that it gave "authentic evidence" of Hiscock's integral part in the ring. Cornelius must have felt vindicated and delighted to find the name of Lieutenant Governor Thomas "Old Salt" Alvord—Hiscock's mentor—in the opening summary of the pickings and the stealings and repeated many times after. Buried several hundred pages later was testimony that Hiscock's brother Frank was paid for "getting [a claim] through." Frank reportedly pocketed perhaps $6,000 for his work, while Alvord skimmed off an unknown sum for having ensured the claim was well received by the canal board.[9]

At last, on page 630, Cornelius found the proof. "And L.H. Hiscock," one witness testified, had leveraged his position as a legislator and "helped all he could."[10] In truth, the report of Hiscock helping "all he could" hardly meant his participation was prominent, or even certain. If anything, he was a mere bit player, not a ringleader, in a vast operation of schemers and grifters.

Cornelius had learned, as a young attorney in California, to divide men into grand opposing camps. Antislavery politics had been his teacher. He had been there in the infancy of the Republican Party in California in the 1850s, cementing relations with other antislavery men—newspaper editors and the soon-to-be railroad titans: Collis P. Huntington, Mark Hopkins, Leland Stanford, and the Crocker brothers. (The corruption of their Central Pacific Railroad dwarfed the misdeeds of the Canal Ring.) In Cornelius's words, he and his Republican allies—one in their promotion of railroads and one in the struggle against the spread of slavery—were "all personal and political friends."[11]

To others, the California Republicans' wedded interests of politics, newspapers, and railroads seemed like a ring. But from within, Cornelius only saw political friends joined in common cause.[12]

Americans of this era used the concept of "rings" to describe metastasizing corruption that seemed to have spread everywhere after the war. The combinations between lawyers, "bought" newspapers, banks, politicians, and commercial interests had grown more complex than Americans, who overwhelmingly hailed from smaller towns and farmlands, could fathom. "Rings" gave a name to the fearsome power and corruption circulating through widening, often impersonal, connections that operated above and beyond small-town alliances and friendships.[13]

The "ring" metaphor oversimplified the nature of the corruption, suggesting a kind of closed simplicity and stability in form. The so-called rings were more like overlapping webs, spun into confused intersecting planes, creating countless points of connection between markets, law, and legislation. Men like Hiscock and Cornelius exploited—or, as they would see it, formed friends and sought opportunity through—the ever-expanding and interconnected gossamer strands between government and American business. The connections were mind boggling. A lineage of friends could be traced, at some point, to rings of enemies. An enemy of an enemy might have been a friend. But this was a world where the friends of friends could be the worst sorts of foes.[14]

★

THE NATION, it seemed, was endangered by its own founding logic. The institution of friendship had held a cherished place in the minds of Americans since independence. The revolution's architects had hoped to replace inherited hierarchies, based on bloodline and dependence, with bonds of affection and equality. Sincere friendships promised to be the new glue that would hold the young republic together—in the aftermath of a war that was waged, after all, to sever older bonds of loyalty.

The Founders celebrated the destruction of traditional vertical bonds, which had led upward to fathers, masters, nobles, and monarchs, and bet that the affection of friends would hold a young republic together horizontally.[15]

Old hierarchies, of course, outlasted the revolution's assault on relationships of patronage and dependence, in part because they were repackaged and sentimentalized as "friendships," a term that softened—and masked—the continuing inequality between fathers and sons, craftsmen and apprentices, husbands and wives, and sometimes even masters and servants. When Americans assured themselves that they were merely advancing or helping friends according to merit, not favor, friendship provided a kind of cloak for old-world relations of favoritism, privilege, aristocracy, and patronage—those relics of monarchy supposedly swept into the dustbin of history. Since the birth of the nation, friendship had been the medicine that merely masked old-world disease.[16]

In an editorial from a Syracuse paper that had been published alongside a report on George's trial, a Syracuse journalist worried that political rings promoted privilege through concentric circles of friendship. The inner circles profited most. In this "wheel within a wheel," the only cardinal rule was that a ring member "must be one who never betrays or 'goes back on' a friend." It was a perverse and unnerving claim: the most loyal friendships, not hierarchical inequality, endangered republican virtue.[17] Rings of friendship threatened to infect the republic.

It was deeply powerful, then, when George's attorneys began painting an image of the prisoner as a friend betrayed. They seized on the fact that right after the killing, the prisoner and various reports had referred to Hiscock as a "bosom friend." The two men had supposedly shared a soulful bond. It was common in the nineteenth century for men, at least younger ones, to form romantic friendships that often entailed hand-holding, honeyed conversation, embraces, bedsharing, and emotional communion.[18] There was, though, little proof that George and Hiscock had shared a friendship so deeply in their bosoms.[19]

Telling the story of the prisoner as a jilted friend created pity. It also emphasized how he had been let down by one of the most comforting promises of the recent past: that the Civil War would purify men of their competitive, greed-based relationships. Combat, it was hoped, would lash Americans together through mutual sacrifice. After the first call for Union troops, Horace Greeley, the most influential editor in America, wrote that before the war, Northerners were "esteemed a sordid, grasping, money-loving people, too greedy of gain to cherish generous and lofty aspirations." But the rush to enlist proved that "in spite of the insidious approaches of corruption, the fires of patriotic devotion are still intensely burning."[20]

Poets, North and South, had welcomed the war for similar reasons. If friendships had been made false by the cold self-interest of commerce, the war would weld a national brotherhood—as 1776 supposedly had—with blood and muzzle fire, burning away enmity and materialism. Walt Whitman idealized war as *the* primal force that would purge America of corruption and the money lust that he found so disturbing in antebellum America. He came to believe in the great promise of war when he rushed to Fredericksburg to find his enlisted brother, George Washington Whitman. (The poet had falsely believed his brother had been badly injured because the *New York Tribune* reported the casualty of another soldier with a similar name, G. W. Whitmore.)

Whitman spent much of the war nursing, consoling, sponging, and reading and writing letters at the bedside of soldiers in Washington, DC, hospitals. For America's poet, war's "ruthless force" erased artificial class barriers, bringing farmers, bankers, and mechanics into a mystical brotherhood. The violence somehow swept away the miasma of capitalism, what

Whitman called "the shallowness and miserable selfism of these crowds of men."[21]

The beauty of such dreams, of American men purged of materialism, along with promises that the war would heal the cankers of patronage and graft, only made uglier the real corruption unleashed in the years during and after the war. Whitman-like visions were hard to reconcile with the ugly truth that for too many "friendship" had become a euphemism for calculating alliance. In the rush for postwar prosperity, railroad tycoons, businessmen, and speculators of all sorts needed favors, special legislation, insider tips, timely news, or favorable reports to keep their complex schemes running and themselves in the best places to reap the bounteous rewards. For this, friends were most dear. Letters that sought such favors or patronage consistently began with the appellation of "friend." "Friend Cole." "Friend Stanford." "Friend Huntington." Cornelius's letter about the secret Canal Ring began, "My Dear Friend."[22]

When Cornelius had failed to keep his promise to Friend Huntington and later reneged on his commitment to secure patronage for a crony of the railroads, Huntington seethed about Cornelius's false affections. "The fact is," Huntington wrote to Hopkins, "there is no good feeling in Cole." In Huntington's eyes, Cornelius's politics were misguided and he was a liar. But what irked Huntington most was that the heart of Cornelius was "cold, and his blood white." He had no warmth. Double-crossed by a senator who would not remain bought, Huntington talked about getting duped as if it all boiled down to the loss of affection: "I do not nor *cannot* like him," he concluded.[23]

Prisoner Cole's letters entertained no Whitman-like hope in a transfigured society rescued from competitive manhood. He was an embattled believer in Abraham Lincoln's "race of life," not a dissenter. His return from war had made clear how the two social relations—bosom friends and virtuous wives—

that were supposed to keep a grasping society knitted together through bonds of affection had conspired to further convert society to "miserable selfism." Hiscock, posing as a friend, had helped Mary Cole legally set her interests apart from her husband's. And his supposed role in the Canal Ring bore witness to how friendship was the fig leaf for corruption. For George, the bonds of affection had ruined him.

IN NOVEMBER 1868, the second trial began. Finding an unbiased jury proved just as difficult as it had been for the first trial.[24] After six days, and hundreds of rejected candidates, the jury was still stocked with at least a few secret admirers of the General. Before arguments began, the prosecution successfully rooted out two. Once revealed, the judge dismissed Richard Betts, an elderly juryman who had frequented the prisoner's cell with his family in tow. Word got out the next morning that juryman Samuel Trull, known as "the Cole man" in his village, had visited George's cell several times since the murder, sometimes with others, including a member of the original grand jury. Before Trull was dismissed, the defense attorneys exploited the moment by reading to him and the court some of the poems that the prisoner had penned for Mary during the war. When prompted, Trull identified it as poetry that the prisoner had shared with him during their cell visits. Trull was then dismissed. George's image as a devoted husband was secured.[25]

In the opening argument of the second trial, the defense lawyer William Hadley laid friendship and false affection at the center. It wasn't hard to do. George's first words in his jail confession were, "I had a friend . . . I thought him the best friend in the world. I have a wife and two children; she is as pure as snow." Hadley pointed out that seconds after the killing, a witness begged the General to tell him what it meant. George's first, raw words, Hadley stressed, were, "That man was my *best* friend, but he has ruined my wife while I was in the army."[26] This said it all, Hadley insisted. The nation that had consecrated intimate relations for the support of aspiring men had not kept its promises.

In the first days there was a notable sag in public fascination, though bets were still tendered in Albany's hotels and streets.[27] Little new was revealed; over the six months between trials, the original arguments had merely cured like cement. Once again, the defense claimed George had started as a private and ended as a "full Major-General." This time, Hadley cut short the war descriptions, claiming that it was in obedience to the wishes of the prisoner to "remain silent" about his military achievements. (Perhaps Olive Cole's warning about saying too much about coolness in battle had finally been heeded.) Hadley doubled down, though, on war as a purifying rite of passage that could never have taught a soldier "to work the death of an *unarmed friend.*"[28]

"What motive then," Hadley asked, had George "to take the life of his *best friend?*"

Hadley returned to the words "friend" and "friendship" over and over. Hiscock truly "*was* his *best* friend." Twice more, George's first words about believing he had a best friend in Hiscock were quoted. How could George kill a friend? The answer was that Hiscock had truly done something so vile that he became for George "the false friend whom he had loved."[29] The death of a true friendship was the original tragedy.

Hadley held up a small locket containing an image of Mary. The prisoner had worn it against his "manly breast" as he lay "crushed" during sleepless nights in his army bed. (If this was true, George wore it alongside his identification disc.) With the locket dangling before the packed courtroom, Hadley vividly fused together the two other losses suffered by the prisoner. George's beloved wife had failed him and so had his body.[30]

Hadley made George out to be the most pitiful of creatures. He depicted a traumatized, numbed veteran, a heap of sorrow just before the murder, bewildered and questioning whether he was lost in a nightmare. Whenever George saw glimmers of light, he was dragged back into his present hell by his "sobbing" children asking, "Father what *is* the matter with mother?"[31]

In the new telling of things, it was suggested that seconds before the murder, the General noticed the silver studs on Hiscock's cuffs and—seeing the cigar puffed on by the libertine—imagined the match that was pulled from George's own silver box that Mary had regifted to the seducer. At this moment, "*insanity smote him.*" He was as helpless "as a worm to arrest the tread of fate." It was "not George W. Cole" who fired the gun but the "wreck of" a man. In discharging the pistol, his hand was enacting motions that were "solely the result of a blind, irresistible impulse" with which reason had as little to do as with the "movements of a new-born infant." The reasoning, self-made general of the first trial had been fully reduced to a worm, a baby without reason.[32] The only course left to him—which he could not resist—was violent impulse. He had been unmade by the universe.[33]

The rancor between the opposing sides boiled over. One of George's attorneys made a personal threat to one of the prosecutors. "I'll hunt you pretty close," he warned. At another point, the prosecution intimated that if the jury was going to acquit the defendant, it should do it quickly so the "gray-haired father of Hiscock" could take his gun and inflict vengeance on the prisoner. The second-to-last testimony came from George's comrade Edwin Fox. In cross-examination, the prosecution badgered him for having murdered Henry Edwards.[34]

It had become a bare-knuckle courtroom brawl. For the first time, George's counsel insinuated that Hiscock had been connected to "the corrupt canal ring" and that Stanwix Hall had served as the ring's headquarters. The defense went on to question why the prosecution needed to hire professional "champions" of adultery, besides the state's paid attorneys. It questioned the propriety of securing lawyers who were also warm "friends" of the deceased.[35]

It had only been three years since George's attorney Amasa Parker had helped carry the casket of prosecutor Lyman Tremain's son, Frederick, into an Albany church echoing with the melancholy bass tones of an organ. And one of Hiscock's pallbearers, Allen Munroe—who had been a witness in the trial—had written a warm letter of recommendation for George during the war in hope of getting George a permanent promotion in the Regular Army. By the end of the trial, any goodwill that had been created by the mystic chords of memory, or by the shared trauma of war, had evaporated.[36]

The legendary James Topham Brady—in what turned out to be his last courtroom drama before dying of some unacknowledged disease—tried to mend fences at the close of the trial by paying compliments to the efforts of both counsels. But he also stated baldly that Hiscock got what he deserved and that, had a lecher done a similar thing to his (Brady's) sister, and had he not responded as the General had done, he would have been "unfit to live among men." In such crises of family, he said, a man could not be governed by the "coldness of the counting-house." Brady then maundered through a half-coherent story about Julius Caesar and closed by asking the jury to restore George to his family with Christmas at hand.[37]

As the first judge had done in the previous trial, Judge Henry Hogeboom tried in vain to make the act of adultery, or the General's war record, irrelevant. As before, Hogeboom suggested the jury consider manslaughter. And just as before, the prisoner's counsel rejected anything between the extremes of execution and acquittal, saying that the prisoner preferred the hangman over state prison. The judge then held forth for over two hours, instructing the jurors in ways that, as before, clearly favored the prosecution, and then left them to deliberate.

Soon, the foreman returned to the judge to tell him the court had made a grave mistake in letting a man who was set in his belief in George's guilt take the juror's box. Cornelius wrote a panicked letter to Olive claiming that the holdout, a "sanctimonious churchman," had been "bought out" by the Canal Ring. Cornelius thought Hogeboom had been influenced too.[38]

By Monday morning, at least ten jurors had joined for acquittal. The remaining one or two wrestled with the concept of temporary insanity and asked the judge for more guidance. The judge admitted—with some cajoling from the prisoner's lawyers—that if the jurors had any reasonable doubt about George's sanity at the time of the murder, they had to give the prisoner the benefit of the doubt.[39]

When the jury announced that it had arrived at a decision, the prisoner was escorted from his cell, leaving behind his home of 552 nights—his books, the bouquets and flowers from his daughters and female admirers, and his white mice that stirred in the little wooden homes he had built for them. He walked down "the bridge of sighs," the connecting walkway that led from the old jail to city hall, into a courtroom that was "crowded to suffocation."[40]

Without ceremony, the foreman arose and announced that the jury had found the prisoner to be innocent. With that, the General's backers stood atop their seats and gave "deafening cheers" as the judge futilely banged his gavel. For two minutes, George Cole's defenders "threw their hats upwards, waved their handkerchiefs and continued cheering." After keeping silent the entire trial, George at last raised his voice, saying, "I thank the Jury for restoring me to the guardianship of my children." As he pushed his way toward his carriage through a crowd of several hundred people, men and women surrounded him, "striving to grasp his hands." The crowd followed the carriage to a hotel where they continued to fete the "hero of a domestic tragedy."[41]

Cornelius wrote to an associate that the verdict "called forth the most tremendous & long continued cheering." The canal ring, at last, had been defeated. "Nothing like it," he wrote. "Gen'l has a host of friends."[42]

CHAPTER 23

SCHEMES and SMOKE

Though it was nearly Christmas, George showed no intention of returning to live with Mary Cole in the family hotel.[1] After the celebrations in Albany, he went straightway to the Empire House, a Syracuse hotel right on the canal at the center of the city's social life. For several days, friends and strangers came to clasp his hands and pay their respects.

He did not know where his home was. For seven years he had slept in a soldier's quarters or in a cell. One paper mocked him as George "Coal," a dig at his command over Black soldiers. Another claimed that he would be "branded" with the "mark of Cain." That is, because he was a killer, like the Bible's first murderer, he would be expelled from his family and doomed to wander the earth.[2]

Wander he would. He visited his daughters in Trumansburg, in the home of his brother-in-law, Henry Barto Jr., who, George concluded, was determined to get his hands on Mary's estate. Soon after, he was seen on the streets of Albany, where he tapped the shoulder of a childhood friend who was gazing at art through a window. The General told him that he had decided to leave the girls under the care of their mother, with whom he had no plans to reunite.[3]

In late January 1869, he passed through Elmira, just a few miles south of Horseheads near his childhood home, where soldiers in the American Revolution had slain their horses. A local newspaper mockingly wondered whether he was temporarily insane at the time of his visit there. That spring, another paper reported that he was seen in a hotel in Seneca Falls, the cradle of American women's rights.[4]

Weeks later he likely attended the commencement exercises of Wesleyan University, where his youthful ambitions were once stoked by promises that any strong-willed man could make something of himself. He was elected as "co–vice president" of the school's Army and Navy Union, a title that likely entailed little responsibility, given to him by fellow Methodist veterans who admired or pitied him, or both.[5]

In news accounts, George became a mere sidenote in updates about Daniel Sickles, the *full* general who had recently been appointed minister to Spain. Because both men had killed supposed seducers, the two murders were mocked as the new path to political appointments. Once a cynosure, George quickly became little more than a shadow that tracked the movement of a famous man closer to the sun.[6]

One newspaper recalled that, after the murder, George worked at the post office in Cortland, New York, though if he did, it was not for long.[7] In late 1869 he relocated to Washington, DC, the hub of American patronage, where he hoped to secure a clerkship in the US Senate. Cornelius Cole had told the public that he would not further aid his brother. George had become a political and financial liability to him.[8]

By the summer of 1870, he had made his home in the Fourth Ward of Washington, DC, with Eliza Bruce, a Black illiterate woman, born in Maryland, who was roughly his age. A census worker labeled her as a cook and him as a physician. George evidently took her for his wife, a guarded, poorly kept secret within the Cole family.[9]

He failed to secure his "place" in Washington as he had done after the war.[10] He then fixed his hopes on the fringes of America's expanding empire. He first plotted to go to Santo Domingo, the island nation on Haiti's border that President Ulysses S. Grant planned to annex. George obtained recommendation letters from a friend who vouched for the General's "pure" war promotions. When Congress rejected annexation in 1871, he was forced to adjust his sights.[11] He soon set them on America's unfinished empire in the West.

DURING THE WAR, Republican congressmen, freed from the obstructions of slave drivers and their Democratic allies, muscled through their vision of a market-centered nation that stretched from the Atlantic to the Pacific. They approved the construction of the transcontinental railroad (which favored the North, and Cornelius's friends) and, to incentivize its rapid construction, supplied railroad corporations vast land grants that, if lumped together, roughly totaled the size of Texas. The party of Abraham Lincoln figuratively and—thanks to the toil of Irish and Chinese workers—literally laid the rails for America's industrial and capitalistic future.[12]

In the decade following the war, Republicans converted the remaining Union army into capitalism's frontline troops. As Northerners lost the will to shield freedpeople from terror in the unrepentant South, the army shifted its energies to putting down labor uprisings in the North and West, crushing strikes and revolts in mines, mills, and the railroad industry. Other units were sent to conquer Indians in the Great Plains and Southwest, forcing the migration of Blackfoot, Crow, Lakota, Sioux, Comanche, and many others to reservations. The sad destiny for frontier Indians was made more certain with the laying of each railroad tie.[13]

Laborers completed the transcontinental railroad five months after George's acquittal. Sometime between late 1871 and 1873, George journeyed to the West, likely taking the Atchison, Topeka and Santa Fe train to its western terminus in Colorado territory, and then making his way southward to the red alkali highlands of northern New Mexico. His destination was Fort Union in Mora Valley, a key military post built a decade before the war to house soldiers who protected settlers and traders along the Santa Fe Trail from raids by outlaws, resistant Hispanos, and Native peoples.

George had at least one vital friend there. His nephew Gilbert Cole Smith, a captain who had risen to assistant quartermaster of the US Army. Gilbert was the surviving son of George's older sister Emeline, whose death twenty-five years before had plunged young George, home from college, into deadly depression.[14]

Gilbert used his post as quartermaster to employ George in some way. It wasn't nepotism exactly. It was policy at the fort to offer veterans first dibs on employment and contracts.[15] George worked for a time on a sheep ranch, perhaps as a hired hand alongside Mexican merchants and laborers. He probably sold mutton and wool to the fort. If he owned the land he worked, there was no record kept and preserved of its purchase.[16]

★

IN A SIX-DAY SPAN from April 29 to May 4, 1873, George sent off three desperate letters to Cornelius. They are his last surviving words to family. He had not retired to the frontier to sell wool or live the life of a shepherd. He wrote as if time were running out. It was. The pace of railroad building had recently reached its peak. At their fastest pace, the approaching Atchison, Topeka and Santa Fe Railroad crews in southern Colorado laid track at the dizzying rate of three miles a day. The fast-approaching rail would soon penetrate New Mexico territory. He believed this was his last main chance.[17]

His plan was to make a bid to the federal government to operate a postal route between Fort Union and Granada, Colorado, the most westerly railhead town along the line. He believed he could get ahead of the game. He just needed some friends.

He made elaborate calculations of the costs to run the 280-mile route, including the outlays for ponies, feed, and wages for hands. He could make a small fortune if he had the winning bid (or won two smaller contracts for which he had recently submitted bids). The capital required to get the enterprise running was beyond his reach. Cornelius responded to George's flurry of dreams with doubts and warnings, apologizing for "chopping off" George's imagination. But imagination was what made poor men prosperous. There was "no other road to bread," responded George. He added a postscript at the end of the inked letter. "There is no time to spare," he warned in pencil.[18]

Days later, George started another restless letter. He had just improved his route plans and claimed to have a strong lead for another investor. He feared someone—a competitor with "friends in W.[ashington]"—would cause his more competitive bid to be thrown out as an "informal bid," the shady methods used by Luther Harris Hiscock's cronies in the Canal Ring.[19]

He scrawled out multiple pages of details on how he would lower the costs by, among other tactics, subletting sections of the route to Mexicans. "This letter holds a fortune if you can make the <u>ripples</u>," he wrote. He needed his brother to make those ripples in Washington at once because Cornelius's tenure as a senator had just ended two weeks before. George was desperate and believed he couldn't afford to play by the rules any longer. "You and I well know that <u>no</u> bids are awarded on merit any more," he fumed. He was ready to do the very

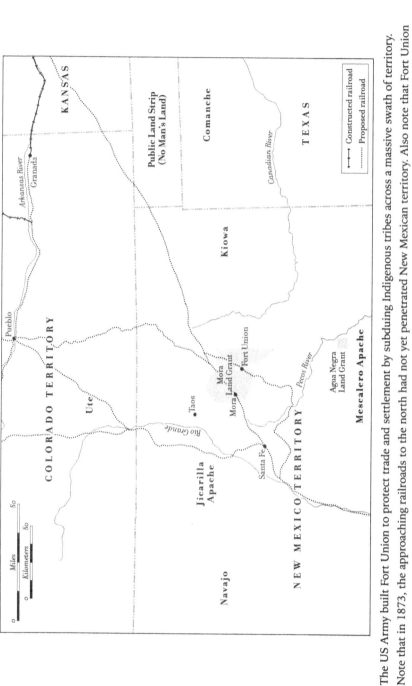

The US Army built Fort Union to protect trade and settlement by subduing Indigenous tribes across a massive swath of territory. Note that in 1873, the approaching railroads to the north had not yet penetrated New Mexican territory. Also note that Fort Union and Mora (where George's grave would be located) are within the boundaries of the Mora Land Grant. *Drawn by Mapping Specialists*

thing he had so long denounced: lay pipe and pull wires. "I believe $1000 judiciously applied will secure my two bids now in, & $1000 more secure the Grenada bid." If he was going to compete in the game, he had to play by its universal rules.[20]

He believed he could come up with most of the bribe money and, with Cornelius's help, entice US vice president Henry Wilson and Congressman Benjamin Butler to aid in securing the bids. He had always known that Butler could be bought. Now, out of desperation, and with some borrowed dough, he hoped to do the buying. He had reasons to believe that Wilson, a lion for the antislavery movement, could also be bribed. Wilson had recently had his upstanding reputation sullied by the Crédit Mobilier scandal, in what was just coming to light as one of the largest scandals in American history.[21]

Playing by the rules made failure certain. There were other schemes already in operation where lucrative mail routes in the West, like the "Star Routes," were gained by crookery.[22] Blind in so many ways, George saw clearly how the nation was entering an era of unmatched corruption. The rise of national corporations meant the consolidation of agriculture, ranching, and mining into fewer and fewer hands. These consolidating powers were steadily making their way toward northern New Mexico. He was only a fool in thinking he could beat them.

In his final letter, after sensing that Cornelius wasn't going to prop up his plans, he mentioned a "second consideration" of becoming a trader near the fort. As he darted from one angle to the next, he questioned why his brother had lost faith in him. "I seem to have a faculty of making others believe I can be somebody far more readily than I can you," wrote George. His words betrayed his deepest fear. He would die a nobody.[23]

He promised to send Cornelius the contract's first pile of cash, as he felt anxious to pay off the massive debts from the two trials. The debt "hangs over me as a life obligation," he wrote.

★

GEORGE HAD ANOTHER PLAN TO free himself from his debts. He was wide awake to the fact that speculators, like swarms of buzzards, were circling around New Mexico's greatest treasure, the Spanish and Mexican land grants. The lands had been granted generations before by Spanish and Mexican governors. Over one hundred of them in the northern part of New Mexico alone, they were a tangle of overlapping claims, customary laws, local tradition, Mexican law, and Spanish *fueros* (special privileges for different social groups, a system tracing as far back as the days of Hernán Cortés and the conquistadores).[24]

After the United States defeated Mexico in 1848 and wrested away the northern third of Mexico's land, Congress committed, in the Treaty of Guadalupe Hidalgo, to honor the property rights of its newly absorbed Spanish-speaking citizens. Instead, Americans essentially saddled locals with the burden of proving land ownership in the language and logic of American law, a process that required land surveys and drawn-out litigation in American courts. It was hardly in Hispanos' favor when Congress established the Office of Surveyor of New Mexico, which was woefully understaffed and often headed by notorious speculators. When the office called on Hispanos who were largely illiterate to bring proof of their grants before agents in Santa Fe, the farmers were helpless in fending off the disciples of legalistic, materialistic individualism.[25]

New Mexico was a land grabber's paradise where cunning men with some legal training could coin confusion. American justices of the peace and government surveyors often had poor understanding of, and little interest in learning about, Mexican land laws and customs. The voices of claimants fell on the ears of willfully deaf judges. The getting was good for those who were part of what many called the "Santa Fe Ring," a shadowy cabal of lawyers, judges, indispensable Hispano middlemen, sympathetic journalists, Masonic brothers, mercantile capitalists, and politicians (including nearly every governor of New Mexico's territory).[26]

George arrived in Mora Valley when the ring was just coming to light in the press. It reportedly traced back to the formation of the Republican Party in the territory. Its members dreamed of replacing what they saw as backward and primitive farming methods and stock raising with American ingenuity and private property.[27]

The ringleaders, Stephen B. Elkins and Thomas Catron, were attorneys, politicians, and devotees of the land grants. In 1873 (the year that George wrote his desperate last letters), Elkins and his friends helped European investors acquire the 1.7-million-acre Maxwell Grant and began evicting its inhabitants. The land that most interested Elkins and Catron, though, was the Mora Land Grant, an enormous, indeterminate expanse that encompassed much of the valley, including Fort Union. While George had lived in his cell, Elkins began acquiring portions of the grant in exchange for legal services for Hispanos. George wouldn't have known it when he arrived in New Mexico, but he lived on land that was half swallowed up by a scheme that, if successful, would constitute one of the nation's largest, and most flagrant, conspiracies in land speculation.[28]

Elkins had been freshly elected New Mexico's territorial delegate in the US Congress. If George wanted in on the grabbing, he had to gain his confidence. He was confident that Elkins would help with his plans. He also counted on getting help from a local Hispano judge named V. Romero, an agent for a gigantic swath of real estate called the Nolan Land Grant in Colorado. George, in some way that isn't clear, had helped Romero in legal matters and believed that it would earn him one-third interest in the Nolan Grant, which, he figured, was "really worth" millions. Its "gold & lead & silver" promised wealth, he wrote, "but the coal is the thing" that would make him a somebody. All he needed was to get his third and then wait a year for the railroad to reach the mines.[29]

The ailing veteran knew the drama. He was saying all the right lines. He asked Cornelius to tell Elkins to "send speeches," and to remind Elkins that George would try to "push him ahead." He asked his brother to "leave the wires laid" with some other important players in the schemes. Owning the land would turn his fortunes around. He would hold it for a time until he could entice "some capitalists to gobble it up." He would outsmart the moneyed speculators. Perhaps he could sell it to Butler, he added. "I can climb up here."[30]

George's last letters were the final spasms of failing ambition, like the twitching of an animal after its slaughter. He knew he was in decline and that the stench of failure followed a man through life. He worried that his poverty would doom his efforts. He was out of work, "in the dark," and nearly out of money. His clothes were too ragged to make himself "appear creditably even." How he wished, he said, that he could follow his brother's mantra that a man should "push [his] way to honor & position." He had exhausted his life pushing. Yet he sensed honor was beyond his grasp because "a poor Devil is in no way to win here."

George wanted to know if he was the reason for his own poverty. If he failed in New Mexico, he figured, he would at least "feel sure" that it had been God's will, as it clearly had not been his own. Perhaps he had not been free to determine his own destiny. If he needed to, he would accept his fate, and would gather his "scanty" possessions and move along to hire himself out again "to secure bread." He couldn't depend any longer on his nephew Captain Smith to feed him. Time was running out. "Ye Gods," he cried. "Can all my schemes end in smoke?"

In this last letter, he mentioned Butler one more time as a possible connection, then closed by saying that it made him curse to be "nailed fast" to his fate. He was trying in vain to make his mark but was forced to watch "progress coming like a RR train," chugging along only to "leave [him] by the wayside as it now looks." If George hadn't quite figured it out yet, "progress" was that irresistible cultural force that secured its grip on Americans not by delivering on its promises so much as by constantly threatening to leave its deepest believers behind.

CHAPTER 24

BURIED *on the* BROW *of a* HILL

GEORGE COLE NEEDED SOMEONE to believe in his "schemes" the same year that confidence in the American economy was turning to smoke. Five months after his frenzied letters, the Panic of 1873 began, one of the deepest depressions in American history.

How George got by for the next year is unclear. Even more unclear is how, by the summer of 1874, he scraped together nearly $1,200 to buy his first interests in a land grant. Mary Cole, who had a deep well of guilt, must have sent it to him from her dwindling estate. He bought what he believed was an "undivided fifth" of the 1,700-acre Agua Negra Grant, a property nearly one hundred miles south of Fort Union. It was a peculiar investment. Perhaps George figured he couldn't compete with capitalist combinations that sought property near the Colorado border and the approaching rail lines.[1]

IN LATE 1874, he reached out to the local Masons because he wanted into their secretive brotherhood.[2] He risked rejection. A new brother had to win unanimous approval through a secret ballot in which members slipped white or black balls into a box. A single black marble would sink his candidacy. Just months before, Thomas Morris, a soldier from the army post, had petitioned to join but was "black balled."[3]

Masons were supposed to only accept whole-bodied men because in their rituals a missing finger or foot diminished the symbolic power. George's hidden injuries were fortuitous. Nobody had to know about his asymmetrical rib cage, his jumbled bowels, or his occasional inability to feel his extremities. He appeared to be whole.[4]

His real problem would be what the brothers knew about the murder. Eddies of rumors from the sensationalized trials certainly followed him to the frontier. But if there was a place within America's expanse where a man could shed his past, George had found it. Recent arrivals in borderlands could assume new lives and reinvent themselves. Silence about past sins—not confession—was how man could be born again.

Maybe none of the Masons needed to be jawboned into looking past his checkered life. They had recently experienced a similar murder among their own. In the same year of Luther Harris Hiscock's murder, William Logan Rynerson, a war veteran in New Mexico (and a brevet lieutenant colonel), gunned down a justice of the territorial high court, shooting him in a hotel lobby in Santa Fe. Rynerson, who in a handful of years would ascend to grand Mason of all New Mexico, claimed self-defense. The "arm of the law," it was said, had pulled a Derringer on Rynerson first. George, though, had shot an unarmed attorney standing in his slippers.[5]

Despite George's past—or maybe because of it—in January 1875, the lodge's rawhide-handed soldiers and laborers voted him in on the first ballot.[6] He wasted no time, attending the monthly rituals to move up and through the first two degrees.

The lodge had been converted from a quartermaster's clerk office at Fort Union. In their "moonlight lodge," the fraternity performed initiation rituals once a month, on Saturday nights just before a full moon—so that after the late-night ceremonies the men could make their way home in the sulfur moonlight.

In March 1875, George journeyed to the lodge to be "raised" to a full Mason, the third and highest degree. The windows in the twenty-seven-inch-thick adobe walls were covered for secrecy. A man, armed with drawn sword, guarded the door. The ceremony ritual was as thick as the walls. George was stripped half naked and blindfolded while pretending to be the central character of the ceremony, Hiram Abiff, a master builder of the ancient Temple of Solomon. His brothers coiled a rope around his torso three times. He put on special aprons, learned secret sayings and hand grips, and knelt at an altar to kiss an ornate bible.

He was warned by the master Mason that on that night he would have to prove his reliance on God and on himself in the most trying ordeal. Somebody dimmed the lamps before soldiers playing jealous killers symbolically beat George to death; they pretended to crush his skull with a mallet and laid him in a makeshift imaginary grave made from chairs and tables.

After the participants declared that his rotting flesh had begun to stink, they pretended to carry George's corpse, laid out on a cloth stretcher, up a hillside and buried him on the "brow of the hill." They planted an evergreen sapling near his head to mark the secret spot. Eighteen hundred miles from his abandoned wife and daughters, George pretended to be a murdered worker from an ancient Hebrew temple. There he waited for some power or friend to symbolically resurrect him.

During the ceremony, George had been warned to curb his ambitions and to only measure brothers by character, not money. They made oaths to one another to never violate the chastity of one another's wives, daughters, and sisters. He learned that man had wrecked the world—and therefore needed straightening. The master Mason finally lifted George's rotting cadaver from the grave, raising him while drawing him close. The two men pressed their bodies together in a symbolic embrace of fraternity. Then, with cheek pressed to cheek, they whispered a secret phrase into each other's ears.[7]

As George returned to his bed that night, he could take comfort that he had found friends who swore on their lives to be true to him. His failing body was at last ensured a decent burial. He wouldn't have to worry that his cadaver would be abandoned or left in a shallow grave in the valley where it would be clawed up by coyotes. His brothers' hands would prepare his body. He would be given an honorable funeral.[8]

★

HIS FINAL YEAR OF LIFE is puzzling and sparse in detail. In the same period that he ascended the Masonic degrees, he made large purchases of land. Ten days after attaining the second degree, on February 10, 1875, he bought the remaining interests of the Agua Negra Grant from Luciano Roival.[9] George paid Roival an extraordinary sum of $6,000 for "four undivided fifths" of the grant. Added to his first "one-fifth" from the previous summer, George had supposedly become the sole owner of the distant Agua Negra Grant.[10]

A few days after he was raised to the third degree, he visited the county recorder twice and produced the contracts from his previous transactions, making official his ownership of the grant.[11]

It may not have been clear to him what he was buying or who the true owners of the contested land grants were. Negotiations were likely, at least in part, in Spanish. The lands were entangled in a skein of conflicting community memories, deeds, grants, and the designs of ring men. It appears that George had been taken. Either he held deeds from men who sold him land

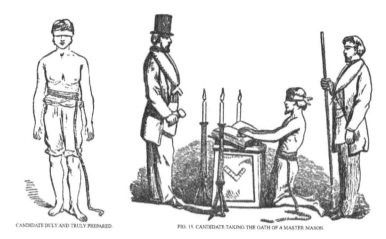

Illustrations of Masonic rituals. *Malcom C. Duncan*, Duncan's Masonic Ritual and Monitor, *1866. Public domain. Internet Sacred Text Archive, https://sacred-texts.com/mas/dun/dun04.htm*

FIG 18. MASTER GIVING THE GRAND MASONIC WORD ON THE FIVE POINTS OF FELLOWSHIP.

COFFIN, GRAVE, AND ACACIA

they did not own or, sometime after he died, those claims would be stolen by friends of friends. With the details lost in the confused historical records of clashing empires, time would not bring clarity. (His wife, Mary, and other family would learn this when years later they tried unsuccessfully to claim the lands.)[12]

There are no surviving letters from George in his final months and days. He may have believed that he had finally seized his main chance; that he had outstripped ring members and wire pullers by securing rights to an entire, if small and remote, land grant. There was a lucrative wool trade in that region; an investment there promised to rake in a fortune once the railroad cut its way down the middle of the New Mexican territory. If he could live that long, he could ship his wool or minerals to the markets in Old Mexico and the Southwest. As obsessed as he was with connections and exploiting markets, George had surely kept abreast of the wild schemes of American investors, including some Civil War generals, like William Rosecrans, who were buying up lands in Mexico and lobbying to connect the United States by rail to places like Mexico City, Veracruz, and Acapulco.[13]

George's injuries at last caught up with him. The Masonic rituals had warned him that men's days were numbered. A fellow doctor, and Mason who had participated in George's "raising," recalled that George had to administer daily shots to himself to stimulate his bowels into activity. Edwin Fox traveled to Mora and witnessed George's dying days. The General's "second wife"—most likely Eliza Bruce, the Black domestic worker who had lived with him in Washington, DC—came to nurse him sometime near the end.[14]

He moved to the small town of Mora about the time he requested to join the Masons. There is evidence that he began practicing medicine again. According to his obituary, and to his sister who made a pilgrimage to his grave decades later, he rented a space on the main street that he used as a doctor's office and storage for medicines. He was remembered for treating the town's poor for free.

★

ON DECEMBER 9, 1875, he died. The Masonic brothers posted an obituary in the local newspaper and sent word to Mary. Somebody obtained permission to have his body interred on a hill, right beside a small private cemetery where a prominent Mason from another lodge had been buried.

His funeral took place on the upper floor of the courthouse in Mora. In the eulogy, a master Mason moved through the ritualized questions. His cold words reverberated off cold walls.

"What man is he that liveth and shall not see death?"

"Man walketh in a vain shadow," the fellow Masons chanted back. "He heapeth up riches, and can not tell who shall gather them."

And when a man dies, added the master, "he shall carry nothing away; his glory shall not descend after him."

"Naked he came into the world, and naked he must return," the chorus droned.

When the rote phrases and gestures ended, the fraternity filed off toward the body. The same hands that had recently raised him fastened the white apron around the hips and groin of his cadaver, now three days stiff. The casket was probably marked with Masonic signs—a builder's compass, a square, perhaps a pentagram.[15]

With the corpse in tow, in the crisp December air, a train of white-gloved men, led by a man gripping a drawn sword, clambered up a foothill set against the abrupt face of the nearby Sangre de Cristo Mountains—a chain of peaks to the west that early Spanish colonizers had named after the blood of Christ. A man carried the Holy Bible on a cushion draped with black cloth.[16] Once the men reached the hilltop cemetery, overlooking the Mora Valley, they formed a hollow square around the hole, standing in their Masonic aprons.

The presiding Mason again mined life lessons from death. "Here we view a striking instance of the uncertainty of life and the vanity of all human pursuits," he warned. Frightening death awaited every man. Yet, he said, "through some unaccountable infatuation, we forget that we are born to die. We go on from one design to another."

The master warned onlookers to fix their eyes on the pitiful end at hand—and to hear the silence of the grave. Maybe then they would "be convinced of the futility of those empty delusions." He continued, "In the grave, all fallacies are detected, all ranks are leveled, and all distinctions are done away." The tomb would erase all the work that men had done to outpace their fellows.

Not every tomb. An elaborate grave on the same hilltop belonged to Ceran St. Vrain, an esteemed Mason who had been a successful newspaper editor, fur trader, and millowner. After St. Vrain had brutally crushed an uprising of Hispanos and Taos Indians in the 1840s, he made a fortune selling flour and supplies to the US military fort. The hilltop was his land.[17]

The Masons dropped sprigs of evergreen onto the General's remains and filed down the hill. They did not provide a headstone; the rough-hewn rocks they used to cover his grave contrasted sharply with the stonework in the cemetery. George's resting place did not seem like a place of rest. Strangely, the men had dug the grave so that his corpse would teeter, in a kind of eternal disquietude, on the brow of the hill. They buried their troubled brother on a slant, like Hiram Abiff from the ritual, as if telling George that he would have to wait again for a brother to raise him and whisper the secrets.

The tilted remains of George Washington Cole still lie on the brow of that hill. His family later had a gravestone placed at his head. It proudly bears the name of his Black regiment, the Second United States Colored Cavalry, etched beneath his name and his military title. The experiment with the Black army had brought him his greatest worldly honors. It likely gave him the only path he had to reach *actual* colonel. His Black soldiers brought him face-to-face with the most profound contradictions of American freedom. Today, their colonel, and the stone that bears the name of their regiment, lies a few feet outside a fence that encloses St. Vrain's graveyard, a place reserved for the family and friends of men who proved their worth.[18]

EPILOGUE

In 1873, the year that George Cole penned his most desperate letters, Cornelius and Olive Cole buried their three-year-old son, Frederick. Reeling in grief, Cornelius sought help from a renowned spiritualist, Charles Foster. He met with him in a Sacramento hotel and at least once convinced Olive to join him. Cornelius had strayed from the Methodist path and had come to doubt there was an afterlife. He wanted to believe Foster's claims yet worried that his grief made him susceptible to chicanery. During the séances, he grew convinced of Foster's powers. The dead were speaking with him. He learned that his ancestors and deceased siblings were well; they said they were watching over little Freddy.

The séances moved from family matters to political connections. Cornelius began receiving messages from a man described by Foster as an imposing, broad-shouldered figure who had been "badly shot." Cornelius first believed it to be Senator David Broderick, who had died in a duel; but Cornelius never liked Broderick's politics and soon learned that instead it was an antislavery colleague, a bullet-gashed E. D. Baker, the only senator who had been slain on a Civil War battlefield.

Cornelius continued these communications after George's death. In one séance, George's spirit emerged and invited

Cornelius to pose a question. "Dear George," Cornelius responded. "Have I a good or poor prospect for worldly prosperity & happiness or not?" George, who was flanked by two deceased men—one linked to hotel money in California—assured his brother likely success. "I will tell you how it looks to me," George said through Foster. "To me your chances are about 4 in a scale of 5." The other two spirits concurred. The race of life continued into the next realm.[1]

HALF A DECADE AFTER GEORGE'S DEATH, Mary Cole began writing despairing letters to Cornelius. She claimed she badly needed a widow's pension and didn't say where all her money had gone. She needed George's closest friends to testify that his war wounds had killed him and that he had "entered the army an unusually strong man and left it a perfect wreck, mentally and physically." Unfortunately for her, his wounds had not been clearly documented in official records, and she couldn't track down the transcripts from the trials. "I believe women are nothing but a trouble," she wrote.

She spent decades troubling other men to help her get a pension that was doomed to be rejected. Her youngest daughter, Alice, died in her late thirties. Mary said that she grew sick from "anxiety about our affairs." Mary eventually moved, with her senile mother, to Milwaukee to live with her oldest girl, Fannie, who wore her life out caring for her aging mother and grandmother. Fannie had married a traveling salesman, Jack Brown, who sold cigar boxes door to door. When Fannie died in 1910, in her midfifties, Jack sent Mary to a sanatorium, where she died the same year.[2]

★

EDWIN FOX, George's orderly and nurse after the fall, had personal knowledge about George's injury that Mary needed in her pension application.

Fox struggled after the war like many White officers who had served in the Black military.[3] Before the war he had been trained as a machinist; he and his family expected a bright future. But he returned home a shattered killer with bloody hemorrhoids, a torn shoulder, and an eardrum that had been blown out at Bull Run (he learned to read lips). His aunt would testify to his demise. "One thing is certain," she said, "he came from the war with a broken constitution, sickly, nervous and irritable." The sweet nephew who left for war was not the man who returned from war. Her "charming, bright, healthy boy who left home" was as different from "the wreck" he returned "as day was from night."[4]

Fox came back to Rochester after Benjamin Butler dismissed him and soon discovered that he didn't belong at home. After he went to Southeast Texas to be with his old regiment, and George and the troops mustered out of service, Fox crossed the border into Matamoros to serve as a commander in the Mexican Army.[5]

He drifted the rest of his life from New York to the Mexican borderlands. In Southern California he lived in a home with some widows who helped him get by. He applied in vain for a pension starting in the 1880s. He had a reputation as a "cutthroat" and "desperado" in El Paso where he made subsistence money hauling and trading scrap wood across the Mexican border. Though he ended his time in the US Army as a second lieutenant, he was known in Southern California as Colonel Edwin Fox.

In the final years of his life, he sent furious, rambling letters to the federal government insisting that he had only been doing his duty when he executed Henry Edwards Jr. below the plum trees.[6]

★

EDWARDS'S BODY WAS NOT returned to his illiterate father, Henry Sr., and his mother, Hannah, who were still enslaved on a plantation in North Carolina. Edwards had somehow sent some or all of his soldiering money to help his parents and his younger siblings—two sisters, Margaret and Lizzie, and three brothers, Solomon, Drew, and Jack. The family seems to have not known for decades exactly what happened to their son and brother who never returned.[7]

A few of Edwards's comrades leveraged their war sacrifice into successful postwar careers, joining many hundreds of formerly enslaved men who, in the hopeful years of Reconstruction, were elected to local and national public office. Many of George's soldiers, though, dissolved into lives of obscurity and poverty. Their pension records offer glimpses into their struggles during and after the war: the often fruitless search for a White officer who remembered them and was willing to testify of their wounds; their struggle to find steady work; their bloody hemorrhoids; and most especially their suffering during their service in Texas.[8] Mostly filed some twenty to thirty years after the war, their pensions bear testimony to distressed freedom after the bold work of Reconstruction was abandoned.

BENJAMIN BUTLER had tirelessly fought so that the work of Reconstruction would not be abandoned. The war had changed him into a defender of the enslaved and the newly freed. Once, after a failed charge outside Petersburg, he was moved by the faces of his Black soldiers strewn in death poses on the ground. White soldiers, he wrote, had "patriotism, fame, love of country, pride, ambition" to spur them on. But the dead Black soldiers—

their determined faces turning "ghastly tawny blue"—were driven into the teeth of death by the pure love of freedom.[9]

He admired them and joined with Radical Republicans to ensure that the blood of Union soldiers had not been spilled in vain. He and Republicans empowered the Freedmen's Bureau to protect the rights of freedpeople; they carved up the defeated South into occupied military districts to ensure a new birth of freedom. They were freed families' staunchest allies.

Unrepentant Confederates, though, countered with brutality and terror. By the time of George's death in 1875, even President Ulysses S. Grant—ever determined like Butler to convert war deaths into meaningful freedom—had grown weary of protecting Southern Blacks from cyclical terror and intimidation. Within two years of George's death, the last Federal troops were pulled from the South, leaving freedpeople to fend for themselves in what would become some of the darkest days of Black American life.

In one of America's most tragic ironies, Reconstruction was abandoned, in part, because of intense loathing for men like Butler. In less than a decade after the war, many Republicans believed that formerly enslaved Americans had become dependent pawns of southern Republican governments that were accused of corruption, runaway taxes, and gross budgetary mismanagement. The new Liberal Republican Party concluded that Southern freedmen, like Irish immigrants in New York City and Boston, needed to work out their own destiny. The term "Butlerism" was used to decry any alliance, north or south, between the dispossessed and politicians who seemed to promise special favors for political loyalty. As one critic wrote in a Boston newspaper, Butlerism was an appeal to the "sordid motives of men" who believed that political duties should bring "prompt reward from the henchmen whom they serve."[10]

Unfairly, Butler's reputation for graft and cronyism eclipsed his remarkable record of protecting the civil rights of America's weak. (It didn't help his reputation when, in the decade following the war, he built a political machine in Massachusetts from men largely drawn from his war staff.)[11] Butler's name, as much as any other, evoked fears of self-dealing and special favors. It became shorthand for the alarmism that sealed the death of Reconstruction.[12] In 1877, the party of freedom and self-made manhood abandoned millions of Black Southerners because it believed that they had been given ample time to prove themselves.[13]

In 1887, Butler published an advice letter to young men on how to obtain wealth. It was printed a second time alongside similar essays in a book entitled *How to Get Rich*. By this last decade of his life, he had amassed dizzying wealth from his legal practice, his ownership of textile and lumber mills, and his concerns in the manufacturing of ammunition and American flags. He owned quarries and coal and mineral interests. "He lives well," the book's introduction claimed, "is very generous and has one of the finest yachts on the Massachusetts coast." Butler advised young men to put their money into improved property and reap the cumulative rewards of a landlord.[14]

Butler bolted from the Republican Party when he concluded it had aligned itself with monopolists and corporate interests. He believed both Republicans and Democrats were enslaved to the same national ring. He ran for president in 1884 as a Greenback Party candidate, hoping to unite the nation's Black and White laborers against capitalists, but lost in humiliating fashion. Nearly blind, and with his political career finished, he spent his waning energies dictating to an aid his massive autobiography—most of which forcefully defended his time in uniform.[15]

On his last day of life, he visited the Washington, DC, office of Secretary of War Stephen B. Elkins, the accomplished land-grabber who had wrested the Mora Land Grant from its New

Mexican inhabitants. This was the same Elkins who, twenty years earlier, George had written about enthusiastically in his final flurry of letters.[16] Elkins had helped form the Santa Fe Ring made up of lawyers, politicians, and speculators, many affiliated with the Santa Fe Masonic lodge. (George had belonged to the humbler lodge associated with Fort Union soldiers.)

Elkins and his friends had sold the Mora Land Grant, some six hundred thousand acres, to Butler and his family, adding to Butler's vast tracts of western lands, especially in Colorado. George had been right that Butler would have wanted in on the land grabbing.[17]

It is doubtful that Butler or Elkins knew there was a little hill on the Mora Land Grant where George Cole had been buried. Even in his grave, George could not escape his old commander or the grasp of ring men.[18]

Butler died in his Washington, DC, mansion with his beloved Black servant tending to him. Black Americans, Irish Americans, aging veterans, women's rights advocates, and members of the labor movement mourned his passing.[19] His family buried him beneath a stately granite monument. They etched on it one of his most cherished sayings:

> THE TRUE TOUCHSTONE OF CIVIL LIBERTY
> IS NOT THAT ALL MEN ARE EQUAL
> BUT THAT EVERY MAN HAS THE RIGHT TO BE
> THE EQUAL OF EVERY OTHER MAN—IF HE CAN

Butler died one of the staunchest champions of dispossessed Americans. He proved himself a lifelong adversary to privilege and exploitative powers. Yet he boiled liberty down to a contest between men who were required to prove their equality. His epitaph captured America's greatest, and least interrogated, paradox: the country's dual devotion to equality and self-making turns even its most compassionate actors into guardians of earned inequality.

★

WHEN I DECIDED to find George Cole's grave years ago, I only knew that it was in northern New Mexico, on a hill overlooking Mora Valley.

I consulted two photocopied pictures of his youngest sister, Mary Cole Stewart, posing beside the grave. In 1910, sister Mary, who had been a witness in the trial, had made a pilgrimage to find his resting place. She was an old woman by then. In one photograph, she kneels at his grave, a look of pity and reverence on her plump face. She had decorated his grave with two American flags by jamming the wood dowels into the crevices between the crystal rocks that covered him. She had lovingly tucked a small bunch of wildflowers into the rocks over his head.[20]

She must have located his resting place during her research in New Mexico into what had happened to George's murky claims to land grants. Perhaps she had some clues from her nephew Gilbert Cole Smith, the soldier who kept George fed in his lowest times around Fort Union. A village local probably led her to the place, as it had no headstone at the time.

With the help of Google Maps and the photocopies at hand, I drove with my dear friend Bryan through hailstorms and rain on I-25. We were on a quest into the enchanted and sparsely populated plateau where America's high plains cede to the jutting Sangre de Cristo Mountains.

Before I disclose what happened when I found George's grave, I want to be clear about my state of mind. I knew that his loved ones had understandably wanted to tell his story in a way that rescued him from his pitiful end. There were hopeful scraps to cling to. After her visit to find George's grave, sister Mary wrote that in his final days he returned to the art of medicine and cared for the poor. She wrote on the back of

In 1910 Mary Cole Stewart, George's baby sister, trekked across the United States to New Mexico to honor the unmarked grave of her brother. The grave lies just on the brow of the small hill; one can see the sudden sloping downward at the very edge of his grave, which is clearly set apart from the cemetery atop the hill. *UCLA Library Special Collections*

one of the grave photographs that she had learned from locals that when George died, there was an outpouring in Mora village. "It was the largest and saddest funeral ever there."

A generation after George's death, a nephew wrote that the General was his "ideal of a man—poet, soldier, and physician." He wished that God would still make his kind. Compared with George, men everywhere seemed "selfish and full of self-centered ambition."[21]

I wanted it to be true. After Bryan (not I) discovered on microfilm that George had joined the Masons before his death, I imagined the lodge rituals and stern warnings shaking George from his delusions. A broken soldier, a strayed Methodist boy— the story might have gone—had been driven to a kind of madness by the American race of life but was transformed in the final hour. He was poetically buried in a valley nested within mountains named after the blood of Christ.

I didn't believe the story I wanted to tell. I suspected that he had died with voices still hectoring him to grasp for more. I concluded that he had gotten the money for his dubious shares in the land grant from guilt-ridden Mary Cole, who by the end of her life seems to have lost her entire fortune.

I knew from the sources that I had to tell a bleak story, not only about the troubled American whose grave I was tracking down but about the larger national forces that had shaped him. To my mind, America is the greatest social and political experiment in the history of the world; I cherish the ideals of freedom and equality and feel indebted to the Union soldiers—and the self-made president who presided over their fates—who rescued the United States from ruin and, in so doing, altered the fate of nearly four million Americans in bondage.

Even so, America's halting, but world-changing, commitment to equality and meritocracy, shored up by Abraham Lincoln, presents one of the most vexing moral problems in the modern world. I can't conceive of a better system of organizing society than by the tests of merit. The meritocratic creed is nearly irresistible; it appears to be aligned with nature and to have no reasonable alternative. For these reasons, it is rarely questioned as an ideal. The meritocratic creed so rife in the nineteenth century did not get eradicated or purified by some inevitable march toward progress. Instead, it has spread through corporate culture, modern sports, political rhetoric (particularly from the moderate left), and, especially, prestigious universities—the modern temples of merit.

In his striking work *The Tyranny of Merit*, Michael Sandel demonstrates how American meritocracy in the past thirty years has functioned as a vast sorting machine that creates its own credentialed, hereditary ruling class; it diminishes the worth of poor or less educated citizens; and it devalues ordinary work. It perversely maps worth onto station. Think of it this way: meritocracy is a uniquely problematic ideal in that the closer a society comes to reaching this seemingly beautiful end, the more morally repulsive its outcomes. What would it mean to live in a society whose citizens have somehow truly come to deserve their inequality, their success and failure, their wealth or poverty?[22]

★

AS WE DROVE TOWARD GEORGE COLE'S GRAVE, I was wrestling with the problems of merit—and its relationship to freedom, ambition, community, individualism, and the measure of the self. I had recently experienced, in an inconsequential way, the pain of unrealized ambition. For two years I had been on the market trying to land a job as a history professor. After I finished extensive research that would become part of this book, I sent out hundreds of applications. I had worked hard for my university credentials and was eager for life's rewards.

When I almost landed several jobs but came up short each time, I began to wonder if I'd ever find employment in my field. When I barely missed my shot at a prestigious university, I began nursing self-pity. On one hand, I doubted that I was worthy of the job; on the other, I was smitten by my own self-made story: I had barely made it through public high school; my father had no college degree; my mother and I worked an early-morning paper route to help make ends meet. "Son of a tire salesman turned Ivy League professor." It was a precious conceit, one hard to resist because I had come to believe in the central tenet of meritocracy: success and failure were reflections of one's value to society.

I had suffered no serious setback or meaningful loss; no injury, insult, or discrimination. Still, as so often happens in any supposed meritocracy, once faced with a record of failure, I teetered between self-loathing and nursing grudges against a rigged system.[23]

My petty problems helped me glimpse how a man like George Cole could have been so driven by the delusions of self-making. I was beginning to make out some of the broader connections in George's story: the promotion-begging letters everywhere in the army; the flood of brevets; the daguerrean galleries; the keen focus among women's rights advocates on selfhood; the theology that men were the makers of their own destinies; the men who saw rings everywhere except in their own circle of friends; the contempt for dependence in refugees; the White officers' disregard for the bonds of community within enslaved families.

These all seemed to hang together, to be connected to a pervasive worldview in which more and more Americans, no longer subject to unjust constraints of inherited station, stumbled into the beauty and confusion of freedom, unaware of its new moral traps. When bundled with a new Christian theology and the disfiguring powers of the marketplace, this new American freedom rendered its citizens less capable of respecting parts of every human life: the mystery of fate, ordinary work, weakness, and cradle-to-grave dependence.

WHEN BRYAN AND I ARRIVED in Mora Valley, we pulled over on the side of the road. I was dizzy with anticipation. With my photocopied pictures in hand, we spent a few hours comparing the mountain lines while we swept through decaying graveyards and trespassed private fields. We climbed over fences and clambered through icy, muddy gullies. My pants got tangled in barbed wire. After regrouping and starting from another angle, we eventually found ourselves standing at the foot of a hill that seemed to have a graveyard, enclosed in wire fence, on its crown. It had to be where they buried him!

I started up the hill to see the grave. Bryan stayed back. He probably knew I was after something that I'd never find. I had openly fantasized about readers of my book someday posting a sign on a nearby road that reads, "Here lies George Washington Cole, a true American." Maybe students of American culture, or those who had been dinged by failure, would make a pilgrimage to glimpse a true relic of America's founding faith.

I morbidly fantasized that if we could just open his casket, we might find George with a tattered copy of *Amelia* on his chest, or a love letter from Mary, or her picture, somehow preserved atop a heap of bones and a Masonic apron. Then I could tell the most compelling story! Maybe that would land me a job.

I walked up through the brown scrub oak and frozen weeds, dreaming as I went. When I reached the grave, I stood there panting thin air, staring at the jumble of rocks.

There was no voice speaking from the grave. There would be no traces of *Amelia*. The flags placed by his sister were gone. The stones piled on him were covered with dull gray and green lichen. His grave, placed just outside the fence, seemed to be slipping down the sorry hill. It was anticlimactic. I felt blunt sadness.

Who was this man? What was it that I hoped to find here?

"George Washington Cole . . . ," I said to the pile of rocks. "Those spirits, those voices you heard, that long ago taunted you and goaded you—to this hill. . . . They drove me here too."

NOTES

Prologue

1. I have used, and will use, dozens of accounts to sketch out what happened around the time of the slaying. See RTAC; NYW, 6/7/1867; NYH, 6/7/1867, various testimonies; and LN, 6/12/1867. Also see TS, 6/6/1867. The story I tell will reflect the general narrative taken from various newspaper reports and the court record.
2. The timing and meaning of the "market revolution" has provoked fierce debate among historians. Like John Lauritz Larson, I believe the "tipping point" happened in antebellum America and that it brought extraordinary material prosperity and hope for many, even as it disturbed, dislocated, and exploited new populations. By the eve of the Civil War, though, many who benefited from it materially had profound worries about its effects on American society. See MRA.
3. Read more about the revolution's long legacy and its seminal commitment to self-making in, ‡.
4. The questions I ask in this book were inspired long ago by a seminal essay from Edward Ayers: WACW.
5. For starters, see the works of Frances M. Clarke (WS), Drew Gilpin Faust (ROS), and James Oakes (FN).

Chapter 1. America, Republic without Grace

1. For more on the potent, widespread effects of revolutionary mythology, ‡.
2. For more on how a young George Cole would have learned about land, money, and ideal manhood from his childhood environment, ‡.

3. James Madison, "The Federalist No. 10," *New York Packet*, November 23, 1787, Library of Congress, https://guides.loc.gov/federalist-papers/text-1-10.
4. For more on the revolution, meritocracy, and ambition, ‡.
5. MRA, esp. 98–140.
6. MCC, 1-9-2; CCCP, 13; ‡.
7. According to a short sketch of George's life (written after his death, probably by Cornelius); see UB, 1–6.
8. Luther Hiscock had a similar education. ‡.
9. AOA, 36–37; CMC, 169–70.
10. AOA, 1–48; MMS, 228–57.
11. MCC, 1–2; CCCP, 16–19. A short biography about George says that he labored "severely" on his father's farm in the summer and attended school in the winters, though it is unclear to which phase of George's schooling this refers. In later years he walked three miles each way daily to attend his village school. See UB, 1–2.
12. For more on education in antebellum America and self-made men, ‡.
13. *Blackwood's* magazine, quoted in MMS, 246. Also see MMS, 226, 228–29, 230–33, 235, 244.
14. ACFA, 17–23.
15. CRJG. ‡. This is the earliest direct source by George Cole that I have been able to locate.
16. CRJG.
17. CRJG.
18. RF. For more on friendship and ambition in early America, ‡.
19. For more on Calvinism and grace, ‡.
20. For more on revivals around the Erie Canal, ‡.
21. SFN, 1–24, 135–40.
22. For more on the Cole family religion, ‡.
23. For more on methodism and American ambition, ‡.
24. SOE, 9–12. For more on Fisk's tenure and curricula he implemented, ‡.
25. For more on this shift toward business, ‡.
26. WU, 32.
27. CCCP, 19–21.
28. EP, 13, 14, 15. For more on Olin, ‡.
29. EP, 16, 19.
30. EP, 22–23.

31. EP, 29–30.
32. EP, 30, 24.
33. HWB. While denouncing these spirits, the preacher, Henry Bellows, celebrated that a system of merit helped fill all of the republic's stations.

Chapter 2. To See Ourselves as Others See Us

1. CCCP, 54–55. This may be because of the antislavery sentiments of their "tender hearted mother." ‡.
2. MCC, chap. 3.
3. MCC, 11.
4. Mary Barto claimed that her husband had practiced medicine in her town of Trumansburg starting in 1849. See PRGWC, December 1882, affidavit of Mary Cole.
5. For descriptions of Mary, see AEJ, 6/6/1867; TS, 6/13/1867; and CC, 6/13/1867. For more about her birth, ‡.
6. GVAS, 394–96. For more on family, ‡.
7. EHH, 101, 113–16, 120, 131; ‡.
8. UB, 2; RTAC, 213.
9. HJ. See almost any issue from 1852 to late 1854. For more on his store and images of inventory he purchased for it, ‡.
10. For this transition to acquisitive liberalism and the flood of objects, see especially ROA, TRR, and NNG. For more on this refinement in frontier villages and the centrality of possessions, ‡.
11. ROA, xiv; ‡.
12. ROA, 405–7. See advertisement for George's store in HJ, years 1852–54; ‡.
13. One sees the crucial place of owning books in popular books themselves. ‡.
14. MCC, 10–11.
15. ROA, 270–78; ‡.
16. HJ, 4/30/1853; CAC, 102–3.
17. ER, 5/5/1852.
18. Advertisement in HJ, years 1852–54.
19. For other images pertaining to Cole's gallery, including Brown's advertisement, ‡.
20. HJ, years 1852–54.
21. SJ, 4/25/1868; EHH, 12, 22, 183–84.
22. MRF.

23. For more on the agricultural colleges and new technologies celebrated in the new farming sciences, ‡. For the kinds of crops grown at midcentury, see MRF, 366.
24. SJ, 4/25/1868.
25. ROA, chap. 9, esp. 309–12.

Chapter 3. The False Dawn of Seneca Falls

1. The family seems to have been firmly in the Democratic camp, largely opposed to reform. ‡.
2. See IEL; and MWA, esp. 93–135.
3. For more on the property acts, ‡.
4. IEL, 187–97; ‡.
5. IEL, 200–207; ‡.
6. IEL, 209–12.
7. RT, 6/10/1867.
8. See LWTHB; ‡.
9. LWTHB: Because the father detailed an alternate way of supporting his wife (Mary's mother), one might conclude that his plans for the rest of the money were deliberate.
10. LWTHB.
11. RTAC, 214–15.
12. RTAC, 214–15; SJ, 4/25/1868; UB, 1–2.
13. SDS, 11/3/1851.
14. LSSO, 266–67. For more on the office of surrogate and its amenability to corruption, see SDJ, 10/29/1851.
15. See obituary in SDC&U, 2/26/1861.
16. Quote here and next paragraph in SDC&U, 5/3/1861.
17. Lincoln "race of life" quote from his address to Congress, in ALSW, 259; messages to Union troops, 623–24, 626–27. LEAD, esp. chap. 19; BL, 189–225. Jim Cullen argues that at the end of the war Lincoln backed away somewhat from the belief that men controlled their fate. AD, 92–102. More on self-making and the war, ‡.
18. MOC; FSFL, 291–300.
19. Nobody captures this crucial change in America's "categories of human worth"—from freedom and slavery to winners and losers—better or more beautifully than Scott Sandage: see BL, 189–225. Though perhaps dated, see PHD for a provocative case that the Civil War served as a pressure valve for mounting ambitions in antebellum America. ‡.

20. For more on war and gender, ‡.
21. IEL, 207; ‡; FPR, 81–84.
22. Office of the Country Clerk in Syracuse County Court House, New York. See Deeds and Mortgages, in Deed Books, 1799–1933. Mary shows up on dozens of mortgagor and mortgagee records, before and during the war. George's name appears on only some of them.

Chapter 4. Fog of War

1. For a more detailed account of this early disaster, ‡.
2. For an account of a soldier who was representative, if unusually eloquent, in his obsession with how his organization was depicted in the papers, see MRFR.
3. Soldiers wanting out are discussed in the article "War Correspondence" in SDS, 9/18/1861; letter to Brig. Gen. Stoneman, chief of cavalry, 8/26/1861, in CSRGWC, 12th New York Volunteers. ‡.
4. See letter signed by Walrath and Simon Mix in CSRGWC.
5. His company became Company K; it brought some confusion in the records because another captain in Company G, named "George W.," transferred with his infantry to the regiment. ‡.
6. UCCW, xi–xii; MRCW, 11–18. For more on perceptions of calvary, ‡.
7. ROS, chap. 4, esp. 119–29. I am indebted to David L. Burrows for helping me figure out, after years of misdirection, that this object, written about and partly described by someone who later found it, had been an identification disc and not a medal. ‡.
8. Comrade quoted in TKS, 80–82.
9. PCCJ, esp. chap. 6.
10. See WAE; atrocities claimed by John Timmerman in PCCJ, chap. 6.
11. George's fall is best described in dozens of testimonies found in RTAC, and in court transcriptions in local newspapers. See especially the accounts of Guy David and others in SJ, 4/25/1868; also see affidavit by Lodewick Wooden in PRGWC.
12. NYH, 6/7/1867; PRGWC, various affidavits; ‡.
13. For his wounds and related problems, see various testimonies and affidavits throughout PRGWC and RTAC; and ‡.
14. For more on these raids, ‡.
15. New York soldier Charles Mosher quoted in CMCW, 114–15; ‡.
16. SJ, 7/11/1863.
17. Many of these accomplishments, not the darker aspects, were reported in NYH, 12/20/1862.

Chapter 5. George Washington, Town Destroyer

1. CSRGWC, Third New York Cavalry; ‡.
2. See nearly every entry in JME. For more about Sullivan's Raid, ‡. The powerful lust for the land is undeniable throughout the soldiers' diaries.
3. Cornplanter quoted in HATP, 156–57.
4. MCC, 6–7; CCCP, 14; SWL, 1–6. For more on relics and George's neighborhood, ‡.
5. MCC, 7. For more on the violence and lust for land, ‡.
6. I could not have told the story that follows without the careful contextual work of David Norris and others. See DANPR; DANTY; and CWNC, 162–67.
7. Correspondent quoted in WSJ, 9/1/1863. See also WSJ, 8/12/1863.
8. DANPR, 100; WD, 8/12/1863 and 7/28/1863. See also CWN, 7/24/1863.
9. OR, ser. 1, vol. 20, pt. 2, p. 970. The citizens later joined with Southern soldiers to salvage the bridge. Potter's Raid may have been one of the most daring raids in eastern North Carolina. Yet, because of timing and other factors, it was largely ignored in the press. For more on this, ‡.
10. OR, ser. 1, vol. 27, pt. 2, p. 968; CWN, 7/24/1863; WD, 7/28/1863.
11. Report of Col. S. L. Fremont in OR, ser. 1, vol. 27, pt. 2, p. 976.
12. NYT, 7/25/1863.
13. NYT, 7/25/1863; VC, 89–113.
14. WD, 7/14/1863.
15. The raiders' focus on women's and their children's clothing was unmistakable. In a similar raid in August, other soldiers dashed mirrors and slashed paintings, then "tore up the ladies' and children's clothing." WSJ, 8/12/1863.
16. White and Black soldiers had distinct but overlapping reasons to steal Confederate women's clothing. For more on clothing in refugee camps and the different treatment of male refugees and their families, see EF, 157–73. ‡.
17. UMH, 7/23/1863; CWN, various clippings; DANPR, 140–41.
18. CFP, George Cole to Cornelius, 11/20/1863.
19. DANPR, 139–40.
20. OR, ser. 1, vol. 27, pt. 2, pp. 970–71.

21. See OR, ser. 1, vol. 27, pt. 2, pp. 968–69; and DANTY, 20–21. Also see various clippings, especially CWN, "The Great Cavalry Raid in North Carolina." Like so many soldiers in battle, George was confused in his own reports about the specifics of the raid; ‡.
22. Nearly four decades later, Ellington provided a detailed account of the event as if it had been burned into his mind. His quotes can be found in HSR, 3:174–75.
23. KJC, 13; HSR, 3:174–75.
24. HSR, 3:174–75. Though Ellington said the soldier was a captain, Black men could not become captains except in extremely rare cases. Perhaps Ellington confused an ordinary soldier for an officer. The man may have been a White officer over the Black troops as well. Ellington recalled this even decades later; the detail he recalls, though, is striking.
25. Ellington quotes in HSR, 3:174–75. Another vague report stated that both "Yankees and negroes" had been killed in the violence. See WSJ, 7/29/1863; WD, 7/28/863.
26. See CWN, *Utica Morning Herald*, 7/23/1863, and "Fourth Day's Advance" in "The Great Cavalry Raid in North Carolina."
27. Quotes from George's official report. See OR, ser. 1, vol. 27, pt. 2, pp. 970–71.
28. OR, ser. 1, vol. 27, pt. 2, pp. 970–71.
29. A New York reporter wrote that besides the Union's persistent problems with rebels at the rear, "several times before they arrived at Newbern they were compelled to cut their way through vastly superior numbers." CWN, *Utica Morning Herald*, 7/23/1863.
30. OR, ser. 1, vol. 27, pt. 2, pp. 965–66.
31. NYT, 8/5/1863; DANPR, 121–22, 141. For Black guides, ‡.
32. KJC, 13; WSJ, 7/29/1863, several places; WD, 7/28/1863.
33. ‡. Confederate reports confirm that rebel soldiers anticipated discarded booty when they chased Yankee soldiers after raids. WJ, 8/27/1863. Also see HSR, 4:80–81.
34. HSR, 3:174–75.
35. Quote from WSJ, 8/5/1863. The fate could have been execution. For a letter revealing one master's intention to hang a refugee who had betrayed him, see DANPR, 140.
36. For George's official report, see OR, ser. 1, vol. 27, pt. 2, pp. 970–71. Also see CWN, "Our Army Correspondence," 7/24/1863, esp. "Fourth Day's Advance."

37. SJ, 7/27/1863. In other New York papers, there is no mention of how the contrabands were lost to the Confederates. Nor is much said about the plundering. But in one account it is mentioned that gold and some $40,000 in North Carolina scrip were taken from Southerners. See NYT, 8/5/1863.
38. For more on the absolute dependence of Union raiders on the local knowledge of enslaved people and freedpeople in the area, ‡.

Chapter 6. Below the Beast

1. AD, 61–65.
2. Butler's brother was named after America's self-made president, Andrew Jackson.
3. For our purposes, the Army of the James is the term used to describe the evolving military structures in southeast Virginia and coastline North Carolina from 1863 until 1865. ‡.
4. I am deeply indebted to Edward Longacre and his various publications about the Army of the James. I am more interested in contemporary perceptions of the army than actual military contributions. See EGLAOA, xi. And for disagreement about the importance of the Army of the James, ‡.
5. On the incompetence of the Army of the James, ‡.
6. EGLAOA, 45.
7. EGLAOA, xi–xii; ALSW, 258–59.
8. For more on trying to remove Butler, ‡. Also, for more on Butler before he commanded the AOJ, ‡.
9. CSRGWC.
10. There is a trace of the lawsuit against George in SNYDC, 1/27/1864, "Philander W. Fobes vs. George Cole."
11. Butler response found in CMGWC.
12. BB, 63.
13. CMGWC.
14. On his complaints about inconsistent seniority rules and his attempts to get what he thought was his earned seniority, see CWHC, 33–35; CSRGWC; and ‡.
15. CFP, George Cole to Cornelius Cole, 11/20/1863. The date on the letter is not fully legible. It could be 11/29.
16. CFP, George Cole to Cornelius Cole, 11/20/1863.
17. Davis quote in EDW, 14–15; CFP, George Cole to Cornelius Cole, 11/20/1863.

18. CFP, George Cole to Cornelius Cole, 11/20/1863.
19. CFP, George Cole to Cornelius Cole, 11/20/1863.
20. ‡; CFP, George Cole to Cornelius Cole, 11/20/1863.
21. CFP, George Cole to Cornelius Cole, 11/20/1863.
22. For more on pipelaying, ‡.
23. H. W. Halleck to John M. Schofield, 11/28/1862, in OR, ser. 1, vol. 22, pt. 1, pp. 793–94; "little better than murder" in OR, ser. 1, vol. 34, pt. 3, pp. 332–33.
24. ‡; H. W. Halleck to John M. Schofield, 11/28/1862, in OR, ser. 1, vol. 22, pt. 1, pp. 793–94.

Chapter 7. Tears for Uncle Tom

1. CFP, George Cole to Cornelius Cole, 11/20/1863.
2. I will draw from this rich, effusive letter extensively. CFP, George Cole to Cornelius Cole, 2/15/1864, 2/16/1864.
3. The Confederates, who lived in the shadow of Fort Monroe and who could not keep enslaved people from running to the fort, which was soundly in the hands of the Union army, decided to bolt northward into Virginia and destroy possible living quarters for Black people or Yankee soldiers.
4. PI, 8/8/1861.
5. ‡; BFB, 130–34; FFG, 33–34. See the full General Order No. 46, published in NYT, 12/12/1863. Also see CR, 2/13/1864.
6. CFP, George Cole to Cornelius Cole, 2/15/1864, 2/16/1864.
7. ‡. Many White troopers wore buckskin gauntlets. Later in the war, he showed interest in helping his men invest in homes.
8. CFP, George Cole to Cornelius Cole, 2/15/1864, 2/16/1864.
9. EOB, 15–19. For more on Black soldiers and literacy during the war, ‡.
10. This and the next five paragraphs draw from this extended letter: CFP, George Cole to Cornelius Cole, 2/15/1864, 2/16/1864.
11. ‡. His brother Cornelius Cole read, with key alterations, parts of George's letter to Congress.
12. ‡. Dollard had first tried unsuccessfully to be commissioned with another colonel.
13. RCW, 8–9, 98.
14. Dollard held a lifelong adoration for George, though George would grow deeply frustrated with his drinking problems and abuse of the Black soldiers.

15. In 1860, less than 1 percent of Massachusetts's population was Black. And only a fraction of Northern free Black people lived outside large towns and cities. UW, 42–43.
16. Story of returned hound found in untitled newspaper clipping, OHA, 2/11/1863.
17. ‡. For more details about the viciousness of those interactions and the broadly shared disgust that the rural Massachusetts men held for Black humans, as well as more on Robert Dollard's early war, ‡.
18. As a historian of the Twenty-Third Massachusetts put it, soldiers "ostracized" those men who had hopes of gaining a promotion by joining Butler's swelling Black army. Serving with the Black troops "was not popular." He wrote that joining "required no little moral courage to gratify ambition by way of a commission in the 'nigger regiments.'" ROTT, 139–40.
19. USCT2, General Order No. 4, 1/1/1864, from headquarters of Second United States Colored Cavalry, Camp Hamilton, Fort Monroe, VA. See Butler's "General Order, No. 46" in BME, 135–38.
20. MIC, 97–98; New York and Massachusetts soldiers quoted in LBY, 109–10; ‡.
21. LBY, 114.
22. RCW, 80–81. For more on Dollard's treatment of his servant, ‡.
23. For more on this color line, ‡.
24. RCW, 99–100.
25. ‡; USCT2, General Order No. 28, 7/13/1864, from headquarters of Second United States Colored Cavalry, near Petersburg, VA. This was not unique to George's regiment.
26. One of George's young officers falsely believed that the enlisted men were free Black men in the South; ‡.
27. MOM; FFG, xvii.

Chapter 8. A Good Deal of Trouble

1. WDNTP, 36–39. For more on the historical literature that I relied on here, as well as other atrocities perpetrated on Black soldiers, ‡.
2. ‡. Reports mostly in OR, ser. 1, vol. 33, pp. 237–39; SJ, 3/16/1864. The SJ report reminded readers that "Col. Cole is our townsman, and a truly gallant officer he is." The editor believed that Syracusans needed reminding that George was from their city.

3. Many, especially in the South, dismissed the reports as fabrications by abolitionists designed to push Northerners toward more radical politics. See FPM and ‡.
4. Whatever transpired in Plymouth will remain partly obscured by ensuing silence, conflicting reports, and soldiers who assumed new identities (to avoid execution). See CRYW, 135–47. I could not have written what follows without the careful sleuth work found in MP. ‡.
5. Butler's introduction and Johnson's entire sworn testimony found in OR, ser. 2, vol. 7, pp. 459–60. The next three paragraphs draw from this source.
6. For a detailed defense of my claim that "Samuel Johnson" was created by the brilliant, scheming, justifiably impatient Butler, see ‡. I am not the only person to arrive at a similar conclusion.
7. Some records erroneously have French's name as "George N." But in French's compiled service records there is a desperate letter from his mother in which she asks officers what happened to her son and calls him "George W." His mother, too, likely named him after America's first president.
8. USCT2, General Order No. 19, 4/22/1864, from Fort Monroe, VA. For more on drinking under George's command, ‡.
9. Out of some eighty thousand recorded general courts-martial in the Union army, over fourteen thousand listed alcohol as an inciting agent in the alleged crime. For more on alcohol and courts-martial, see NACWR; LBY, 252–55; and SBG, 96–101.
10. Butler stated, "Drunken officers are the curse of our Colored soldiers and I will reform it in this Department, if I can, in spite of . . . the Devil." Quoted in EGLBT, 3.
11. CMRD. For more on the probability of needing to abate malaria, ‡.
12. Quotes from Dollard's court-martial, CMRD. As Dollard's actions suggest, some White officers believed that Black soldiers were interchangeable. Because they commanded some Black enlisted men, they felt their authority simply extended over any of them. One witness suggests as much in the testimonies.
13. CMRD.
14. CMRD.
15. CMWHP. Major Anil A. Dennison was appointed to try all regimental courts-martial, ordered by George. See USCT2, Special Order No. 16, 7/4/1864, "near Petersburg," VA.

16. Partial court-martial for mutiny included in Ray's compiled service record, CSRSR. The complete records from the subsequent trial have not survived. It is not clear whether Ray was found guilty of mutiny. ‡.
17. USCT2, General Order No. 26, 7/4/1864, "near Petersburg."
18. We can never be sure about the accuracy of Dollard's stories. It's a mistake, though, to dismiss them outright, as all of them reflect realities seen in other regimental records. One illuminating, but almost certainly embellished, story is about a conflict that began with a Black noncommissioned officer going to tie up an enlisted man. In this story, Dollard suspiciously finds his ever-loyal Uncle Tom. For more about this story, ‡.
19. CMRD. Dollard's court-martial provides the evidence for the rest of this story.
20. RCW, 130–31; CFP, George Cole to Cornelius Cole, 12/7/1864, 1/12/1865 (from Chapin's Farm).
21. For more on George's conflicting testimony, ‡.
22. CMRD.

Chapter 9. No Return

1. He was not an alienated soldier, isolated in an all-male world, far from the safety of family and hearth. For more on this crisscrossing, ‡.
2. ‡. Her comings and goings were frequent, though the precise dates are impossible to know for sure. Report of suicide in SJ, 1/24/1868.
3. CFP, George Cole to Cornelius Cole, 5/2/1864; the threat came from a joint resolution from the Confederate Congress, 5/1/1863. ‡.
4. CFP, Mary Barto Cole to Cornelius Cole, 5/11/1864.
5. This and the next two paragraphs are from CFP, Mary Barto Cole to Cornelius Cole, 5/11/1864.
6. CFP, Mary Barto Cole to Cornelius Cole, 5/11/1864; FBS, 99, 351–53.
7. Dollard does not mention Fox in his memoirs. But he does seem to cast blame on him for an assault of the enemy. ‡.
8. The quotes in this paragraph and the next four are from PRHG, 33–34. The details of this story are taken from Edwin Fox's court-martial. From several testimonies, I have re-created the tragic event. The best copy of the trial is a typed, paginated version found in the pension file for Henry Edwards (PRHG). After the

war, his father tried to secure a pension, as he had been a dependent parent. The trial (with different page numbers) can also be found in CMERF. The most detailed testimonies are those of Lieutenant Edwin Fox, PRHG, 33–37; Sergeant Samuel Brown, PRHG, 24–27; Private Owen Dennis, PRHG, 29–32; and First Lieutenant Benjamin Swarthout, PRHG, 3–14.
9. Details of Edwards found throughout PRHG.
10. PRHG, 24, 34, 25.
11. PRHG, 34, 29–30, 25–28.
12. PRHG, 25–26.
13. See, for example, PRHG, 26, 28–29, 32.
14. PRHG, 25, 20.
15. Bucking and gagging was a form of corporal punishment widely used throughout the military where a soldier's limbs were tightly bound, his knees drawn up between his arms, and his body locked into a painfully hunched posture on the ground by running a pole under the folded knees and over the arms. A rag or rope was usually tied into an open mouth.
16. PRHG, 35, 3, 30.
17. PRHG, 17.
18. PRHG, 30–31.
19. PRHG, 22, 25–26.
20. PRHG, 20–23, 35.
21. PRHG, 26, 36.
22. PRHG, 36, 13.
23. The quotes in this paragraph and the next two are from PRHG, 36–37.
24. Butler's report and summary of 9/13/1864 in CMERF. ‡.
25. PRHG, 3–4.
26. PRHG, 29.
27. PRHG, 11–14, 25. For more on the three soldiers furtively "looking at" the book, ‡.
28. Butler's report and summary of 9/13/1864 in CMERF. Similar cycles of violence could be found in White regiments throughout the military. This was different. ‡.

Chapter 10. The Resurrectionists
1. ‡; letters to superiors in CSRGWC.
2. CFP, George Cole to Cornelius Cole, 10/22/1864.

3. CFP, George Cole to Cornelius Cole, 10/24/1864.
4. OR, ser. 1, vol. 42, pt. 3, pp. 97–98. George believed, but could not prove, that several brigadier generals had leapfrogged him in promotion.
5. CFP, George Cole to Cornelius Cole, no date [approximately fall of 1864]. By 1864, George had lost his grip on reality when it came to the merits of other men. He had grown desperately jealous and nursed legitimate complaints until they became delusions. For more, ‡.
6. SP, 190–93; SBB, 136; BFB, 136–38.
7. EGLAOA, 62–63, 74–75, 82–83; SBB, 115–20; OR, ser. 1, vol. 46, pt. 1, p. 19, General Report of Richmond Campaign, from U.S. Grant, 7/22/1865.
8. WWU, 118–21, 300; BFB, 141–44. For more on his inner circle and the stoking of Butler's ambitions, and his wife's, ‡.
9. Part of the regiment had already been sent to Deep Bottom, at least by July 1864. The regiment's battle records do not list Dutch Gap, but in many of the pension records, veterans of the Second Colored Cavalry traced their wounds to Dutch Gap. George also drew a detailed map of the region. See ‡.
10. BCWC, 137, report from Deep Bottom, VA, 9/24/1864.
11. The use of rebel prisoners at the project inflamed Confederate leaders, leading to further racial tensions. BFB, 152–53; FBS, 390–93; OR, ser. 2, vol. 7, pp. 1010–12. See ‡.
12. BCWC, 137.
13. BCWC, 137.
14. BCWC, 138, 136–39. Grant had recently issued Circular No. 31, which was designed to encourage rebel soldiers to desert into Union lines. The circular promised deserters money, amnesty from possible charges of treason, and transportation home. Chester did not elaborate on how, exactly, George would be able to capitalize on the order.
15. BCWC, 139.
16. BCWC, 139. For more examples of this curious blindness, ‡.
17. OR, ser. 1, vol. 42, pt. 2, pp. 349–50.
18. EGLBT, 1.
19. The Twenty-Fifth Corps did have White artillery regiments. The Twenty-Fifth was formed on December 3, 1864. See CS, 401–3; and

FBS, 401–2. For the formation of the corps, see OR, ser. 1, vol. 42, pt. 3, pp. 761, 791.
20. Ord's policies toward the families of Black soldiers were especially heartless. See ‡.
21. OR, ser. 1, vol. 42, pt. 3, pp. 800–801, 819.
22. FBS, 403–5; BFB, 150–52; CFP, George Cole to Cornelius Cole, dated 1/2/1864 [actually 1865].
23. EGLAOA, 258–59; CFP, George Cole to Cornelius Cole, dated 1/2/1864 [actually 1865]. George misspelled a few of the Latin words and mistakenly swapped the places of *parturient* and *montes*.
24. SBB, 149–53; BCF, 819–20.
25. EGLAOA, 245–59; SBB, 152–53; BFB, 153–54.
26. Butler's speech in NYT, 1/23/1865.
27. Admiral Porter to Lieutenant General Grant, 1/3/1853, in OR, ser. 1, vol. 46, pt. 2, p. 20; General Sherman to Admiral Porter, 1/21/1865, in OR, ser. 1, vol. 47, pt. 2, pp. 104–5.
28. CFP, George Cole to Cornelius Cole, dated 1/2/1864 [actually 1865].
29. CFP, George Cole to Cornelius Cole, dated 1/2/1864 [actually 1865]. For more on the letter and how Butler had unsuccessfully tried to get George his promotions, ‡.
30. Resignation letter in SCFP, George Cole to Major General Ord, 1/7/[1865]; Wild to Cole in SCFP; CFP, George Cole to Cornelius Cole (private), 1/3/1865. For more on the letter and Wild, ‡.
31. CFP, George Cole to Cornelius Cole, 1/7/1865.
32. CFP, George Cole to Cornelius Cole, 1/12/1865 (from Chapin's Farm). Draper, like Butler, was one of the officers most committed to Black soldiers; George was right, though, that Draper cultivated a political alliance with Butler. See ‡.
33. For more on his desperate ideas at the close of the war, ‡.
34. Butler was never convicted for any of the many war crimes accusations. See ‡.
35. CFP, George Cole to Cornelius Cole, dated 1/2/1864 [actually 1865].
36. AGO, Microfilm #C173 CB1866, Benjamin Butler to Colonel Cole, 2/28/1865.
37. The quotes in this paragraph and the next three are from CFP, George Cole to Cornelius Cole, written on paper with letterhead of

"Inspector General's Office," estimated to be January 1865 but almost certainly mid-March. See ‡.
38. This literary allusion is rich with possible meanings. See ‡.
39. For more on Butler's visionary plan, which he claims he pitched to a receptive Lincoln days before the assassination, ‡.

Chapter 11. Mutiny

1. FBS, 411–13.
2. OOS.
3. FBS, 411–13; OOS, 585.
4. Charles Francis Adams Jr. (HQ, Fifth Massachusetts Cavalry, Point Lookout, MD) to father, 11/2/1864, in CAL, 2:216–17. Adams at this time was at Point Lookout in Maryland. This only suggests how widespread the sickness was. He would soon join the other Black regiments outside Richmond, Virginia.
5. SFF; IH. For more on this, ‡.
6. OOS. A similar report on Black troops in Louisiana can be found in LMW, 437–38. For more on the conditions of White and Black soldiers, ‡.
7. RTAC, 331. See ‡.
8. OOS; EGLBT, 6. For the inconsistent documenting of soldiers' sickness, ‡.
9. CS, 412–16. George, a trained physician, might have written about the health problems of his Black soldiers. But none of his surviving letters carry a whiff of diagnosis. For more, ‡.
10. For more on this controversy, ‡.
11. For more on Richmond and the fate of Black troops, see the controversy surrounding Richmond's fall, ‡.
12. Birney quoted in EGLBT, 6. For more on the profound hatred for Black people held by various officers left behind after Butler's departure, ‡.
13. AA, 9, 103–4; the combining of Colored Cavalry units into George's brigade in OR, ser. 1, vol. 46, pt. 2, p. 144. For more on retaining Black troops, ‡.
14. OR, ser. 1, vol. 46, pt. 3, sec. 2, p. 1253. For his promotion by brevet, see AGO, Microfilm #C447 CB1865.
15. CFP, George Cole to Cornelius Cole, 6/10/1864 [actually 1865]; EGLD, vol. 4, chap. 12, pp. 978–79.

NOTES TO PAGES 134–139   327

16. MSUS, 11–13; correspondent in *Philadelphia Inquirer* quoted in NYT, 6/16/1865; AAHCW, 38–39; FBS, 424. For the purported reasons for sending the troops to Texas, ‡.
17. NYT, 6/16/1865. Few newspapers continued to report on the experiences of Black troops, especially with the war "over." Various court-martial transcripts, though, along with a few soldiers' accounts, reveal a sweeping mutiny that took place on various ships at roughly the same time. Evidence reveals that the anger and violence in George's calvary were not an exception in the Black army. The uprisings appear to have been orchestrated. See ‡.
18. OR, ser. 1, vol. 46, pt. 3, p. 1199, Circular from Headquarters Twenty-Fifth Army Corps, Camp Lincoln, VA, 5/22/1865.
19. MSUS, 11. Frederick Browne, who served as an officer in the First United States Colored Cavalry, gave the most detailed account of the mutiny. In the following account I weave together his memory of the events with many courts-martial of soldiers accused of being the lead mutineers. For more on how I compiled evidence for this mutiny, ‡.
20. Quote from James Linier court martial, MCM; MOM, 63–98.
21. CMWC.
22. PI quoted in NYT, 6/16/1865. In his memoir, officer Browne said nothing about the families at the wharf.
23. PI quoted in NYT, 6/16/1865. The *Inquirer* report conflicts in some key details with the account by Browne. Also, one anti-Black paper reported the mutiny included the soldiers keeping their guns and terrorizing a local town. Some did take advantage of the confusion and desert. See ‡.
24. RCW, 147–51.
25. RCW, 147.
26. Trial of Oliver Jones in MCM. For the resistance among the band, see Compiled Service Record of Guion Souther, Microfilm Roll #22, National Archives and Records Administration, Washington, DC.
27. BBGG; RCW, 150.
28. Trial of Spencer Edwards in MCM; RCW, 149–50.
29. Trial of Spencer Edwards in MCM; quote in RCW, 150.
30. MSUS, 12.
31. MSUS, 12.

32. Quotes from the trials of John Carr and Henry Washington in MCM; MSUS, 12–13.
33. MSUS, 13.
34. MSUS, 13. The man lived for two more days.
35. RCW, 150–51.
36. CFP, George Cole to Cornelius Cole, 6/10/1864 [actually 1865].
37. Testimony of Captain Ells in SJ, 4/28/1868; Pension Affidavit of Mary Barto Cole, probably 1884, in PRGWC; CS, 419.

Chapter 12. Family, the Inflammatory Stimulus

1. For more on why these women and elderly were likely desperate, ‡.
2. BBGG. This source can also be found, with rich context, in FF, 126–29; and BME, 723–25.
3. RCW, 147.
4. BBGG; BME, 724.
5. I infer this because of a speech that his brother gave that drew heavily from George's own experiences with Black soldiers: SHC. See ‡.
6. BBGG; BME, 724.
7. BBGG; BME, 724.
8. CMJB; NYT, 6/23/1865; PI, 6/13/1865.
9. See documents 314a–314c in BME, 721–23.
10. For a nuanced exploration of material realities and conditions of refugee camps, see EF; Letter on behalf of Thirty-Sixth United States Colored Troops quoted in FF, 125–26.
11. CMWR; CMWC.
12. EGLBT, 4; FF, 30–33, 46–48. For why tidewater enslaved people understood freedom and family differently from enslaved people from other regions, ‡.
13. FF, 5–7, 95–96.
14. I find in the Black military evidence of what Jacqueline Jones calls the "ethos of mutuality" in her work on Black women after the Civil War. See LL.
15. CFP, George Cole to "Dear Brother" Cornelius, 11/19/[1863]. The phrase was something the father often repeated to his children. For more about this, ‡.
16. For a few examples of his tenderness toward home, see the testimony of Frank Spaulding in SJ, 4/28/1868; CFP, George Cole to "Dear Brother," 11/19/[1863].

17. BCWSI, 154. See ‡.
18. OOS.
19. IH, 119–25, 139.
20. OOTB, 79–80; S29, 33; IH, 124–25.
21. At the same time that the Twenty-Fifth Corps began mobilizing toward Texas, the Sanitary Commission was in Washington, DC, issuing fresh vegetables to White soldiers returning to their homes. See ‡.
22. IH, 10–11, 126–27; FBS, 442–43.
23. FBS, 441–42.
24. IH, 131, 140–41; S29, 38–39.
25. The tedious hell of Texas can be carefully gleaned fragment by fragment from the piles of soldiers' pension records. See, for example, PRDH; PRPF; PRFH; and esp. PREN. Also see ‡.
26. FBS, 437; Grant and Weitzel exchange in OR, ser. 1, vol. 46, pt. 3, p. 1193.
27. Anonymous letter in FAL, 533–34. See ‡.
28. For proof that Mary went to Texas, see Testimony of James Ells in SJ, 4/28/1869. Other testimonies and sources corroborate that Mary was on one of the ships: CFP, especially the typed copy of affidavit by Mary B. Cole, 3/12/1884. Also see ‡.
29. Edwin Fox quoted in SJ, 4/25/1868; RTAC, 243; more on his health in Texas from Frank Garrett in RTAC, 243–44.
30. Quote from Frank Garrett in RTAC, 244. Clark did get him breveted a brigadier general in late January. This and the following discussion of George's various recommendations for promotion, brevets, and promotions are drawn from the following: CWHC, 180; CSRGWC, 2nd U.S. Colored Cavalry, Microfilm #M1817; AGO, Microfilms #C1346 CB1865, #C173 CB1866, and #C180 CB1866.
31. AGO, Microfilm #C173 CB1866.
32. Davis wrote, "I believe he made a good I may say an excellent record. He is about being mustered out of service." AGO, Microfilm #C173 CB1866.
33. For details on Stanton's recommendation, ‡.
34. CFP, F. B. Alderice to the Civil War Veteran Bureau, 2/22/1935. Much mystery remains about this medal, how he lost it, and who possesses it today. See ‡. I had a strange, almost cosmic, personal experience tracking down the meaning of this letter.

Chapter 13. Homecoming

1. I have created a short sketch of some of their postwar lives through what I gleaned from regimental pensions. For more on these soldiers' postwar experiences, ‡.
2. For more on this backlash, ‡.
3. See, for example, the testimony of Mary Cuyler in RTAC, 291.
4. Testimony of George Raynor in SJ, 4/25/1868. The "boy" was likely a refugee or common soldier converted into a personal servant for the war and after: See ‡. For more about the house, ‡.
5. Quote from George Raynor, RTAC, 249. The fact that his friends recalled the Black boy and the children while reflecting on the General's postwar troubles suggests that his peers thought it odd that a war officer would spend personal time with small children or a Black boy or "colored man." There is not a whiff of accusation that George sexually molested these boys. There is no evidence of pederasty. For more, ‡.
6. Garrett quoted in RTAC, 244.
7. Garrett quoted in RTAC, 246. Like so much of the war, this detail about a bullet in his leg does not line up with the military records. See ‡.
8. FGAW, 26–28; OHAB; EWMC. For more on the company, ‡.
9. Quotes from treasurer of the company, Henry L. Duguid, in SJ, 5/1/1868, and SDS, 5/1/1868. Perhaps the General took advantage of military connections and sold some windmills on credit to a few of his Black soldiers. After what he and his comrades had done to the foothills of North Carolina, there certainly would have been a need for windmills.
10. NYH, 5/1/1868; various trial witnesses found in SJ, 4/25, 4/30, 5/1, and 5/7/1868. See also testimonies of Allen Munroe and Harman W. Van Buren, as well as summary of defense, RTAC, 301–2, 316.
11. CFP, George Cole to Cornelius Cole, 1/28/1867.
12. CFP, George Cole to Cornelius Cole, 1/28/1867.
13. CFP, George Cole to Cornelius Cole, 1/29/1867. The loose "place" ads appear to belong to this letter.
14. The war itself indeed created unprecedented growth in government positions and jobs. See ‡.
15. CFP, George Cole to Cornelius Cole, 1/29/1867.
16. Joshua K. Rogers in SJ, 4/25/1868.

NOTES TO PAGES 162-168

17. CFP, George Cole to Cornelius Cole, 2/11/1867. The outside of the letter has been incorrectly marked as 1866.
18. Joshua K. Rogers in SJ, 4/25/1868; RTAC, 246–47.
19. Information about George's appointment in SJ, 4/25/1868; and testimony of William Barrows, SJ, 11/25/1868.
20. William C. Fink in SJ, 4/25/1868, and RTAC, 249–50.
21. Testimony of George Raynor in SJ, 4/25/1868; testimony of Dr. Roberts in RTAC, 241; Rowland M. Hall quoted in RTAC, 255–54; and in SJ, 4/27/1868. George often wandered in and around hotels, the nexus of sociality and business in towns like Syracuse. See ‡.

Chapter 14. Killing for Union

1. See SJ, 4/25, 4/30, and 5/7/1868, for various testimonies about George's employment at the windmill company. For more on the company and other prospects, ‡.
2. SJ, 6/18/1867, 4/25/1868; AOT, 12–13.
3. According to one paper's report, George originally suspected that Hiscock had been cheating him in money matters pertaining to Mary's large estate. SJ, 1/24/1868.
4. His first suspicions, SJ 1/24/1868; on the bazaar, Elizabeth Wyman and Harriet D. Lee in RTAC, 253–54; AOT, 13.
5. Various testimonies during trial; quote from Frank B. Garrett, SJ, 11/23/1868; Henry L. Duguid, RTAC, 300; AOT, 13.
6. CFP, George Cole to Olive Cole, 4/1 and 4/2/1868; AOT, 11–12.
7. Quote in RTAC, 222; SJ, 4/25/1867; AOT, 11–12.
8. SJ, 4/25 and 11/28/1868; testimony of Mary Cuyler in SJ, 4/30/1868, and in RTAC, 290–91.
9. Letter to Montgomery Pelton reported in SJ, 11/30/868. George also wrote in this same letter, "Now, I have less confidence in [my wife's] discretion than in her integrity. She has no discretion and but little care for people's opinion, as you probably know. . . . You will thus do her a kindness as well as myself and perhaps save a scene unpleasant and disgraceful."
10. SJ, 6/18/1867.
11. Testimony of James Hutchinson in SJ, 4/27/1868.
12. See several witnesses in SJ, 4/25, 4/29, 4/30, and 12/2/1868; SJ, 6/18/1867. See esp. the testimonies of Ransom W. Green and John Cuyler in SJ, 4/25/1868; and RTAC, 252, 280–81.

13. Confession in SJ, 4/30/1867. The newspaper version and published trial report vary slightly. See ‡.
14. Testimony of Mary Cuyler in RTAC, 289–93.
15. SJ, 6/13/1867; testimony of John Cuyler in SJ, 4/29/1868; testimony of Mary Cuyler in RTAC, 292–93, and SJ, 4/30/1868.
16. See testimony of Mary Cuyler in SJ, 4/30/1868, and RTAC, 289–91.
17. See testimony of Edmund B. Cole in RTAC, 258–59; and testimony of Mary Cuyler in SJ, 4/30/1868.
18. See testimony of Mary Cuyler in SJ, 4/30/1868. See also testimony of William Tifft in SJ, 4/28/1868. See ‡ about the revolver.
19. See testimonies of Elizabeth Wyman and Harriet D. Lee, a mother and daughter who lived in the hotel, in RTAC, 253–54; and SJ, 4/23/1868.
20. Letter introduced in trial by George's attorney, SJ, 4/30/1868, and RTAC, 296. This letter may have been fabricated just after the murder. See ‡.
21. PDCC, 17–18.
22. Quote from James M. Gould in RTAC, 295.
23. John Cuyler in RTAC, 281–83. In Cuyler's recollection, George asked him to go and amend the entry to "Dr. and Mrs. George. W. Cole." Other sources say George did it. See SJ, 6/6/1867; and BDU, 6/6/1867.
24. NYTr, 6/10/1867 (clipping also found in OHA). If this note had been sent to Hiscock, it would have probably been in his possession when he died; had his attorneys had such evidence, I believe they would have used it in the trial to prove Mary's complicity and George's premeditated deed.
25. The prosecuting attorney, Henry Smith, made a case that George hoped to slay Hiscock on the floor of the Constitutional Convention. SJ, 4/4/1868.
26. SJ, 12/3/1868; newspaper clipping "Gen. Cole's Syracuse Letter," 6/17/1867, OHA. For more on a central testimony, ‡.
27. George quoted in Mary Cuyler's testimony in RTAC, 292. Mary Cole would earn a reputation among George's family as a woman who preferred to play solitaire over studying the Bible. Neither George nor Mary seems to have been deeply engaged with the religions of their upbringing. George's sister, Mary Stewart, would later call Mary a "great card fiend." CFP, Mary Stewart to Cornelius Cole, 4/29/[no date, must be 1910].

28. For the signing of the registry, see SJ, 6/6/1867; and BDU, 6/6/1867. For the duel, see SJ, 1/24/1868. George likely planned to use the Derringer; see SJ, 11/25/1868, where a fellow customs worker testified that George criticized the worker's revolver for its lack of range and power.
29. See extensive testimony of John Cuyler in RTAC, 280–86.
30. RTAC, 350.
31. TS, 6/6/1867; LN, 6/12/1867; NYW, 6/7/1867.
32. SJ, 1/23/1868; RTAC, 206–8; NYW, 6/7/1867.
33. Moses Summers in SJ, 11/28/68; TS, 6/6/1867.
34. Moses Summers must have opened the letter and read it on his way to delivering it to Mary. See his original testimony, particularly in TS, 6/6/1867; and LN 6/12/1867.
35. Telegraph in CFP.

Chapter 15. Rising Men (Who Nearly Needed God)

1. See TS, 6/6/1867. Though some reports suggest he gave his statement the next morning, in other reports, like ALA, 6/6/1867, George delivered his speech hours after the murder without reading it. It was also reported that he stopped once to suggest that maybe he should just hang if it would save his poor Mary from her sorrows.
2. SJ, 6/5/1867. The statement was published widely throughout New York State and beyond.
3. NYT, 6/6/1867; NYTr quoted in SJ, 6/13/1867. The *Tribune* reported a "strong under-current of opinion in favor" of the prisoner.
4. SJ, 6/13/1867. George indeed began the war as a captain. See, for example, HOC, 406; CSRGWC; CWHC, 180. In a resignation letter, he claimed, "I entered the service in April 1861 as Capt. 12th N.Y.V." SCFP, George Cole to Major General Ord, 1/7/[1865].
5. At issue was a potent story about self-made manhood that gained enormous power by the middle of the nineteenth century, especially in politics. ‡.
6. BU, 6/5/1867. The following quotes in tribute of Hiscock's achievements are from various speeches found in SJ, 6/6/1867.
7. Various speeches in PDCC, 26–27; SJ, 6/10/1867.
8. George must have hoped that few locals would have had the will or wherewithal to check old newspapers, sift through army records,

or think to interrogate his personal record from the beginning of the war. For more on George's promotions, ‡.
9. Butler quoted in DAE, 353–54. The world of military authority did not offer the kind of hierarchical precision that one might imagine. Take, for example, rank versus grade. Even officers at the top of the army at times wrote or spoke confusedly about the differences between grade (the degree of officer) and rank (the relative priority, often by date of promotion, of an officer within the grade itself). See CWHC, 33–34.
10. When postwar soldiers returned to the dense ranks of the Regular Army, officers climbed back down the ladder into significantly lower ranks. Though George Custer had obtained the grade of major general in the volunteer army, he returned to the duty of captain in the Regular Army after the war. CWHC, 196.
11. Quote in SJ, 6/15/1867.
12. NYW, 6/7/1867, emphasis added. About the confusion in the closing months of the war, see CWHC, 34–35. This purposeful use of confusing titles was not unusual. ‡.
13. For more on the army's records of his promotions, ‡.
14. HLEB, 224.
15. For more on the flood of promotions, ‡.
16. See BU, 12/10/1867.
17. The confusion is clear in the Cole family letters. ‡.
18. SJ, 6/6/1867.
19. NYH, 6/7/1867; SJ, "Second Edition" in 11/24/1868; and a report from unknown newspaper, marked "11-24-68," all loose clippings in OHA.
20. This was reported after Hadley's death in AE, reprinted in SJ, 4/26/1879.
21. See especially the questioning of John Eddy in SJ, 6/7/1867; SJ, 6/8/1867 (clipping from folder in OHA); RT, 6/10/1867.
22. Frank Hiscock may have simply wanted to secure his brother's dignity by preventing millions of Americans from vicariously rifling through his brother's pockets. Still, had they been sentimental notes and pictures of family, it seems he would have been eager to hand them over in order to rescue his brother's reputation.
23. SJ, 6/7/1867.
24. ELS, 221; BMR, 52–56. For more on Canfield, ‡.

25. For suicidal intentions, see UDO, 6/5/1867; SJ, 6/8/1867; and NYTr, 6/10/1867. In one of Olive's earliest letters, she notes, "It is my opinion that he felt perfectly desperate and intended to commit suicide afterwards." CFP, Olive Cole to Cornelius Cole, 6/6/1867. Another report claimed he hid another pocket knife with "G.W. Cole" engraved in a pearl handle: SJ, 6/10/1867.
26. EWM, 16–17, 32. For more on Mundy, ‡.
27. On Dimmock, Beecher, and sexual controversy, ‡.
28. OA, 162. See ‡.
29. This and following quotes from Dimmock's sermon are in SJ, 6/8/1867.
30. ALA in NYTr, 6/7/1867; CFP, George Cole to Olive Cole, 6/13/1867. For more on reformers and experimentation with sexual and marital mores, see HGNYT, chap. 5. For more, ‡.
31. As a result, the two opposing sides painted each other as consumed by "maudlin appeals" and "sickly sentimentalism." See AEJ, 6/17/1867. On feelings, love, and their place in Victorian marriage, see STH, chap. 5; and MAH. See also ‡.
32. On the alliance between Christianity and the cult of femininity, see FAC.
33. SJ, 6/8/1867.
34. Quote in PDCC, 27.

Chapter 16. The Domesticated Prisoner

1. DAC, 12/16/1868; SJ, 11/23/1868.
2. CCCP, 66–67, 73.
3. CFP, George Cole to Olive Cole, 6/22/1867.
4. CFP, Olive Cole to Cornelius Cole, 6/20/1867.
5. CFP, George Cole to Olive Cole, appears to be 7/1/1867. Testimony of Bernard Kavanagh in SJ, 11/21/1868; RTAC, 373–74.
6. CFP, George Cole to Olive Cole, appears to be 7/1/1867.
7. Those letters between Mary and George have not survived. Lost is any of the tenderness shared between them, his flood of sentimental poetry, or her ardent and worried responses. CFP, George Cole to Olive Cole, appears to be 7/1/1867. For more on this odd quote, ‡.
8. Quotes here and in the next four paragraphs in CFP, George Cole to Olive Cole, 7/5/1867.

9. Clipping in CFP, *Albany Express*, [month clipped off]/8/1867; RT, 6/10/1867, in CFP; undated letter in CFP, top of letter marked "Room 'B'" [appears to be one week after the murder]; quote from Cornelius Cole to Olive Cole, 6/11/1867. Also see SJ, 11/21/1868.
10. For the report that George occupied Hartung's cell, see NYTr, 6/10/1867, found in OHA. Quote in DAC, 12/21/1867.
11. NAR, 30–39, 333–36.
12. NAR, 30–39, 333–36.
13. Smith quotes and report in BCHA, 99; last quote in NAR, 33, 333–36. For more on the Albany jail, ‡.
14. FC, 6/4/1868; quotes in DAC, 12/21/1867; CFP, Olive Cole to Cornelius Cole, 8/3/1867.
15. CFP, Cornelius Cole to Olive Cole, 11/7/1867.
16. CFP, Cornelius Cole to Olive Cole, 11/7/1867; testimony of Bernard Kavanagh in SJ, 11/21/1868. There were many reports of frequent visits by female sympathizers—for example, SJ, 11/23/1868.
17. Quotes in TDW, 8/5/1867, and NPG, 8/17/1867; NPG 6/15/1867. The *National Police Gazette* copied and slightly altered the story from the *Troy Daily Whig*.
18. SDC&U, 8/13/1867. Because this and other accounts did not describe the soldiers' race, I assume that these were White soldiers. George had control over who entered his cell. A paper reported that he wanted Mary's visits and that he had given orders "that if she appeared for admission to the jail to grant it." SJ, 1/24/1868.
19. Quotes in TDW, 8/5/1867, and NPG, 8/17/1867; NPG, 6/15/1867.
20. PUF, 4–6; quotes in TDW, 8/5/1867, and NPG, 8/17/1867; NPG, 6/15/1867. The *Troy Daily Whig* emphasized that George especially read the *New York Tribune*, a paper largely sympathetic to his plight, at least initially. A Brooklyn paper reported in August 1867 that he was "spending his time reading religious books and Shakespeare." BDE, 8/16/1867.
21. Quotes from DAC, 12/21/1867. For some descriptions of the cell, see SJ, 1/24 and 11/21/1868; NPG, 8/17/1867; and newspaper clipping of AE, no date, looks like 11/9/1867, in CFP. Also see DAC, 12/21/1867.
22. Quote in DAC, 12/21/1867, and TDW, 8/5/1867.
23. Reports on ring: NN, 12/14/1867; AE, 11/15/1867.

24. Even as the apocalyptic battles raged, Americans trafficked in the war's death relics. See LWS.
25. For descriptions of the anchor of hope and all related quotes, see DAC, 12/21/1867; meaning of dried white flowers taken from an antebellum floral dictionary referenced in CTW, 154.
26. DAC, 12/21/1867.

Chapter 17. Confessions
1. The quotes from the anonymous letter in this paragraph and the next two come from SJ, 6/8/1867.
2. SJ, 11/21/1868; GG, 6/14/1867; TDT, 6/10/1867; VH, 6/22/1867. See ‡.
3. The following treatment of rape in the nineteenth century draws from the works of Estelle Freedman and Sharon Block: RR, esp. chaps. 1–2; RSPEA. See ‡.
4. RR, esp. chaps. 1–2; RSPEA.
5. SJ, 4/30/1868. Testimonies conflict about when this amendment was made. See ‡.
6. STH.
7. LSSO, 266–69.
8. Testimony of Mary Cuyler in SJ, 11/28/1868.
9. Quote from Mary Cuyler, SJ, 11/28/1868; RTAC, 378–79. For more on the jewelry, ‡.
10. Testimony of John De Mill in SJ, 6/30/1868 (summarized in two places).
11. Testimony of Mary Cuyler in SJ, 4/28/1868; and RTAC, 291, 377. For more on these diagrams, see TDW, 1/20/1866; and AEJ, 3/1/1864.
12. John Cuyler's testimony about how the letter was given to him can be found in SJ, 4/29/1868.
13. SJ, 4/30/1868.

Chapter 18. Mary. Wife. Self.
1. Quotes about sex between Mary and George here and in the next two paragraphs from CFP, George Cole to Olive Cole, 12/5/[1867].
2. Stanton quoted in CAA, 5. Also see CAA, 134–35, 150–51. For more, see ‡.
3. MLID; USM.
4. AO, chap. 4; HR, chap. 4. See ‡.
5. CAA, 112–19. See ‡.

6. Contraceptives offered a confusing array of often ineffective options. See ‡.
7. SDU, 2/18/1868. Report from Syracuse in SNYDU, 1/30/1868.
8. CFP, Olive Cole to Cornelius Cole, 11/5/1867.
9. WAWAC, 1–8.
10. CAA, 57–86.
11. This and the next paragraph, see AIA, 3–19; WAWAC, 8–11; CAA, 118–19.
12. In his bookstore, George carried something called the Universal Catholicon for "female complaints." The advertisement often appeared next to his ad for his "Daguerreian Gallery." For the image, ‡; AIA, 3–19; WAWAC, 8–11; CAA, 118–19.
13. AIA, 13–19; WAWAC, 11–14. See ‡.
14. See testimony of Elizabeth Wyman, RTAC, 253. On the timing of the move, see ‡.
15. For more on family hotels, ‡.
16. AT, 14–26; SJ, 11/27/1868. In the decades after the war, family hotels would allow upwardly mobile Americans to enjoy the newest technologies of gas lighting, heated water, elevator cars, and plumbing while releasing wives from domestic drudgery.
17. See ‡.
18. SJ, 3/17/1862 (clipping in "Hotels & Inns" folder, OHA); SJ, 4/23/1858 (clipping in "Syracuse Block 113" folder, OHA). The saloon was eventually converted to a cigar shop. SJ, 7/7/1869 ("Syracuse Block 113" folder, OHA).
19. SAIE, 318–19. Also see "A Short History of the Cobleighs" in "Social Life, Cobleighs" folder, OHA. See ad for Dr. Williams in SDC&U, 4/18/1862; or for Ernest Held in SDC&U, 9/2/1863; "Electropathy" in SDJ, 4/13/1861.
20. See BTD, 135–51; MHOS, 681–82; SAIE, 318–19; and GDR, 69–77.
21. PNYB, 165–72.
22. NYT, 3/15/1864.
23. CFP, Mary Stewart to Cornelius Cole, 4/12/1868.

Chapter 19. Life Imitates Art

1. Cornelius described Cuyler as "so far <u>gone</u>" during her illness that she seemed as if she were on death's doorstep. CFP, Cornelius Cole to Olive Cole, 11/9/[1867].

2. The private letters used to tell this story reveal how much Americans like George, who had aspirations beyond the hardscrabble farms of their parents, shared an inclination toward seeing themselves through the prism of literature. See ROA, 280–312. For more on *Amelia* and the prisoner, ‡.
3. For more on Fielding and *Amelia*, ‡.
4. Unless stated otherwise, all quotes in this section are found in George's proposed defense. His defense was copied word for word from *Amelia*. The novel's original words can be found in HFA, 418–19. Compare with George's defense in CFP, no date, no signature (in George Cole's hand), on longer sheets of paper like today's legal pads. See ‡.
5. When George got to the word "subject," he wrote in the left margin of his copied version, "Substitute citizen for s[ubject]."
6. For more about his copying the word "possess," ‡.
7. CFP, Cornelius Cole to Olive Cole, 8/14/1867.
8. CFP, Cornelius Cole to Olive Cole, 11/8/1867.
9. CFP, Cornelius Cole to Olive Cole, 11/8/1867. See ‡.
10. CFP, Olive Cole to Cornelius Cole, 11/9/1867; SDU, 10/22/1867. See ‡.
11. All quotes from Olive's letter to Cornelius over the next several paragraphs are in CFP, Olive Cole to Cornelius Cole, 11/9/1867. This story is merely referenced in the letter. The actual publication can be found in SDU, 10/22/1867.
12. NPG, 8/17/1867; WW. See ‡.
13. WW; FP; LG, 89–92. See ‡ on the ineffectiveness of antiobscenity laws.
14. The pointed feet might have been a reference to the popular depictions of refined individuals (especially women and children) who, in Victorian drawings and literature, were portrayed as feathery-light creatures whose delicate feet hardly touched the dirty earth. See ROA, 294–96.
15. See ‡ for more on the interpretations of Mary's sexuality.

Chapter 20. Some Magnetic Power

1. CFP, Olive Cole to Cornelius Cole, 8/3 and 10/11/1867; NYH, 5/1/1868. Mary Cole still seems to have footed a large part of the mounting legal bill. ‡.
2. SJ, 6/6/1867; FC, 6/27/1867.

3. CFP, George Cole to Olive Cole, 6/15/1867.
4. ‡. Compared with the pro-Lincoln sentiments in upstate New York, Albany was a bastion of Democratic politics.
5. PBFB, Olive Cole to Benjamin F. Butler, 6/14/1867; CFP, Olive Cole to Cornelius Cole, 6/20/1867.
6. CFP, Benjamin F. Butler to Olive Cole, 6/19/1867.
7. PBFB. For fanfare letters to Butler, ‡.
8. EE, 85, 418–19. See ‡ for Cornelius's connections to the California railroads.
9. EE, 418. For more on similarities between the Sickles and Cole cases, see ‡.
10. For more on Brady, ‡.
11. PH, 434–44. For Parker's antiemancipation credentials, see ‡.
12. BAB, 238–39, 270–71; AGA; GF, 435–47.
13. For more on the prosecution, ‡.
14. The quotes here and in the next two paragraphs are in CFP, Olive Cole to Cornelius Cole, 11/5/1867.
15. See ‡.
16. The quotes from the circular found in CFP, untitled, four-page pamphlet; CFP, Cornelius Cole to Olive Cole, 11/8/1867.
17. For early reports of George's coolness, see NPG, 6/15/1867; and LN, 6/12/1867.
18. LN, 6/12/1867.
19. EC, 73–79. On cool murder, ‡.
20. The quote here and the extended one below in CFP, Olive Cole to Cornelius Cole, 11/10/1867.
21. CFP, Olive Cole to Cornelius Cole, 11/10/1867.
22. SJ, 4/22/1868 (loose clipping from OHA). Among other things, the trial had been postponed until the adjournment of the Court of Oyer and Terminer.
23. SJ, 4/22/1868 (loose clipping from OHA).
24. Deputy sheriff in RTAC, 382; admirer David Freedlander in SJ, 4/23/1868; CFP, George Cole to Cornelius Cole, 5/25/1868.
25. Because the attorneys asked so many questions about newspapers of choice, it is clear that they believed reading habits could predict a candidate's view of the murder. See ‡.
26. Thomas Bedell in SJ, 4/23/1868. See ‡.
27. HDS, 5/3/1871.
28. SJ, 4/23/1868; RTAC, 203–5.

29. Compare question in SJ, 4/24/1868, and in RTAC, 209.
30. RTAC, 209.
31. Testimonies of Egbert Whittaker and Cornelius Allen in RTAC, 210–11; SJ, 4/24/1868. George's exclamation was remembered in various ways. But the accounts generally make the same points: that Hiscock was supposed to be a friend, Mary was an innocent wife, and all this happened while George was in uniform. See ‡.
32. Hadley's speech in RTAC, 211–38.
33. Hadley quoted in RTAC, 211–13, 231–33; SJ, 4/24/1868.
34. RTAC, 216. In none of the various trial transcriptions have I seen "the Army of the James" printed. Nor was its official name, the Department of Virginia and North Carolina, mentioned. Butler was unavoidably mentioned at various points in discussing George's ascent up the chain of command. See ‡.
35. RTAC, 217–18; SJ, 4/25/1868. For more on Northern states' desperate strategies to meet these quotas, see BC, 270; and FS, 19–20.
36. RTAC, 217.
37. SJ, 4/28/1868.
38. See esp. argument of Parker in RTAC, 322–23.
39. IUL; LMD; LHR. See ‡.
40. TS, 6/13/1867.
41. RTAC, 233–35.
42. RR, chap. 2, esp. text relevant to footnotes 33 and 34. See ‡.
43. RTAC, 235.
44. Testimonies of Lewis Post, Frank H. Hamilton, and John Townsend in RTAC, 264–69, 374. See ‡.
45. TCB; CI. See ‡.
46. SJ, 5/2/1868.
47. IUL, 166–67; TDW, 6/25/1870.
48. MMF.
49. RTAC, 228.

Chapter 21. Heroic Wounds

1. RTAC, 216–17; "great" used in transcription in SJ, 4/24/1868, and RTAC, 217; on 1862, see RTAC, 241.
2. The town had been called Kinston, not Kingston, since the American Revolution.

3. See testimonies of Lodewick W. Woodin and Edwin R. Fox in RTAC, 241, 243, and SJ, 4/25/1868.
4. Quotes from testimonies of Fox and Garrett in SJ, 4/25/1868; RTAC, 242–44; W. H. Palmer in RTAC, 287–88; Frederick Douglass, RTAC, 269. Neither do the official records often agree. See ‡.
5. Hall in SJ, 4/27/1868; Palmer in RTAC, 274, 287–89.
6. MSH, iii–ix, 336–92; testimonies of Jacob S. Mosher and John Swinburne in SJ, 5/2/1868. See ‡.
7. James F. Boshall and John F. Moschell in RTAC, 302–3; Barnum in SJ, 5/1/1868, and RTAC, 303–4.
8. OPW, 18–19; SDS, 10/18/1862.
9. OPW, 18–19.
10. Barnum testimony in SJ, 5/1/1868.
11. RTAC, 302–4. See also ‡.
12. Frederick Douglass in RTAC, 270, and SJ, 4/28/1868; J. Marcus Rice in RTAC, 261; Frank M. Spaulding in SJ, 4/28/1868. Also see James Ells in RTAC, 270–71, and SJ 4/28/1868; and various testimonies of army doctors in RTAC, 259–62, 270–71, 287–89. See ‡.
13. Testimony of General Weitzel, SJ, 4/25/1868.
14. CFP, George Cole to Cornelius Cole [family marked letter as July 1862]; Martha Cole to "Brother & Sister Corn + Olive," 12/9/1862.
15. Private letters, testimonies, and service records all confirm that something grave happened to him. See ‡.
16. Brady in SJ, 5/5/1868; on Olive's insight on the fears of jurymen, ‡.
17. These specifics are not found in the published trial but only in the newspaper reports. See SJ, 5/7/1868.
18. RTAC, 359.
19. RTAC, 360–62.
20. RTAC, 362.
21. RTAC, 365–67; CFP, George Cole to Cornelius Cole, 5/25/1868.
22. Visit in his prison cell in SJ, 5/9/1868; RTAC, 228, 362–67. See also CFP, newspaper clipping dated 6/11/1868. For more on the hung jury, ‡.

Chapter 22. Rings and Friends

1. CFP, Cornelius Cole to James McClatchy, 5/31/1868.
2. CFP, Cornelius Cole to James McClatchy, 5/31/1868.

3. An Albany paper spoke for many when it claimed that "a more profligate misuse of public moneys was never made" than with the canal's "prevailing contracts." AEJ, 6/17/1867; ECR.
4. SDC&U, 4/15/1867. See ‡.
5. SDC&U, 9/10/1867; OHA, "The Cole-Hiscock Case," newspaper clipping of report from Philadelphia paper; SDR, 9/19/1867.
6. SJ, 6/15/1867. Hiscock's close ally Thomas G. Alvord is generally understood to have been an ally to the ring. ECR, 413. See ‡.
7. The report was published as RSC. Quote in RSC, 2.
8. RSC; HCS, 270–73; DES, 1/4/1867. See ‡.
9. CFP, Cornelius Cole to James McClatchy, 5/31/1868; Alvord found in RSC, 11; quotes about Frank Hiscock in RSC, 628–29.
10. RSC, 630. In a later interrogation, Hiscock is mentioned briefly for suspicious activities in interviewing claimants and drawing up unauthorized checks for them. See RSC, 966–79.
11. CCCP, 79.
12. See ‡.
13. SFO, 1–10.
14. See ‡ on the strange overlapping connections within the courtroom itself.
15. RAR, 74–77.
16. OF, 193–97; RAR, 74–77, 327–28.
17. SJ, 4/28/1868.
18. RF; OF, 192–96. See ‡ on romantic friendships.
19. See ‡.
20. NYDT, 4/17/1861.
21. WWA, 383–447; Whitman quoted in ICW, 66–67.
22. RTT, 93–133; CFP, Cornelius Cole to James McClatchy, 5/31/1868. See ‡.
23. Huntington quoted in EE, 418–19. See ‡.
24. See ‡.
25. AEJ, 11/18/1868. See ‡.
26. AOT, 7–8.
27. SJ, 11/23/1868.
28. AOT, 5, 8.
29. SJ, 11/30/1868; AOT, 8, 15. See ‡.
30. AOT, 10.
31. AOT, 18.
32. AOT, 22–28, quotes on 23.

33. See ‡.
34. Threats in SJ, 11/19/1868; RTAC, 393, 382.
35. AOT, 23; RTAC, 386.
36. MFLT, 67; SCFP, typed manuscript, undated, p. 20. See ‡.
37. RTAC, 390–91.
38. CFP, Cornelius Cole to Olive Cole, 12/5/1868; CFP, Cornelius Cole to Olive Cole, undated; SJ, 12/5/1868. Cornelius was certain that the oft-inebriated Brady had failed to convert or convince anybody with his "drivel."
39. RTAC, 415–18. See CLNY, 987n5.
40. CLNY, 987n5; CFP, newspaper clip in Folder 7 (newspaper unknown).
41. RTAC, 419–20; SJ, 12/7/1868.
42. CFP, Cornelius Cole to C. K. McClatchy, 12/9/1868.

Chapter 23. Schemes and Smoke

1. WE, 12/17/1868; OHA, TDW, no date.
2. AEJ, 12/9/1868; The allusion to Cain may have also been a jab at his time commanding in the United States Colored Cavalry and his antislavery politics. See BIWM, 87–89; and ‡.
3. VWWS, 1/30/1869, taken from a correspondent from the *Seneca Falls Reveille*. Henry clearly had some sort of indirect control over Mary's money; in one letter, George told Olive that Henry and Mary had promised to support one of his (George's) business plans and then pulled out. CFP, George Cole to Olive Cole, 12/5/1867.
4. WE, 1/21/1869, 4/15/1869. George was spotted in a Seneca Falls hotel in April 1869: WE, 4/15/1869. See ‡.
5. NYH, 7/16/1869.
6. BI, 6/14/1867; BDA, 11/11/1869; GG, 7/19/1867. See ‡.
7. CCD, 1/21/1876.
8. WE, 1/27/1876; DES, 11/15/1869; AJ quoted in WE, 11/25/1869; CT, 11/18/1869; NHP, 11/24/1869. See ‡ about what he was doing in Washington, DC.
9. CFP, C. H. Stewart to Cornelius Cole, 7/19/1912; US Census, 1870. On Eliza Bruce, see ‡.
10. See ‡.
11. SCFP, James E. Taylor to Paul Augervard, 5/3/1871. See ‡.
12. GNE; YL. See ‡.

13. OHFG, 8–13; As Megan Kate Nelson writes, the Union's war aims, a reflection Republican commitments to free labor, "simultaneously embraced slave emancipation and Native extermination in order to secure an American empire of liberty." See TCW, 252.
14. See ‡.
15. FU, 552, 555–60. See ‡.
16. Sparse details of George's existence in Mora found in typed manuscript in SCFP; MLG, 60–61. See ‡.
17. RTT, 50. See ‡.
18. CFP, George Cole to Cornelius Cole, 4/29/1873. Cornelius is quoted in this letter.
19. CFP, George Cole to Cornelius Cole, 5/2/1873.
20. CFP, George Cole to Cornelius Cole, 5/2/1873.
21. See ‡.
22. See ‡ for more on the Star Route Frauds; PCA, 308–9; and SRC.
23. The quotes in this paragraph and the next are in CFP, George Cole to Cornelius Cole, 5/4/1873. For why a decorated veteran like George would view himself as not yet "somebody," see BL; and ‡.
24. ISM.
25. LGL, 28–39. See ‡.
26. For more on the incompatible ways of using and seeing land, see CU; and ISM.
27. ISM; CSFR, 17–25, 85–88.
28. MLG, 64–65; CSFR, 111–12. See ‡.
29. The quotes in this paragraph and the rest of the chapter come from CFP, George Cole to Cornelius Cole, 5/4/1873.
30. See ‡.

Chapter 24. Buried on the Brow of a Hill

1. SMCA, Fernando Nolan & Wife to George Cole, 7/3/1874, p. 9. According to the 1870 federal census, Mary still had significant wealth. She seems to have been the last person to believe in George's visions. See ‡.
2. Thanks to Dan Irick and Bryan J. Pickett for making this chapter possible. For this and other comments on Masonry, see ‡.
3. FURC.
4. SR, 141–43. On George's numbness, see RTAC, testimony of Frank H. Hamilton, 264–65. For more on bodies, ‡.

5. CSFR, 21–22, 26–28.
6. FURC. See ‡.
7. For a more detailed version of this fascinating ceremony, see ‡.
8. FU, 570–78. His military honors probably would have secured him a grave. See ‡.
9. LGL, 249–51. Also spelled Roybal, it was a name that traced back to one of the earliest Spanish families to colonize northern New Mexico.
10. SMCA, Luciano Roibal (Roybal) to George Cole, 2/10/1875, p. 11.
11. See SMCA, index for deeds.
12. For more on the confusion of this grant, and land grants in general, see ‡.
13. RTT, 53–55. See ‡.
14. PRGWC, various depositions and affidavits of Edwin Fox, Mary Cole, and Dr. Bowmer. On George's secret second wife visiting him, see CFP, C. H. Stewart to Cornelius Cole, 7/19/1912. Stewart wrote, "Now can you tell me anything in regard to ever hearing of Uncle George's <u>second</u> wife. (the one that came West when he was sick and died?)." See ‡.
15. Here and below, the description of the rituals and liturgy for Masonic funerals in the mid-nineteenth century is taken from WFM, 142–48.
16. See ‡ on weather.
17. St. Vrain was buried by Masons from all over New Mexico and with full military honors. There are unsubstantiated rumors that his real grave is somewhere else. See entry under "1870" in CST.
18. See ‡. See CSFR, 17.

Epilogue

1. CFP, spiritualist notes in brown notebook (Box 60) and transcriptions of séances (Box 22).
2. CFP, Mary Cole to Cornelius Cole, 11/7/1879, 2/17/1881; Mary Stewart to Cornelius Cole, 4/29/[no date, must be 1910]; entry for Jonathan C. Brown and Fannie Brown, 1900, in "United States Census, 1900," FamilySearch, accessed October 5, 2023, https://www.familysearch.org/ark:/61903/1:1:MMVV-81Z; entry for Jonathan C. Brown and Fannie H. Brown, 1910, in "United States Census, 1910," FamilySearch, accessed October 6, 2023, https://www.familysearch.org/ark:/61903/1:1:MPVF-NWB.

3. FIB, 237–42.
4. PRERF, general affidavit by Addie Mitchell, 12/10/1884.
5. What follows is from PRERF.
6. See comments from pension agent in PRERF; and his obituary in *Los Angeles Herald*, 5/22/1909. Curiously, Fox believed that the Black men he commanded had been free before the war. For why he might have believed this, ‡.
7. HGP. For more on Edwards's family and their not knowing the details of his death, ‡.
8. See ATG: Donald Shaffer emphasizes Black veterans' persistence and use of military connections to persevere and demand dignity. See ‡ on the lives of George's Black soldiers after the war.
9. For Butler's emotional experience seeing slain Black troops after another stymied attack, see BFB, 147–49.
10. DOR; BIM, 186.
11. BIM. On patronage in Massachusetts, ‡.
12. RAUR, 491–92; DOR, 141; HGNYT; BBVB.
13. It was a tragedy in the making: FSFL, esp. 290–300; DOR; HGNYT.
14. First publication in HTGRSA, 209; HTGR, 16–17; BFB, 261–62. Quotes in HTGR, 17.
15. Butler quoted in BFB, 253, 268–73.
16. CFP, George Cole to Cornelius Cole, 5/4/1873.
17. HTGR, 17.
18. BFB, 273.
19. BFB, 268–73.
20. PRGWC, various testimonies; CFP, various letters and photographs from sister Mary and her son E. C. Stewart, 1910–12.
21. Stewart quote in SCFP.
22. TOM.
23. See ‡.

KEY TO SOURCES CITED

AA Gregory P. Downs, *After Appomattox: Military Occupation and the Ends of War* (Cambridge, MA: Harvard University Press, 2015)

AAHCW Cassandra L. Newby-Alexander, *An African American History of the Civil War in Hampton Roads* (Charleston: History Press, 2010)

ACFA Charles Francis Adams, *The Autobiography of Charles Francis Adams* (Boston: Houghton Mifflin, 1916)

AD Jim Cullen, *The American Dream: A Short History of an Idea That Shaped a Nation* (New York: Oxford University Press, 2004)

AE *Albany Express*

AEJ *Albany Evening Journal*

AGA I. Edwards Clarke, "A Great Advocate: James T. Brady," *Galaxy* 7 (May 1869): 716–29

AGO Letters received by the Commission Branch of the Adjutant General Office, 1863–70, M1064, National Archives and Records Administration, Washington, DC

AIA James C. Mohr, *Abortion in America: The Origins and Evolution of National Policy* (New York: Oxford University Press, 1978)

AJ *Albany Journal*

ALA *Albany Argus*

ALSW Abraham Lincoln, *Speeches and Writings, 1859–1865: Speeches, Letters, and Miscellaneous Writings, Presidential Messages and Proclamations*, 2 vols., edited by Don Edward Fehrenbacher (New York: Literary Classics of the United States, 1989)

AO Carl N. Degler, *At Odds: Women and the Family in America from the Revolution to the Present* (New York: Oxford University Press, 1980)

AOA Theodore R. Sizer, ed., *The Age of the Academies* (New York: Bureau of Publications, Teachers College, Columbia University, 1964)

AOT *Albany Oyer and Terminer: The People vs Geo. W. Cole, Indictment—Murder: Opening Argument of Wm. J. Hadley, Esq., of the Second Trial of Maj. Gen. George W. Cole for the Murder of L. Harris Hiscock* (Albany: Charles Van Benthuysen and Sons, 1868)

AT Elizabeth Collins Cromley, *Alone Together: A History of New York's Early Apartments* (Ithaca, NY: Cornell University Press, 1990)

ATG Donald Robert Shaffer, *After the Glory: The Struggles of Black Civil War Veterans* (Lawrence: University Press of Kansas, 2004)

BAB Lucien Brock Proctor, *The Bench and Bar of New-York: Containing Biographical Sketches of Eminent Judges, and Lawyers of the New-York Bar, Incidents of the Important Trials in Which They Were Engaged, and Anecdotes Connected with Their Professional, Political and Judicial Career* (New York: Diossy, 1870)

BB Hans Louis Trefousse, *Ben Butler: The South Called Him Beast!* (New York: Twayne, 1957)

BBGG Brevet Brig. General Geo. W. Cole to [Twenty-Fifth Army Corps Headquarters], [June 1865], Miscellaneous Letters, Order, Reports and Circular Letters Received, Ser. 518, 25th Army Corps, RG 393, Pt. 2, No. 9, National Archives and Records Administration, Washington, DC

BBVB Margaret S. Thompson, "Ben Butler versus the Brahmins: Patronage and Politics in Early Gilded Age Massachusetts," *New England Quarterly* 55 (1982): 163–86

BCF James M. McPherson, *Battle Cry of Freedom: The Civil War Era* (New York: Oxford University Press, 1988)

BCHA George Rogers Howell and Jonathan Tenney, *Bi-centennial History of Albany: History of the County of Albany, N.Y., from 1609–1886* (New York: W. W. Munsell, 1886)

BCWC Thomas Morris Chester, *Black Civil War Correspondent: His Dispatches from the Virginia Front*, edited by R. J. M Blackett (Baton Rouge: Louisiana State University Press, 1989)

BCWSI Edward A. Miller, *The Black Civil War Soldiers of Illinois: The Story of the Twenty-Ninth U.S. Colored Infantry* (Columbia: University of South Carolina Press, 1998)

BDA *Boston Daily Advertiser*

BDU *Brooklyn Daily Union*

BFB Elizabeth D. Leonard, *Benjamin Franklin Butler: A Noisy, Fearless Life* (Chapel Hill: University of North Carolina Press, 2022)

BI *Bedford Inquirer*

BIM William D. Mallam, "Butlerism in Massachusetts," *New England Quarterly* 33, no. 2 (1960): 186–206

BIWM George M. Fredrickson, *The Black Image in the White Mind: The Debate on Afro-American Character and Destiny, 1817–1914* (Middletown, CT: Wesleyan University Press, 1987)

BL Scott A. Sandage, *Born Losers: A History of Failure in America* (Cambridge, MA: Harvard University Press, 2005)

BME Ira Berlin, Joseph P. Reidy, and Leslie S. Rowland, eds., *Freedom: A Documentary History of Emancipation, 1861–1867*, ser. 2, *The Black Military Experience* (Cambridge: Cambridge University Press, 1982)

BMR Edward Elbridge Salisbury, *Biographical Memoranda Respecting All Who Ever Were Members of the Class of 1832* (New Haven, CT: The Class, 1880)

BTD Gwendolyn Wright, *Building the Dream: A Social History of Housing in America* (New York: Pantheon Books, 1981)

BU *Brooklyn Union*

CAA Janet Farrell Brodie, *Contraception and Abortion in Nineteenth-Century America* (Ithaca, NY: Cornell University Press, 1994)

CAC Katherine C. Grier, *Culture and Comfort: Parlor Making and Middle-Class Identity, 1850–1930* (Washington, DC: Smithsonian Institution Press, 2010)

CAL Worthington Chauncy Ford, ed., *A Cycle of Adams Letters, 1861–1865*, 2 vols. (New York: Houghton Mifflin, 1920)

CC *Clinton Courier*

CCCP Catherine Coffin Phillips, *Cornelius Cole, California Pioneer and United States Senator: A Study in Personality and Achievements Bearing upon the Growth of a Commonwealth* (San Francisco: J. H. Nash, 1929)

CCD *Cortland Country Democrat*

CFP Cole Family Papers, Collection 217, Library Special Collections, Charles E. Young Research Library, University of California, Los Angeles

CI Norman Dain, *Concepts of Insanity in the United States, 1789–1865* (New Brunswick, NJ: Rutgers University Press, 1964)

CLNY Alden Chester and Edwin Melvin Williams, *Courts and Lawyers of New York: A History, 1609–1925*, vol. 3 (New York: American Historical Society, 1925)

CMC Mary Ryan, *Cradle of the Middle Class: The Family in Oneida County, New York, 1790–1865* (Cambridge: Cambridge University Press, 1981)

CMCW Wayne Mahood, ed., *Charlie Mosher's Civil War: From Fair Oaks to Andersonville with the Plymouth Pilgrims (85th N.Y. Infantry)* (Hightstown, NJ: Longstreet House, 1994)

CMERF Court Martial of Edwin R. Fox, NN2550, National Archives and Records Administration, Washington, DC

CMGWC Court Martial of George W. Cole, NN 916, National Archives and Records Administration, Washington, DC

CMJB Court Martial of John Burkley, OO-1394, National Archives and Records Administration, Washington, DC

CMPW Karen Halttunen, *Confidence Men and Painted Women: A Study of Middle-Class Culture in America, 1830–1870* (New Haven, CT: Yale University Press, 1982)

CMRD Court Martial of Robert Dollard, NN2543, National Archives and Records Administration, Washington, DC

CMWC Court Martial of William Carter, MM 3144, National Archives and Records Administration, Washington, DC

CMWHP Court Martial of William H. Perrin, NN 2543, National Archives and Records Administration, Washington, DC

CMWR Court Martial of William Respers, MM 3144, National Archives and Records Administration, Washington, DC

CR *Christian Recorder*

CRJG George W. Cole to James Griffing, August 11, [1848], in "Grant Power to Break Guadama's Chain," *Private Letters: The Correspondence of Rev. James S. Griffing & J. Augusta Goodrich* (blog), accessed June 27, 2024, https://privatelettersjsg.wordpress.com/1846-1852-college-years/grant-power-to-break-guadamas-chain/

CRYW George S. Burkhardt, *Confederate Rage, Yankee Wrath: No Quarter in the Civil War* (Carbondale: Southern Illinois University Press, 2007)

CS John Dwight Warner, "Crossed Sabres: A History of the Fifth Massachusetts Volunteer Cavalry, an African American Regiment in the Civil War" (PhD diss., Boston College, 1997)

CSFR David L. Caffey, *Chasing the Santa Fe Ring: Power and Privilege in Territorial New Mexico* (Albuquerque: University of New Mexico Press, 2014)

CSRERF Compiled Service Record of Edward R. Fox, National Archives and Records Administration, Washington, DC

CSRGWC Compiled Service Record of George W. Cole, National Archives and Records Administration, Washington, DC

CSRSR Compiled Service Record of Sylvester Ray, National Archives and Records Administration, Washington, DC
CST Louis Bramch, "Ceran St. Vrain and His Molino de Piedra in the Mora Valley," manuscript, New Mexico State Records Center and Archives
CT *Chicago Tribune*
CTW Barbara Welter, "The Cult of True Womanhood: 1820–1860," *American Quarterly* 18, no. 2, pt. 1 (Summer 1966): 151–74
CU Clark S. Knowlton, "Causes of Unrest among the Rural Spanish-American Village Population of Northern New Mexico," n.d., New Mexico State Records Center and Archives
CWHC John H. Eicher and David J. Eicher, *Civil War High Commands* (Stanford, CA: Stanford University Press, 2001)
CWN Civil War Newspaper Clippings, New York State Military Museum and Veterans Research Center, accessed December 29, 2022, https://museum.dmna.ny.gov/unit-history/cavalry/3rd-cavalry-regiment/civil-war-newspaper-clippings
CWNC John Gilchrist Barrett, *The Civil War in North Carolina* (Chapel Hill: University of North Carolina Press, 1963)
DAC *Daily Alta California*
DAE Thomas Leonard Livermore, *Days and Events, 1860–1866* (New York: Houghton Mifflin, 1920)
DANPR David A. Norris, *Potter's Raid: The Union Cavalry's Boldest Expedition in Eastern North Carolina* (Wilmington, NC: Dream Tree Books, 2007)
DANTY David A. Norris, "'The Yankees Have Been Here!': The Story of Brig. Gen. Edward E. Potter's Raid on Greenville, Tarboro, and Rocky Mount, July 19–23, 1863," *North Carolina Historical Review* 73, no. 1 (1996): 1–27
DES *Daily Evening Star* (Washington, DC)
DOR Heather Cox Richardson, *The Death of Reconstruction: Race, Labor, and Politics in the Post–Civil War North, 1865–1901* (Cambridge, MA: Harvard University Press, 2004)
EC Gerald Linderman, *Embattled Courage: The Experience of Combat in the American Civil War* (New York: Free Press, 2008)
ECR Thomas J. Archdeacon, "The Erie Canal Ring, Samuel J. Tilden, and the Democratic Party," *New York History* 58, no. 4 (October 1978): 408–29

EDW Thomas Treadwell Davis, *Eulogy on Daniel Webster, Delivered in Syracuse, N.Y., Nov 13, 1852* (Syracuse: printed at the Daily Star Office, 1852)

EE David Haward Bain, *Empire Express: Building the First Transcontinental Railroad* (London: Penguin Books, 2000)

EF Amy Murrell Taylor, *Embattled Freedom: Journeys Through the Civil War's Slave Refugee Camps* (Chapel Hill: University of North Carolina Press, 2018)

EGLAOA Edward Longacre, *Army of Amateurs: General Benjamin F. Butler and the Army of the James, 1863–1865* (Mechanicsburg, PA: Stackpole Books, 1997)

EGLBT Edward G. Longacre, "Black Troops in the Army of the James, 1863–65," *Military Affairs* 45, no. 1 (1981): 1–8

EGLD Edward G. Longacre, "The Army of the James, 1863–1865: A Military, Political, and Social History" (PhD diss., Temple University, 1988), 4 vols.

EHH Wayne E. Morrison, *Early History, &c., the Village of Havana, N.Y.* ([Ovid, NY?]: W. C. Morrison, n.d.)

ELS Gurney S. Strong, *Early Landmarks of Syracuse* (Syracuse, NY: Times, 1894)

EOB James D. Anderson, *The Education of Blacks in the South, 1860–1935* (Chapel Hill: University of North Carolina Press, 1988)

EP Stephen Olin, *Early Piety, the Basis of Elevated Character: A Discourse to the Graduating Class of Wesleyan University, August 1850* (New York: Lane and Scott, 1851)

ER *Elmira Republican*

EWM *Ezekiel Wilson Mundy: A Book of Loving Remembrance* ([Syracuse, NY]: Syracuse Public Library, 1917)

EWMC Empire Windmill Manufacturing Company, *Illustrated Catalogue of the Empire Wind Mill Manufacturing Company of Syracuse, N.Y., for 1870* (Syracuse, NY: Daily Journal Presses, 1870)

FAC Ann Douglas, *The Feminization of American Culture* (London: Macmillan, 1996)

FAL Ira Berlin, Barbara J. Fields, Steven F. Miller, Joseph P. Reidy, and Leslie S. Rowland, eds., *Free at Last: A Documentary History of Slavery, Freedom, and the Civil War* (New York: New Press, 1992)

FBS William A. Dobak, *Freedom by the Sword: The U.S. Colored Troops, 1862–1867* (Washington, DC: U.S. Army, Center of Military History, 2011)

FC *Farmer's Cabinet* (Amherst, NH)
FF Ira Berlin and Leslie S. Rowland, eds., *Families and Freedom: A Documentary History of African-American Kinship in the Civil War Era* (New York: New Press, 1997)
FFG Robert Engs, *Freedom's First Generation: Black Hampton, Virginia, 1861–1890* (New York: Fordham University Press, 2004)
FGAW T. Lindsay Baker, *A Field Guide to American Windmills* (Norman: University of Oklahoma Press, 1985)
FIB Joseph T. Glatthaar, *Forged in Battle: The Civil War Alliance of Black Soldiers and White Officers* (Baton Rouge: Louisiana State University Press, 2000)
FN James Oakes, *Freedom National: The Destruction of Slavery in the United States, 1861–1865* (New York: W. W. Norton, 2012)
FP Patricia Cline Cohen, Timothy J. Gilfoyle, and Helen Lefkowitz Horowitz, *The Flash Press: Sporting Male Weeklies in 1840s New York* (Chicago: University of Chicago Press, 2008)
FPM Albert Castel, "The Fort Pillow Massacre: An Examination of the Evidence," in *Black Flag over Dixie: Racial Atrocities and Reprisals in the Civil War*, edited by Gregory J. W. Urwin (Carbondale: Southern Illinois University Press, 2004), 89–103
FPR Christine Stansell, *The Feminist Promise: 1792 to the Present* (New York: Random House, 2010)
FS Ira Berlin, Joseph P. Reidy, and Leslie S. Rowland, eds., *Freedom's Soldiers: The Black Military Experience in the Civil War* (Cambridge: Cambridge University Press, 1998)
FSFL Eric Foner, *Free Soil, Free Labor, Free Men: The Ideology of the Republican Party before the Civil War* (Oxford: Oxford University Press, 1995)
FU Leo E. Oliva, *Fort Union and the Frontier Army in the Southwest*, Southwest Cultural Resources Center Professional Papers No. 41 (Santa Fe: National Park Service, 1993)
FURC Dan Irick, "Union Lodge No. 4, AF&AM: Fort Union Rededication Ceremony: Ft. Union National Monument, New Mexico, July 15, 2006," in the author's possession
GDR Dolores Hayden, *The Grand Domestic Revolution: A History of Feminist Designs for American Homes, Neighborhoods and Cities* (Cambridge, MA: MIT Press, 1981)
GF James D. McCabe, *Great Fortunes and How They Were Made; or The Struggles and Triumphs of Our Self-Made Men* (Philadelphia: George Maclean, 1871)

GG *Geneva Gazette*
GNE Heather Cox Richardson, *The Greatest Nation of the Earth: Republican Economic Policies during the Civil War* (Cambridge, MA: Harvard University Press, 1997)
GVAS John Delafield, *A General View and Agricultural Survey of the County of Seneca* ([Albany]: [C. Van Benthuysen], [1851])
HATP William W. Betts Jr., *The Hatchet and the Plow: The Life and Times of Chief Cornplanter* (Bloomington: iUniverse, 2010)
HCS Minnie M. Beal and Noble E. Whitford, *History of the Canal System of the State of New York: Together with Brief Histories of the Canals of the United States and Canada* (Albany, NY: Brandow, 1906)
HDS *Hudson Daily Star*
HFA Henry Fielding, *Amelia* (London: Penguin, 1987)
HGNYT Adam Tuchinsky, *Horace Greeley's "New-York Tribune": Civil War–Era Socialism and the Crisis of Free Labor* (Ithaca, NY: Cornell University Press, 2009)
PRHG Pension Record for Henry Gaitling, father of Henry Edwards, #614.062, National Archives and Records Administration, Washington, DC
HJ *Havana Journal*
HLEB James B. Fry, *The History and Legal Effect of Brevets in the Armies of Great Britain and the United States: From Their Origin in 1692 to the Present Time* (New York: D. Van Nostrand, 1877)
HOC W. W. Clayton, *History of Onondaga County, New York* (Syracuse, NY: D. Mason, Truair, Smith and Bruce, 1878)
HR Steven Mintz, *Huck's Raft: A History of American Childhood* (Cambridge, MA: Harvard University Press, 2004)
HSR Walter Clark, *Histories of the Several Regiments and Battalions from North Carolina, in the Great War, 1861–'65*, 5 vols. (Raleigh, NC: E. M. Uzzell, 1901)
HTGR Benjamin Franklin Butler, Oliver Ames, Phineas Taylor Barnum, Henry Harwick Faxon, Charles Alfred Pillsbury, Erastus Wiman, Russell Sage, and Asa P. Potter, *How to Get Rich* (Boston: J. F. Spofford, 1888)
HTGRSA Benjamin F. Butler, "How to Get Rich," *Scientific American* 57, no. 14 (1887): 209
HWB Henry W. Bellow, "The Influence of the Trading Spirit upon the Social and Moral Life of America," in *The American Review: A Whig*

Journal of Politics, Literature, Art, and Science (New York: Wiley and Putnam, 1845), 1:94–98

ICW George M. Fredrickson, *The Inner Civil War: Northern Intellectuals and the Crisis of the Union* (1965; Urbana: University of Illinois Press, 1993)

IEL Norma Basch, *In the Eyes of the Law: Women, Marriage, and Property in Nineteenth-Century New York* (Ithaca, NY: Cornell University Press, 1982)

IH Margaret Humphreys, *Intensely Human: The Health of the Black Soldier in the American Civil War* (Baltimore: Johns Hopkins University Press, 2008)

ISM Malcolm Ebright, "Introduction: Spanish and Mexican Land Grants and the Law," *Journal of the West* 27, no. 3 (July 1988): 3–11

IUL Robert M. Ireland, "Insanity and the Unwritten Law," *American Journal of Legal History* 32, no. 2 (April 1988): 157–72

JME George S. Conover, comp., *Journals of the Military Expedition of Major General John Sullivan against the Six Nations of Indians in 1779, with Records of Centennial Celebrations* (Auburn, NY: Knapp, Peck and Thomson, 1887)

KJC Kinchen Jahu Carpenter, *War Diary of Kinchen Jahu Carpenter, Company I Fiftieth North Carolina Regiment, War between the States, 1861–'65*, edited by Julie Carpenter Williams (Rutherfordton, NC: privately published, 1955)

LBY Bell Irvin Wiley, *The Life of Billy Yank: The Common Soldier of the Union* (Baton Rouge: Louisiana State University Press, 2008)

LEAD Gabor S. Boritt, *Lincoln and the Economics of the American Dream* (Urbana: University of Illinois Press, 1994)

LG Donna Dennis, *Licentious Gotham: Erotic Publishing and Its Prosecution in Nineteenth-Century New York* (Cambridge, MA: Harvard University Press, 2009)

LGL Malcolm Ebright, *Land Grants and Lawsuits in Northern New Mexico* (Albuquerque: University of New Mexico Press, 1994)

LHR Hendrik Hartog, "Lawyering, Husbands' Rights, and the 'Unwritten Law' in Nineteenth-Century America," *Journal of American History* 84, no. 1 (June 1997): 67–96

LL Jacqueline Jones, *Labor of Love, Labor of Sorrow: Black Women, Work, and the Family, from Slavery to the Present* (New York: Basic Books, 2009)

LMD Robert M. Ireland, "The Libertine Must Die: Sexual Dishonor and the Unwritten Law in the Nineteenth-Century United States," *Journal of Social History* 23, no. 1 (Autumn 1989): 27–34

LMW Noah Andre Trudeau, *Like Men of War: Black Troops in the Civil War, 1862–1865* (Edison, NJ: Castle Books, 2002)

LN *Lamoille Newsdealer* (Hyde Park, VT)

LSSO Samuel R. Harlow and H. H. Boone, *Life Sketches of the State Officers, Senators, and Members of the Assembly of the State of New York, in 1867* (Albany, NY: Weed, Parsons, 1867)

LWS Michael deGruccio, "Letting the War Slip through Our Hands: Material Culture and the Weakness of Words in the Civil War Era," in *Weirding the War: Stories from the Civil War's Ragged Edges*, edited by Stephen Berry (Athens: University of Georgia Press, 2011), 15–35

LWTHB Last Will and Testament of Henry D. Barto, Sr., March 11, 1857, Tompkins County Surrogate Court, New York State

MAH Stephanie Coontz, *Marriage, a History: How Love Conquered Marriage* (New York: Penguin Books, 2006)

MCC Cornelius Cole, *Memoirs of Cornelius Cole: Ex-Senator of the United States from California* (New York: McLoughlin Brothers, 1908)

MCM Mutiny Court Martial, Brazos Santiago, TX, 8/1865, #OO-1394, National Archives and Records Administration, Washington, DC

MFLT Lyman Tremain, *Memorial of Frederick Lyman Tremain, Late Lieut. Col. of the 10th N.Y. Cavalry: Who Was Mortally Wounded at the Battle of Hatcher's Run, Va., February 6th, and Died at City Point Hospital, February 8th, 1865* (Albany, NY: Van Benthuysen's steam printing house, 1865)

MHOS Dwight H. Bruce, *Memorial History of Syracuse, N.Y.: From Its Settlement to the Present Time* (Syracuse, NY: H. P. Smith, 1891)

MIC Brian P. Luskey, *Men Is Cheap: Exposing the Frauds of Free Labor in Civil War America* (Chapel Hill: University of North Carolina Press, 2020)

MLG Clark S. Knowlton, "The Mora Land Grant: A New Mexican Tragedy," *Journal of the West* 27, no. 3 (July 1988): 59–73

MLID Nancy Schrom Dye and Daniel Blake Smith, "Mother Love and Infant Death, 1750–1920," in *Women and Health in America: Historical Readings*, 2nd ed., edited by Judith Walzer Leavitt (Madison: University of Wisconsin Press, 1999), 91–110

MMF Karen Haltunnen, *Murder Most Foul: The Killer and the American Gothic Imagination* (Cambridge, MA: Harvard University Press, 2009)

MMS Elmer Ellsworth Brown, *The Making of Our Middle Schools: An Account of the Development of Secondary Education in the United States* (New York: Longmans, Green, 1902)
MOC Frederick Douglass, *Men of Color to Arms! Now or Never!*, photograph, ca. 1863, retrieved from the Library of Congress, https://www.loc.gov/item/scsm000556/
MOM Calvin Schermerhorn, *Money over Mastery, Family over Freedom: Slavery in the Antebellum Upper South* (Baltimore: Johns Hopkins University Press, 2011)
MP Weymouth T. Jordan Jr. and Gerald W. Thomas, "Massacre at Plymouth: April 20, 1864," *North Carolina Historical Review* 72, no. 2 (April 1995): 125–97
MRA John Lauritz Larson, *The Market Revolution in America: Liberty, Ambition, and the Eclipse of the Common Good* (Cambridge: Cambridge University Press, 2010)
MRCW Edward Longacre, *Mounted Raids of the Civil War* (Lincoln: University of Nebraska Press, 1994)
MRF David C. Smith, "Middle Range Farming in the Civil War Era: Life on a Farm in Seneca County, 1862–1866," *New York History* 48, no. 4 (October 1967): 352–69
MRFR Michael deGruccio, "Manhood, Race, Failure, and Reconciliation: Charles Francis Adams Jr. and the American Civil War," *New England Quarterly* 81, no. 4 (December 2008): 636–75
MSH Joseph K. Barnes, *The Medical and Surgical History of the Civil War*, vol. 3 (Wilmington, NC: Broadfoot, 1990)
MSUS Frederick W. Browne, *My Service in the U.S. Colored Cavalry: A Paper Read before the Ohio Commandery of the Loyal Legion, March 4, 1908* ([Cincinnati?]: n.p., 1908)
MWA Hendrik Hartog, *Man and Wife in America: A History* (Cambridge, MA: Harvard University Press, 2000)
NACWR Thomas P. Lowry, "New Access to a Civil War Resource," *Civil War History* 49, no. 1 (2003): 52–63
NAR *Nineteenth Annual Report of the Executive Committee of the Prison Association of New York*, no. 19 (transmitted to the legislature, January 29, 1864) (Albany, NY: Comstock and Cassidy, 1864)
NHP *New Hampshire Patriot*
NN *Nunda News* (NY)
NNG David Jaffee, *A New Nation of Goods: The Material Culture of Early America* (Philadelphia: University of Pennsylvania Press, 2010)

NPG *National Police Gazette*
NYDT *New York Daily Tribune*
NYH *New York Herald*
NYT *New York Times*
NYTr *New York Tribune*
NYW *New York World*
OA Hamilton Child, comp., "Oxygenized Air Institute," in *Gazetteer and Business Directory of Onondaga County, N.Y., for 1868–9* (Syracuse, NY: Journal Office, 1868), 162
OF Richard Godbeer, *The Overflowing of Friendship: Love between Men and the Creation of the American Republic* (Baltimore: Johns Hopkins University Press, 2009)
OHA Hiscock/Cole File, Clippings from Onondaga Historical Association
OHAB Onondaga Historical Association, Bulletin, February 1960, 2, in OHA folder, "Industry-Machinery, Empire Windmill Manufacturing Company"
OHFG Colin G. Calloway, ed., *Our Hearts Fell to the Ground: Plains Indian Views of How the West Was Lost* (Boston: Bedford/St. Martin's, 1996)
OOS S. Hemenway, "Observations on Scurvy, and Its Causes among the U.S. Colored Troops of the 25th Army Corps, during the Spring and Summer of 1865," *Chicago Medical Examiner* 7 (October1865): 582–86
OOTB Alexander Herritage Newton, *Out of the Briars: An Autobiography and Sketch of the Twenty-Ninth Regiment, Connecticut Volunteers* (Philadelphia: A.M.E. Book Concern, 1910)
OPW Alice E. Northrup, Sarah Sumner Teall, and Edwin Platt Tanner, *Onondaga's Part in the Civil War* (Syracuse, NY: Dehler, 1915)
OR US War Department, *The War of the Rebellion: A Compilation of the Official Records of the Union and Confederate Armies* (Washington, DC: Government Printing Office, 1881–1901)
PBFB Papers of Benjamin F. Butler, Library of Congress
PCA Mark Grossman, *Political Corruption in America: An Encyclopedia of Scandals, Power, and Greed* (Santa Barbara, CA: ABC-CLIO, 2003)
PCCJ Private communication with historian Christopher Jones. Here I draw from unpublished chapters written by Jones about the war in North Carolina. Chapters in author's possession
PDCC Edward F. Underhill, *Proceedings and Debates of the Constitutional Convention of the State of New York: Held in 1867 and 1868 in the City of Albany*, vol. 1 (Albany, NY: Weed, Parsons, 1868)

PH   Sidney David Brummer, "Political History of New York State during the Period of the Civil War" (PhD diss., Columbia University, 1911)
PHD   George Forgie, *Patricide in the House Divided: A Psychological Interpretation of Lincoln and His Age* (New York: Norton, 1979)
PI   *Philadelphia Inquirer*
PNYB   Thomas Butler Gunn, *The Physiology of New York Boarding-Houses* (1857; repr., Carlisle, MA: Applewood Books, 2009)
PRDH   Pension Record of David Hill, Invalid: 767.089, National Archives and Records Administration, Washington, DC
PREC   Pension Record of Eli Cross, Widow: 435.305, National Archives and Records Administration, Washington, DC
PREN   Pension Record of Edwards Nelson, Invalid: 759.33, National Archives and Records Administration, Washington, DC
PRERF   Pension Record of Edwin R. Fox. Invalid: 524.581. National Archives and Records Administration, Washington, DC
PRFH   Court Martial of Francis Hyman, Invalid: 729.138, National Archives and Records Administration, Washington, DC
PRGWC   Pension Record of George W. Cole, Widow: 265.854, National Archives and Records Administration, Washington, DC
PRPF   Pension Record of Peter Fuller, Invalid: 768.014, National Archives and Records Administration, Washington, DC
PUF   William Jay, *Prayers for the Use of Families; or, The Domestic Minister's Assistant* (Hartford, CT: S. Andrus, 1830)
RAR   Gordon S. Wood, *Radicalism of the American Revolution* (New York: Knopf Doubleday, 1993)
RAUR   Eric Foner, *Reconstruction: America's Unfinished Revolution, 1863–1877* (New York: Harper, 2011)
RCW   Robert Dollard, *Recollections of the Civil War and Going West to Grow Up with the Country* (Scotland, SD: the author, 1906)
RF   Anthony Rotundo, "Romantic Friendship: Male Intimacy and Middle-Class Youth in the Northern United States, 1800–1900," *Journal of Social History* 23, no. 1 (Autumn 1989): 1–25
ROA   Richard L. Bushman, *The Refinement of America: Persons, Houses, Cities* (New York: Vintage, 1993)
ROS   Drew Gilpin Faust, *This Republic of Suffering: Death and the American Civil War* (New York: Alfred A. Knopf, 2008)
ROTT   James Arthur Emmerton, *A Record of the Twenty-Third Regiment Mass. Vol. Infantry in the War of the Rebellion 1861–1865* (Boston: W. Ware, 1886)

RR Estelle B. Freedman, *Redefining Rape: Sexual Violence in the Era of Suffrage and Segregation* (Cambridge, MA: Harvard University Press, 2013)

RSC *Report of the Select Committee Appointed by the Senate to Investigate into the Management of the Canals of the State of New York, and the Official Conduct of Persons Now or Heretofore Connected Therewith; and the Conduct of Persons Comprising the Canal Contracting Board* (Albany, NY: C. Van Benthuysen and Sons, 1868)

RSPEA Sharon Block, *Rape and Sexual Power in Early America* (Chapel Hill: Omohundro Institute and University of North Carolina Press, 2012)

RT *Richmond Times*

RTAC *Remarkable Trials of All Countries with the Evidence and Speeches of Counsel, Court Scenes, Incidents, &c.*, vol. 2 (New York: S. S. Peloubet, 1882)

RTT Richard White, *Railroaded: The Transcontinentals and the Making of Modern America* (New York: W. W. Norton, 2012)

S29 Isaac J. Hill, *A Sketch of the 29th Regiment of Connecticut Colored Troops* (Baltimore: Daugherty, Maguire, 1867)

SAIE Franklin Henry Chase, *Syracuse and Its Environs: A History* (Syracuse, NY: Lewis Historical, 1924) VOLUME 1

SBB Robert S. Holzman, *Stormy Ben Butler* (New York: Octagon Books, 1978)

SBG James I. Robertson Jr., *Soldiers Blue and Gray* (Columbia: University of South Carolina Press, 1988)

SCFP Smith-Cole Family Papers, typed biography of Cornelius Cole with "Short Sketch of His Brother, General George W. Cole," n.d., in folder pertaining to Cornelius Cole Smith, US Army Heritage and Education Center, Carlisle, PA

SCH *Speech of Hon. Cornelius Cole of California, on Arming the Slaves, Delivered in the House of Representatives, February 18, 1864* (Washington, DC: McGill and Witherow, 1864)

SDC&U *Syracuse Daily Courier and Union*

SDJ *Syracuse Daily Journal*

SDR *Sabbath Day Recorder*

SDS *Syracuse Daily Standard*

SDU *Sacramento Daily Union*

SFF Jim Downs, *Sick from Freedom: African-American Illness and Suffering during the Civil War and Reconstruction* (New York: Oxford University Press, 2012)

SFN T. J. Jackson Lears, *Something for Nothing: Luck in America* (New York: Viking Penguin, 2003)

SFO Robert H. Wiebe, *The Search for Order, 1877–1920* (New York: Hill and Wang, 1967)

SJ *Syracuse Journal*

SMCA Grantee Index, San Miguel County Archives

SNYDC *Syracuse New York Daily Courier*

SNYDU *Syracuse New York Daily Union*

SOE Wilbur Fisk, *The Science of Education: An Inaugural Address, Delivered at the Opening of the Wesleyan University, in Middletown, Connecticut, September 21, 1831* (New York: M'Elrath and Bangs, 1832)

SP Howard P. Nash, *Stormy Petrel: The Life and Times of General Benjamin F. Butler, 1818–1893* (Rutherford, NJ: Fairleigh Dickinson University Press, 1969)

SR Mark Christopher Carnes, *Secret Ritual and Manhood in Victorian America* (New Haven, CT: Yale University Press, 1989)

SRC T. Martin Klotsche, "The Star Route Cases," *Mississippi Valley Historical Review* 22, no. 3 (December 1995): 407–18

STH Karen Lystra, *Searching the Heart: Women, Men, and Romantic Love in Nineteenth-Century America* (Oxford: Oxford University Press, 1992)

SWL Sophia Webster Lloyd, *Poems of Mrs. Sophia Webster Lloyd* (Cincinnati: Standard, 1887)

TCB Chandler Robbins Gilman, James T. Roberts, James Topham Brady, John Alexander Bryan, and Charles Benjamin Huntington, *Trial of Charles B. Huntington for Forgery: Principal Defence: Insanity* (New York: J. S. Voorhies, 1857)

TCW Megan Kate Nelson, Nelson, *The Three-Cornered War: The Union, the Confederacy, and Native Peoples in the Fight for the West* (New York: United Kingdom: Scribner, 2020)

TDT *Troy Daily Times*

TDW *Troy Daily Whig*

TKS Henry Clay Trumball, *The Knightly Soldier: A Biography of Major Henry Ward Camp, Tenth Conn. Vols.* (Boston: Nichols and Noyes, 1865)

TOM Michael J. Sandel, *The Tyranny of Merit: What's Become of the Common Good?* (London: Allen Lane, 2020)

TRR Steven Watts, *The Republic Reborn: War and the Making of Liberal America, 1790–1820* (Baltimore: Johns Hopkins University Press, 1987)

TS *Saratogian*
UB "Sketch of Life of George W. Cole," Sketch #14 in *Universal Biography: Containing Sketches of Prominent Persons of the 19th Century* (New York: New York and Hartford Publishing, 1871)
UCCW Stephen Z. Starr, *The Union Cavalry in the Civil War*, vol. 1 (Baton Rouge: Louisiana State University Press, 1979)
UDO *Utica Daily Observer*
UMH *Utica Morning Herald*
USCT2 2nd USCT Cavalry Regimental Order and Letter Book, Record Group 94, National Archives and Records Administration, Washington, DC
USM Judith Walzer Leavitt, "Under the Shadow of Maternity: American Women's Responses to Death and Debility Fears in Nineteenth-Century Childbirth," *Feminist Studies* 12, no. 1 (Spring 1986): 129–54
UW Gary W. Gallagher, *The Union War* (Cambridge, MA: Harvard University Press, 2011)
VC Reid Mitchell, *The Vacant Chair: The Northern Soldier Leaves Home* (New York: Oxford University Press, 1993)
VH *Valley Herald* (Chaska, MN)
VWWS *Vincennes Weekly Western Sun*
WACW Edward L. Ayers, "Worrying about the Civil War," in *What Caused the Civil War: Reflections on the South and Southern History* (New York: W. W. Norton, 2005), 103–30
WAE Christopher Jones, "Warlords and Entrepreneurs: The Origins of Guerrilla War in Civil War North Carolina," paper presented at the Popular Culture Association/American Culture Association Civil War and Reconstruction conference, April 14, 2014, Chicago
WAWAC Leslie J. Reagan, *When Abortion Was a Crime: Women, Medicine, and Law in the United States, 1867–1973* (Berkeley: University of California Press, 1998)
WD *Western Democrat* (Charlotte, NC)
WDNTP Bruce Suderow, "'We Did Not Take any Prisoners': The Suffolk Slaughter," *Civil War Times Illustrated* 23, no. 3 (1984): 36–39
WE *Watkins Express*
WFM Robert Morris and Thomas Smith Webb, *The Freemason's Monitor: Or Illustrations of Masonry* (Cincinnati: Moore, Wilstach, Keys, 1859)
WJ *Wilmington Journal*

WS Frances M. Clarke, *War Stories: Suffering and Sacrifice in the Civil War North* (Chicago: University of Chicago Press, 2012)

WSJ *Weekly State Journal* (Raleigh, NC)

WU David B. Potts, *Wesleyan University, 1831–1910: Collegiate Enterprise in New England* (New Haven, CT: Yale University Press, 1992)

WW Elliott J. Gorn, "The Wicked World: The National Gazette and Gilded-Age America," in *The Culture of Crime*, edited by Craig L. LaMay and Everette E. Dennis (New Brunswick, NJ: Transaction, 1995), 9–22

WWA David S. Reynolds, *Walt Whitman's America: A Cultural Biography* (New York: Alfred A. Knopf, 1995)

WWU Thomas Joseph Goss, *The War within the Union High Command: Politics and Generalship during the Civil War* (Lawrence: University Press of Kansas, 2003)

YL Richard Franklin Bensel, *Yankee Leviathan: The Origins of Central State Authority in America, 1859–1877* (Cambridge: Cambridge University Press, 1990)

INDEX

abortion, contraception, 217–19, 240
ambition, 14–16, 21–23 passim
American Dream. *See* self-making
American Revolution, 13–15, 265–66
Army of the James, 70–73, 120–27, 245

Barnum, Henry A., 253–56
Blackburn Ford controversy, 47–48
Black troops: desire to read, 82–83; drinking and abuse, 94–97; family, 80–81, 89, 145, 151; Fort Pillow massacre, 91–92; impressing men into personal servants, 87–88; mutiny, 133–41, 143–47; pay inequality, 97, 105; Plymouth massacre, 92–94; Second Colored Cavalry, 79–85, 115, 132, 137; sickness, 130–32, 148–51; Suffolk massacre, 90–91; tying up men, 97–100, 105, 108–9; William Perrin's confession, 96–97

books and literature, 27–28; reading and sharing stories, 129, 224–31
brevets, 113–14, 152, 178–82
Butler, Benjamin F., 70, 72–74, 80–82, 114–15, 180; ambition and the invention of Samuel Johnson, 93–94; blames murder of Henry Edwards on Cole's order, 111–13; bottled up, 114–15; Colombian canal scheme, 129; contacted by Olive for the trial, 236–38; Dutch Gap, 115–20, 123; forms XXV Corps, 120–21; Fort Fisher, 121–23; pushed from war, 124–25; years after war, 301–3

childbirth, fear of death, pressure of motherhood, 215–16
Cole, Cornelius, 9, 16, 24, 75, 191, 227, 238–39, 261–68; communicates with dead, 297–98; everywhere, 261–65. *See also* rings and corruption

Cole, George W.: adjustment after war, 157–64; after acquittal, 275–77; *Amelia*, 224–27; begins in Black regiment, 79–84; birth, 13–14; breakdown at the capitol, 161–63; childhood (education), 15–20, 56–59; death, 292–95; early marriage (in Havana), 25–32; fall from horse and injuries, 51, 251–52; fateful order, 98, 111–12; final promotions, 152–53; first meets Butler, 73–74; jail and cell, 195–203; letter writing & promotions, 74–78, 125–27; love for family, 147–48; masons, 286–89, 293–95; medical training, 25; murder, 172–75; mutiny, 143–45; parents, 13, 17–18; place and patronage, 160–63; plans for land in NM, 282–86, 289, 292; plans for mail routes in NM, 278–81; prison cell statement, 176–77; religious experience in cell, 193–95; resignation letter, 126; second wife (Eliza Bruce), 276; Wesleyan University, 17–23, 276; wounds, 51–53, 160, 240–42, 246, 251–54, 256–57

Cole, Mary Barto, 25, 191, 236; attraction to Hiscock, 209–10; back and forth to front, 102, 127, 141; darkest hour of war, 102–4; death, 298; family hotel (Jervis House), 220–22; inheritance and will, 36–38; love tokens, 210–11; money and Hiscock, 204–5; nearly losing first child, 31–32; rape or coercion, 205–8; sexuality, 214–16, 228–31; visiting George in Norfolk hotel, 127–28; wanting to live in the city, 33

Cole, Olive, 191–95; advice on trial, 239–42; "Husbands at Home" story, 227–31

confessions notes: First, 168–69, 208–9; letter from George, 171; Second, 211–13

coverture, 35–38, 206, 213, 247

daguerreotypes, gallery, 27–31
Dollard, Robert, 84–89, 95–96, 98–101, 137–38, 141–45

education: academies, 15–17; district schools, Wesleyan University, 17–23
Edwards, Henry, 106–11, 300
Empire Windmill Company, 158–59, 165
Erie Canal: corruption and rings, 262–65

family hotels, 220–22
Fox, Edwin, 104–12, 151–52, 251–52, 299
friendship, 18–19, 265–69, 270

Hiscock, Luther Harris, 38–40, 165–67; effects in pockets, 183–84; funeral, 183–90; gravestone, 190

identification discs, 49–50

Johnson, Samuel. *See* ambition; Butler, Benjamin F.

merit and meritocracy, 7–8, 14–15, 113, 127, 279, 306–7
military grade: rank, promotion, 177–79, 180–82
murder at Stanwix Hall, 3, 172–75; woodcut image, 231–35

Native Americans, 56–59, 277

raids. *See* Third New York Cavalry
railroads: magnates, 238–39, 264, 268; New Mexico, 277–79
rape, coercion and consent, 205–8
religion: at Hiscock's funeral, 185–90; Methodism, 16, 17–23, 191; Reverend Sherman Canfield, 184; seances and spiritualism, 297–98; shift from Calvinism, 19–20, 193–95, 216, 249–50
rings and corruption: canal ring, 261–65; railroad, 264; Santa Fe Ring, 282–83

Second Colored Cavalry. *See* Black troops

self-making, 7–8, 76–28, 302–4; tributes to George and Hiscock, 178–80; war and, 40–41
Seneca Falls, 34–35. *See also* women's rights
Spanish land grants, 282–85
Sullivan's Expedition, 56–59

Third New York Cavalry, 48–51; raids, 53–55, 59–69; raids and women, 60–62, 68
Trials: (Defense) Amasa Parker, 239, 272; (first), 242–60; (Prosecuting attorneys), Charles B. Sedgwick, 258; (second), 269–74; bad blood in court, 271–72; emphasis on George's mind, 250; finding attorneys, 236–39; Henry Smith, 196, 243; James T. Brady, 238–39, 249, 258, 272; Lyman Tremain, 244; railroad money, 238; William Hadley, 183, 195, 245–48, 269–70
Twelfth New York Infantry, 47–48
Twenty-Fifth Corps, 120–21, 129, 131–33

wire Pulling, laying pipe, etc., 76–78, 281
women's rights: Seneca Falls, 34–35; war, 42–43

Explore other books from HOPKINS PRESS

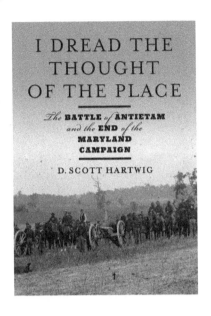

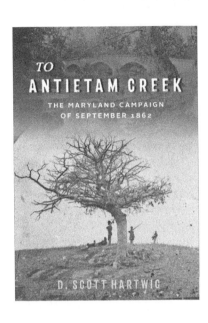

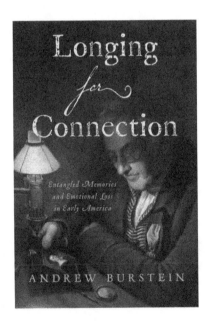

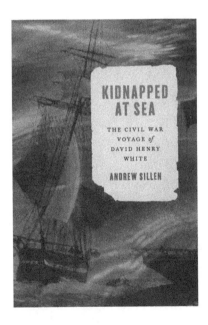

JOHNS HOPKINS UNIVERSITY PRESS | PRESS.JHU.EDU